Photograph by Tony McGrath, courtesy of *The Observer*

Harold
PINTER

an annotated bibliography

A
Reference
Publication
in
Literature

Ronald Gottesman
Editor

Harold
PINTER

an annotated bibliography

STEVEN H. GALE

G.K.HALL &CO.
70 LINCOLN STREET, BOSTON, MASS.

Library of Congress Cataloging in Publication Data
Gale, Steven H.
   Harold Pinter: an annotated bibliography.

   (A Reference publication in literature)
   Includes index.
   1. Pinter, Harold, 1930-   — Bibliography.
I. Series: Reference Publications in literature.
Z8692.55.G34   [PR6066.I53]   016.822'.9'14   78-2782
ISBN 0-8161-8014-8

This publication is printed on permanent/durable acid-free paper
MANUFACTURED IN THE UNITED STATES OF AMERICA

To Kathy and Shannon,
with all my love and thanks

Contents

Introduction

A study of the body of criticism dealing with the work of Harold Pinter is likely to come to two general conclusions: first, the changing tone of critical reactions indicates a growing sophistication among the critics (or the human response of accepting the judgment of others, the "jumping on the bandwagon" syndrome, sometimes with a corresponding blindness); and second, that there is a very real sense of development within the author's canon.

Pinter has described the audience's reaction to several of his early plays. In an interview with Lawrence M. Bensky (The Paris Review, 1966, see no. 427), Pinter recalls that The Birthday Party was forced off the London stage after one week, having earned £260 11s. 8d. There were six people at the Thursday afternoon matinee, representing a take of £2 9s. (Pinter has a copy of the box office receipts framed and hanging on the wall of his Regents Park home). The first night performance of the German production of The Caretaker was even more disasterously received. In "Between the Lines" Pinter recounts what happened when he followed the Continental custom of taking a bow with the actors in Dusseldorf: "I was at once booed violently by what must have been the finest collection of booers in the world. I thought they were using megaphones, but it was pure mouth. The cast, though, were as dogged as the audience, and we took thirty-four curtain calls, all to boos. By the thirty-fourth there were only two people left in the house, still booing" (see no. 43).

Critical reaction was quite similar. With the exception of Harold Hobson's review in The Sunday Times of the original production of The Room at the Festival of University Drama held at Bristol University in December 1958, most early criticism followed the lead of The Times of London. "The first act," The Times stated about The Birthday Party, "sounds an offbeat note of madness; in the second the note has risen to a sort of delirium; and the third act studiously refrains from the slightest hint of what the other two may have been about." In the Manchester Guardian M.W.W. grumbled, "What all this means only Mr. Pinter knows, for as his characters speak in non-sequiturs, half-gibberish and lunatic ravings, they are

unable to explain their actions, thoughts, or feelings" (see no.
1465). These derisive opinions are reflected even in the titles of
many of the initial reviews about the London production of The Birthday Party in 1958. John Barber wrote "A Warning Perhaps, But a
Bore!" for the Daily Express (see no. 398), while Alan Dent charged
"Mr. Pinter Misses his Target" in the News Chronicle (see no. 688),
and the Evening Standard's Milton Shulman concluded, "Sorry, Mr.
Pinter, You're Just Not Funny Enough" (see no. 1731).

Clearly, the critics were not prepared for what Pinter had to
say or for the way in which he said it. Charges of obscurity and
lack of meaning were the keynotes of this early body of criticism.
As in the case of Samuel Beckett only a few years previously, however, the critics became accustomed to Pinter's themes and his new
modes of expression. Moreover, the dramas spoke to their audiences
and gained increasing popular support. In the meantime Pinter ex-
plained his concepts and dramatic theories in a series of articles
and interviews. Scholars, overcoming the first shock suffered on
viewing the plays, began to study the works seriously. While first
reviews of even the most recent plays still tend to display puzzle-
ment and a lack of understanding, meaning has begun to emerge for
the critical mind, and as various patterns are identified and reviewers learn what to look for, writers concentrate more and more
on lauding the plays' good points and discussing exactly what the
plays mean (becoming needlessly esoteric on some occasions and down-
right ridiculous on others, as they try to impose their interpretations on the works).

There are certainly those who have appreciated Pinter's writing
from the beginning, just as there are still critics, such as J. C.
Trewin, who consider Pinter a failure. Ironically, though, while a
strong segment of careful, reasoned scholarship has grown up about
Pinter's writing, another, representing an attitude completely opposite to that expressed in the earliest reviews, has also come into
being. Now Pinter's dramas are often met by wholehearted approval
and acclaim, at times from writers who obviously have no idea what
the plays are about or how they work. George Melloan, for example,
reviewed Old Times for the Wall Street Journal in 1971 (see no.
1422). He praised the play highly as a poetic abstract, a drama
which appeals to our emotions and which has no message. Among those
who have applied more judicious criteria in their assessments are
John Russell Taylor ("among British dramatists of our day...in the
long run he is likely to turn out the greatest of them all"--Anger
and After; see no. 1812), Martin Esslin ("indisputably one of the
most exciting and original dramatists to have emerged since World
War II"--The Peopled Wound; see no. 755), Joseph Chiari ("the most
gifted and versatile of the contemporary dramatists"--Landmarks of
Contemporary Drama; see no. 568), J. L. Styan (one of the "most
exciting playwrights in England"--The Dark Comedy; see no. 1784),

and Charles Marowitz ("the most important dramatist in 'the New Wave'"--"New Wave in a Dead Sea"; see no. 1400). Others are sure of Pinter's genius to such an extent that they make claims like that of Andrew Sarris in his study of The American Cinema (see no. 1678), which finds Pinter's screenplays the primary factor in the major film successes of several film directors.

Tracing the subject matter which has been the concern of writers over the years leads to an appreciation of Pinter's stylistic development and thematic evolution because the extent of that development becomes clear as the subject matter of the criticism changes. Loosely speaking, Pinter's writings through the mid-nineteen-sixties tended to become increasingly compact and spare. In the late sixties his style became much more lyric or "poetic" in nature, though it retains the tightness he has been working at from the beginning of his career.

Thematically, Pinter's dramatic writing can be divided into several very general categories. His first group of plays, The Room, The Birthday Party, and The Dumb Waiter, has been classified as "comedies of menace." In these early plays fear or menace is his prime interest; he is concerned with showing the existence of menace in the modern world. Translated into dramatic terms, this menace becomes a mysterious and undefined something which shuffles about outside the door, trying to get in. Those inside the room realize that there is something on the other side of the door and that they are in danger from its intrusion. The constant threat of invasion produces an atmosphere of menace, menace being the disruption of the status quo, though it is more significant than mere change because the inhabitants of the room will be exposed to expulsion and further unknown dangers, with a suggestion of physical harm.

There is an interesting progression in these plays: Rose tries to create a sanctuary in her room, but it is violated; then Stanley tries to run away from his menace, but it follows him to his hiding place; and finally The Dumb Waiter demonstrates that even the menacers are menaced. All three plays depict the disintegration of the individual under the pressure of menace.

In terms of Pinter's development as a writer, it is significant that the threat in The Room remains undefined. In the next two dramas he develops a pattern from the base established by The Room. The Birthday Party hints that the menace which threatens and eventually destroys the individual originates in society. The suggestion that society is the destructive force is brought out more clearly in The Dumb Waiter, though the source is still vague, and no specific facets of society are singled out as being responsible for the threat. While these two plays develop the idea of menace and define Pinter's related concepts of communication and verification, they are really extensions of elements introduced in The Room.

The following set of plays marks a transition. Having established the presence and nature of menace, Pinter begins to search
for its source and A Slight Ache represents the next step in the
dramatist's thematic development. Most of the fundamental themes
are the same as in the previous works, but for the first time Pinter
uses the subject of emotional needs as the hub around which he dis-
plays his ideas, and menace obviously develops from these needs.
What distinguishes A Slight Ache from the plays which precede it is
quite simple--the menace, in the form of a silent, disgustingly
filthy matchseller, is brought into the room by the inhabitants and
turns out to be harmless. As a result of the confrontation, however, Edward is destroyed. His failure to fulfill his wife's psychological and physical demands causes his downfall, but more
importantly, Pinter has demonstrated that menace is not a physical,
external matter, but derives from internal, phychological deficiencies.

The Caretaker continues the thematic direction indicated in A
Slight Ache by focusing on the three characters' attempts to form or
confirm attachments. Pinter has said that this play is "about love,"
and this is, indeed, the clue to understanding those dramas which
follow. Davies needs to establish a viable relationship with another human being but cannot. Mick and Aston struggle to sustain their
relationship with one another, a relationship based on their own
individual psychological needs.

In The Collection the actions of the characters are again aimed
at preserving their relationships with each other. The Lover probes
the difficulties a husband and wife have in reconciling their needs
for sex and their needs to maintain their special concept of marriage. The Homecoming shows what desperate lengths people will
go to in order to establish the relationships they require to achieve
psychological well-being. When psychological inadequacies become a
central concern as a source from which menace derives, Pinter moves
from discussing the symptom to discussing the disease. The movement
from menace to need is paralleled in the dramatist's use of a room
as a metaphor for a place of security and his very titles provide a
hint to the meaning inherent in this shift. The Room deals with a
physical structure, The Homecoming with abstract thoughts.

Having established that the source of menace exists within the
individual, Pinter turns next to an exploration of the nature of
the human mind--which brings him to his latest group of plays. Night,
Silence, Landscape, Old Times, Monologue, and No Man's Land are all
involved with the mind's working to reconcile itself with certain facts.
Where Pinter has been working in the present tense, he now realizes
that the present is a product of the past and his treatment of time
becomes the central feature in his most recent works; how, in fact,
the mind can create a past which alters the nature of the present.

Needless to say, critical subject matter has tended to parallel
Pinter's thematic evolution. From the first plays in the late

1950's through the early 1960's, articles and reviews focused mainly on the "comedy of menace" elements and the room-womb-tomb symbolism.

In the mid-1960's critical essayists became involved with Pinter's social criticism and his concern with the relationships developed between his characters. W. A. Darlington's Daily Telegraph review, "Mad Meg and Lodger Play Revels in Obscurity" (see no. 662), finding Pinter "most determinedly obscure," was typical of this type of criticism.

Pinter's use of language also became a subject of scholarship in the mid to late 1960's, and terms like "poetic" and "symbolic" were to be found with increasing frequency. In Ruby Cohen's "The World of Harold Pinter" (Tulane Drama Review; see no. 601), for instance, "Man vs. the System" with a "central victim-villain" conflict was proposed as Pinter's main theme, while Bernard F. Dukore's "The Theatre of Harold Pinter" (Tulane Drama Review; see no. 718) saw the plays as "a picture of contemporary man beaten down by the social forces around him" and emphasized the characters' avoidance of communication.

The functions of memory and time, and Pinter's lyrical approach to these topics, were the subjects of much of the writing through the mid-1970's, though many critics and scholars still have not satisfactorily come to grips with his latest set of plays. John Russell Brown in "Dialogue in Pinter and Others" (Critical Quarterly; see no. 499), Katherine H. Burkman in The Dramatic World of Harold Pinter (see no. 529), H. A. L. Craig in "Poetry in the Theatre" (New Statesman; see no. 636), Martin Esslin in The Peopled Wound (see no. 755), and Irving Wardle in "There's Music in that Room" (Encore; see no. 1940) have written on these elements.

Interestingly, attention is now being paid to Pinter's screenwriting, too (Enoch Brater's "Pinter's Homecoming on Celluloid," Modern Drama, is a recent example; see no. 478), and this may open up new approaches to his writing as a whole. Thomas P. Adler ("Pinter's Night: A Stroll Down Memory Lane"--Modern Drama; see no. 138), and Francis Gillen ("All these Bits and Pieces: Fragmentation and Choice in Pinter's Plays"--Modern Drama; see no. 873) are among the exceptions who show insights into Pinter's current writings.

While it is impossible to list all references to Pinter (there are literally thousands of film reviews in small town newspapers), an attempt has been made to include as much material as is feasible. Clearly some of the 2,048 entries in this bibliography are more significant than others, but I have included miscellaneous articles and reviews which merely repeat what is in a majority of other reviews with little or no annotation on the grounds that future scholars may find these items interesting simply because they are repetitive.

Generally speaking, the annotations are descriptive, as opposed to being evaluative. There are exceptions to this, in those cases where entries are judged to be especially important or good, or where entries are so weak or misleading that they should be avoided. If the title of an item adequately describes its content, the annotation has been omitted or kept to a minimum unless certain specific points within the work are considered valuable enough to merit special attention. This is especially true of production reviews which are often shallow or repetitive or both, though an attempt has been made to provide representative samplings, as indicated above. Scholarly studies tend to receive more attention than do production reviews. In those items which are more thoroughly annotated, the length of the annotation usually, though not always, may be indicative of the entry's importance. Every effort has been made to examine each entry; entries which have not been examined are marked with an asterisk (*). Several items which have appeared in previous Pinter bibliographies have not been included here for the simple reason that they do not mention Pinter, and several other items refered to in various pieces of criticism seem to be ghosts or they must include errors, for I was never able to locate them as they were described.

In overall structure the bibliography is divided into two parts: "Works by Harold Pinter" and "Literary Scholarship, Critical Articles, and Reviews Concerning Pinter's Work." The primary section is further divided into the categories "Plays," "Film Scripts," "Shorter Writings," "Juvenilia," "Collaborations," "Miscellaneous Interviews with Pinter," and "Translations of Pinter's Plays."

Because so many of Pinter's plays have been reprinted in so many different combinations with his other plays, those entries included in the "Plays" section are arranged chronologically, according to date of publication. If there are two or more entries with the same publication date, they are arranged in alphabetical order. No date is given for reprints by Samuel French and Dramatists Play Service (acting editions), since the copyright date printed is always the same as the play's first copyright date, regardless of the reprint's date of publication. Information about revised editions is contained in the original's entry rather than being listed separately. It should also be noted that Eyre Methuen published Plays: One in 1976 and that Grove Press published the first two volumes of Pinter's Complete Plays in early 1977 and Volume Three in 1978. Since all of the plays will be published in this series, I have not included this information in the bibliographical notations for the individual works.

Film scripts are also entered chronologically. Those items listed under the heading "Film Scripts" represent screenplays written by Pinter, whether they are based on his own stage plays or are adapted from someone else's work (this includes Butley, which Pinter directed on stage as well as on film). Unless otherwise indicated, publication information in this category is for the source of the film script.

Introduction

The "Shorter Writings" category is composed of sub-divisions for "Essays, Prose, and Speeches," "Poetry," "Short Stories," "Correspondence" (letters to the editors of newspapers), and "Miscellaneous." Within these sub-divisions items are arranged alphabetically.

"Juvenilia" and "Collaborations" entries are listed alphabetically (coincidentally, "Collaborations" are also in chronological order). "Miscellaneous Interviews with Pinter" are recorded chronologically because the date of the interview may be of more concern than who conducted the interview.

"Translations of Pinter's Plays" are arranged alphabetically, according to language, and then alphabetically within the language grouping. Incidentally, the translation section is interesting as a measure of Pinter's world-wide importance and popularity. There have been a total of sixty-nine translations of Pinter's plays, representing sixteen dramas and fourteen languages (from Czech to Turkish and everything in between, including Japanese and Serbo-Croatian). The most frequently translated play has been The Caretaker (thirteen times), followed by The Dumb Waiter (ten), The Birthday Party (seven), and The Lover (six). The Collection, The Homecoming, and A Night Out have all been translated five times, while there are four translations of both The Room and A Slight Ache. Night School, Old Times, and Silence have been translated twice, and The Dwarfs, Tea Party, The Basement, and Landscape have each been translated once.

Secondary sources, "Literary Scholarship, Critical Articles, and Reviews Concerning Pinter's Work," are listed alphabetically by the author's name, and when there are more than one item for an author, these are entered alphabetically under the author's name. In those instances where there are two or more entries with the same title by the same author (this is the case especially with reviewers when there is only a column title given), the items are in chronological order. Those listings for which the author's name is not known are placed in alphabetical order under the sub-heading "Anon." Normally this order is determined by the title, though there are miscellaneous articles concerning Pinter (primarily from the New York Times and The Times of London) which are entered by a descriptive title rather than the actual title. These miscellaneous articles are usually only short announcements relating to an upcoming production (ticket price, location, casting, or some similar notice) which contain no critical material, but which may prove of value to scholars interested in production details or history, or some related topic. Finally, those entries which have a letter following their numerical designation (i.e., 657a) are so listed because of when the item was collected (current publications and those from abroad were slow in arriving); the letter does not indicate a relationship with any other entry.

Acknowledgments

I would like to thank my wife, Kathy, for her help in preparing this manuscript. The Modern Language Association and Patricia M. Colling of <u>Dissertation Abstracts International</u> were kind enough to provide me with information regarding entries to be included in their forthcoming publications, insuring that this bibliography would be as up-to-date as possible. Claudia Menza and Grove Press provided me with information about Pinter's works as they were published. Christing Miller of the <u>New Yorker</u> staff, Katherine Osgood of the <u>Vogue</u> staff, Katrine Ames of the <u>Newsweek</u> staff, and Stanley Kauffman and Andrew Sarris all helped me retrieve film reviews. The reference staffs at the University of Florida Research Library and at the Santa Fe Regional Library (Gainesville, Florida) were very helpful in tracing a number of items. Tetsuo Kishi's aid in locating articles on Pinter published in Japan was invaluable. Susan Elliott very graciously passed on information available to her, including her bibliography. Several other individuals were kind enough to send me notices regarding specific titles. And, finally, I would like to thank the Humanities Council for their help in the form of a summer research grant which allowed me some time to put this manuscript into publishable form, Gene Moss for his continuing help, and especially my daughter, Shannon, for taking naps at strategic times.

Further Sources

Note: There are several continuing or annual bibliographical sources
which might be examined for further references to Pinter These include:

Abstracts of English Studies (monthly, September through July).
American Humanities Index (annual).
Annual Bibliography of English Language and Literature.
Arts and Humanities Citation Index (three times a year).
Book Review Digest (monthly).
Book Review Index (bi-monthly).
British Humanities Index (annual).
Cumulative Book Index (annual).
Dissertation Abstracts International (monthly).
English Studies ("Current Literature" section).
Film Literature Index (quarterly).
Film Research in Progress (quarterly).
Humanities Index (quarterly).
Index to Book Reviews in the Humanities (annual).
Index to Theses (London: Aslib; annual).
Journal of Modern Literature ("Annual Bibliography"--February
    issue).
Literature and Essay Index (semi-annual).
MLA International Bibliography (annual; companion is the MLA
    Abstracts of Articles in Scholarly Journals, also annual,
    though currently not being published).
Modern Drama (annual bibliography--September issue).
Reader's Guide to Periodical Literature (monthly).
Theatre Documentation ("Scholarly Works in Progress" and
    individual issues).
Theatre Research (individual issues).
Theatre Quarterly ("Current Bibliography").
The New York Times Index (annual).
The Times Index (London; annual).
Twentieth Century Literature ("Current Bibliography"--Octo-
    ber issue).
The Year's Work in English Studies (annual).

Works by Harold Pinter

1   The Birthday Party. London: Encore, 1959. Revised in
     Seven Plays of the Modern Theatre, edited by Harold
     Clurman. New York: Grove, 1967. Reprinted: London:
     Samuel French (British acting edition); New York:
     Dramatists Play Service (American acting edition).
     See also no. 32.

2   The Birthday Party: A Play in Three Acts. London: Methuen,
     1960. Revised 1962; reprinted: New York: Grove, 1969.

3   The Birthday Party and Other Plays. London: Methuen, 1960.
         Includes The Room and The Dumb Waiter. The Room has
     been reprinted: London: Samuel French (British acting
     edition); New York: Dramatists Play Service (American Act-
     ing edition). The Dumb Waiter was reprinted in: Cohn and
     Dukore, eds. Twentieth Century Drama: England, Ireland,
     the United States. New York: Random House, 1966; in:
     New English Dramatists, No. 3, edited by Tom Maschler.
     London: Penguin, 1961; in: Soule, The Theatre of the
     Mind. Englewood Cliffs: Prentice-Hall, 1974; and re-
     printed: New York: Dramatists Play Service (American
     acting edition). Reviewed: See no. 1976.

4   The Caretaker. London: Methuen, 1960. Revised 1962.
     Reprinted in: Hewes, The Best Plays of 1961-1962.
     New York and Toronto: Dodd, 1962; in Popkin, Modern
     British Drama (originally The New British Drama). New
     York: Grove, 1964; London: Samuel French (British
     acting edition); New York: Dramatists Play Service
     (American acting edition). Recorded on Oriole Records,
     M. G. 20093-4.
         Typedrafts of The Caretaker are held by the Lilly
     Library, Indiana University. Reviewed: See nos. 186,
     371, 1344, 1976.

Plays

5   A Slight Ache. Tomorrow, Oxford, No. 4 (1960). Reprinted:
     London: Samuel French (British acting edition); New York:
     Dramatists Play Service (American acting edition).

6   A Slight Ache and Other Plays. London: Methuen, 1961.
     Revised 1970.
          The 1970 edition includes corrections (the names of the
     actors playing Pete and Mark in the Arts Theatre pro-
     duction were listed in reverse order originally, and the
     photographer's name was misspelled). Includes A Night
     Out, The Dwarfs, and the revue sketches "Trouble in the
     Works," "The Black and White," "Request Stop," "Last to
     Go," and "Applicant." A Slight Ache was reprinted in:
     Spanos, Existentialism 2. New York: Thomas Y. Crowell,
     1976; in: Auburn and Burkman, Drama Through Performance.
     Boston: Houghton Mifflin, 1977; in: Bender, et. al.,
     Modernism in Literature. New York: Holt, Rinehart and
     Winston, 1977. A Night Out was reprinted: London:
     Samuel French (British acting edition); New York: Drama-
     tists Play Service (American acting edition). The Dwarfs
     was reprinted: London: Samuel French (British acting
     edition); New York: Dramatists Play Service (American
     acting edition). Revue Sketches were reprinted: New
     York: Dramatists Play Service (American acting edition).
     The Dwarfs and Eight Revue Sketches were reprinted: New
     York: Dramatists Play Service (American acting edition).
     "The Black and White" was reprinted in: The Spectator,
     205 (1 July 1960), 16, in a prose version. "The Black
     and White" was reprinted in: Flourish (magazine of the
     Royal Shakespeare Theatre Club), Summer, 1965; in Trans-
     atlantic Review, 21 (Summer 1966), 51-52. "Last to Go"
     was recorded on Kenneth Williams, Decca Records, DFE
     8548; on Pieces of Eight, Decca Records, SKL 4084. Re-
     viewed: See no. 596.

7   The Birthday Party and The Room. New York: Grove, 1961.
     Revised 1968.

8   The Caretaker and The Dumb Waiter: Two Plays. New York:
     Grove, 1961. Revised 1965.

9   Three Plays: A Slight Ache, The Collection, The Dwarfs.
     New York: Grove, 1962. The Collection was reprinted in:
     Hewes, The Best Plays of 1962-1963. New York and Toronto:
     Dodd, 1963; New York: Dramatists Play Service (American
     acting edition).

10   The Collection and The Lover. London: Methuen, 1963. Revised
       1964. The Lover was reprinted: London: Samuel French
       (British acting edition); New York: Dramatists Play Ser-
       vice (American acting edition).
           Also includes reprint of "The Examination" (which first
       appeared in Prospect), in prose. See no. 56.

11   "Dialogue for Three." Stand, 6, No. 3 (1963), 4-5.
       Revue sketch.

12   The Dwarfs and Eight Revue Sketches. New York: Dramatists
       Play Service (American acting edition), 1965.
           Includes the revue sketches: "Trouble in the Works,"
       "The Black and White," "Request Stop," "Last to Go,"
       "Applicant," "Interview," "That's All," and "That's Your
       Trouble."

13   The Homecoming. London: Methuen, 1965. Second edition,
       London: Methuen, and New York: Grove, 1966. Reprinted
       London: 1968. Reprinted in: Guernsey, The Best Plays
       of 1966-1967. New York: Dodd, 1967. Reprinted: Lon-
       don: Karnac/Curwen, 1968; London: Samuel French (British
       acting edition). See also nos. 35 and 73. Reviewed:
       See nos. 337, 1765, 1821, 2008.
           The Karnac/Curwen edition is limited to 200 copies
       signed by Pinter and Harold Cohen, the artist who created
       nine lithographs for the volume. Reviewed: See no. 1765.

14   The Lover and Other Plays. New York: Grove, 1967. Includes
       Tea Party and The Basement.

15   The Lover, Tea Party, The Basement. New York: Grove, 1967.

16   "Special Offer." In Hinchcliffe, Harold Pinter (See no.
       1021), pp. 73-74.
       Revue sketch.

17   Tea Party and Other Plays. London: Methuen, 1967.
           Includes The Basement and Night School. Tea Party was
       reprinted: New York: Dramatists Play Service (American
       acting edition). The Basement was reprinted: New York:
       Dramatists Play Service (American acting edition).
           Reviewed: See nos. 677, 1624, 1850.

18   A Night Out, Night School, Revue Sketches: Early Plays by
       Harold Pinter. New York: Grove, 1968.

19   Three Plays: Tea Party, The Basement, and The Lover. New
       York: Grove, 1968.

Plays

20 <u>Landscape</u>. London: Emanuel Wax for Pendragon, 1968. Reprinted in: <u>Evergreen Review</u>, No. 68 (July 1969), pp.
55-61.
The Pendragon publication is a limited edition, copies
1-1000 for Great Britain, 1001-2000 for the United States.

21 <u>Landscape and Silence</u>. London: Methuen, 1969. Reprinted:
New York: Grove, 1970.
Also includes <u>Night</u>. Reviewed: <u>See</u> nos. 682, 684,
1664.

22 <u>Old Times</u>. London: Methuen, 1971, and New York: Grove
(Black Cat), 1971. Reprinted: New York: Grove (Evergreen), 1973; New York: Dramatists Play Service (American
acting edition).
Reviewed: <u>See</u> nos. 281, 1482, 1664.

23 <u>Monologue</u>. London: Covent Garden Press, 1973. Limited
edition.

24 <u>No Man's Land</u>. London: Methuen, 1975, and New York: Grove
1975. Reprinted: <u>The New Review</u>, No. 13, 1975.
Reviewed: <u>See</u> no. 551.

25 <u>Plays: One</u>. London: Eyre Methuen, 1976. Published in the
United States as <u>Complete Works: One</u>. New York: Grove
Press, 1977.
Includes reprints of <u>The Birthday Party</u>, <u>The Room</u>,
<u>The Dumb Waiter</u>, <u>A Slight Ache</u>, <u>A Night Out</u>, "The Black
and White" (prose version), "The Examination," and "Be-
tween the Lines."

26 <u>Complete Works: Two</u>. New York: Grove Press, 1977.
Includes reprints of <u>The Caretaker</u>, <u>Night School</u>, <u>The
Dwarfs</u>, <u>The Collection</u>, <u>The Lover</u>, "Trouble in the Works,"
"The Black and White" (revue sketch), "Request Stop,"
"Last to Go," "Special Offer," and "Writing for Myself."

26a <u>Complete Works: Three</u>. New York: Grove, 1978.
Contains <u>The Homecoming</u>, <u>Landscape</u>, <u>Silence</u>, <u>The Base-
ment</u>, "Night," "That's All," "That's Your Trouble,"
"Interview," "Applicant," "Dialogue for Three," "Tea
Party" (short story), <u>Tea Party</u>, <u>Mac</u>.

FILM SCRIPTS

27 <u>The Servant</u>. Released 1962. From Robin (Sir Robert)
Maugham's novel, <u>The Servant</u>. London: Falcon, 1948.

4

     Reprinted: New York: Harcourt Brace, 1949; London: Heinemann, 1964. Screenplay copyright: Springbok Films, Ltd., 1971.
     <u>See also</u> no. 33.

28   <u>The Caretaker</u> (<u>The Guest</u>). Released 1963. Based on Pinter's original stage play.
     <u>See</u> nos. 4 and 8.

29   <u>The Pumpkin Eater</u>. Released 1964. From Penelope Mortimer's novel, <u>The Pumpkin Eater</u>. London: Hutchinson, 1962. Reprinted New York: McGraw-Hill. Screenplay copyright: Columbia Pictures Industries, Inc., 1971.
     <u>See also</u> no. 33.

30   <u>The Quiller Memorandum</u>. Released 1966. From Adam Hall's novel, <u>The Berlin Memorandum</u>. London: Collins, 1965. Reprinted: New York: Simon and Schuster. Screenplay copyright: Ivan Foxwell Productions, Ltd., 1971.
     <u>See also</u> no. 33.

31   <u>Accident</u>. Released 1967. From Nicholas Mosley's novel, <u>Accident</u>. London: Hodder and Stoughton, 1965. Reprinted: New York: Coward, McCann and Geohegan. Screenplay copyright: London Independent Producers (Distribution), Ltd., 1971.
     <u>See also</u> no. 33.

32   <u>The Birthday Party</u>. Released 1969. Based on Pinter's original stage play. <u>See</u> nos. 1, 2, 3, and 7. Screenplay: Continental Distributors, 1968.
     A copy of the filmscript is held in Special Collections at the University of Southern California Doheny Library (Los Angeles).

33   <u>Five Screenplays</u>. London: Methuen, 1971. Reprinted: New York: Grove, 1974; London: Eyre Methuen, 1977.
     Includes <u>The Servant</u>, <u>The Pumpkin Eater</u>, <u>The Quiller Memorandum</u>, <u>Accident</u>, and <u>The Go-Between</u>. <u>See</u> nos. 27, 29, 30, 31, and 34. Reviewed: <u>See</u> nos. 180, 224, 225, 227, 836, 1623.

34   <u>The Go-Between</u>. Released 1971. From L. P. Hartley's novel, <u>The Go-Between</u>. London: Hamish and Hamilton, 1953. Reprinted: New York: Knopf, 1954; New York: Avon, 1968; New York: Stein and Day. Screenplay copyright: World Film Services, Ltd., 1971.

Film Scripts

> A copy of the filmscript (Columbia, 1971) is held in Special Collections at the Doheny Library, University of Southern California (Los Angeles). See also no. 33.

35 The Homecoming. Released 1973. Based on Pinter's original stage play. See no. 13. Motion picture sound track recorded on Caedmon Records, TRS 361.

36 Butley. Released 1974. From Simon Gray's play, Butley. New York: Viking, 1974. Motion picture sound track recorded on Caedmon Records, TRS 362.
Film directed by Pinter.

37 The Last Tycoon. Released 1976. From F. Scott Fitzgerald's novel, The Last Tycoon. New York: Scribner's, 1941.

UNRELEASED FILM SCRIPTS

38 The Compartment. New York: Grove (Evergreen), 1963. An original screenplay by Pinter. Bound with Eugene Ionesco's The Hard-Boiled Egg.

39 The Proust Screenplay (Remembrance of Things Past). New York: Grove Press, 1977. From Proust's novel, A la recherche du temps perdu (1912-27), edited by Pierre Clarac and Andre Ferré. 3 vols. Paris: Gallimard, 1954. Translated by C. K. Scott Moncrieff and Frederick A. Blasson. 2 vols. New York: Random House, 1941. Reprinted: New York: Vintage, 1970. 7 vols.
Pinter's screenplay of Marcel Proust's Remembrance of Things Past. Joseph Losey and Barbara Bray are cited as collaborators.

40 Langrishe, Go Down. From the novel, Langrishe, Go Down, by Aidan Higgins. New York: Grove, 1966.

SHORTER WRITINGS

ESSAYS, PROSE, AND SPEECHES

*41 "Art as Therapy, Hobby, or Experience." In Essays in Honour of William Gallacher. Berlin, 1966, pp. 234-36.
Cited in Imhof (no. 1098), p. 4.

42 "Beckett." In Beckett at Sixty: A Festschrift, edited by John Calder. London: Calder and Boyars, 1967, p. 86.

6

A short extract from a letter to a friend in which
Pinter declares that Beckett is "far and away the finest
writer working," because of his honest portrayal of life.

43   "Between the Lines." Speech given at the Seventh National
     Students Drama Festival, Bristol; published in <u>The Sunday
     Times</u> (London), 4 March 1962, p. 25.
          An important revelation by Pinter of his concepts of
     verification and the use of language and paralanguage,
     often for defense.

44   "Harold Pinter Replies." <u>New Theatre Magazine</u>, 11, No. 2
     (January 1961), 8-10.
          An answer to the charge that he is not politically in-
     volved in his works.

45   "The Knight Has Been Unruly: Memories of Sir Donald Wolfit."
     <u>The Listener</u>, 79 (18 April 1968), 501.
          Commentary on Wolfit's acting by Pinter included.

46   <u>Mac</u>. London: Emanuel Wax for Pendragon, 1968. Reprinted in:
     <u>Harper's Bazaar</u>, 102 (November 1968), 234-35; in: <u>Good
     Talk 2: An Anthology from BBC Radio</u>, edited by Derwent
     May, 1969. Reprinted: New York: Grove, 1977.
          A brief reminiscence of Pinter's association with the
     Irish actor-manager Anew McMaster. The Pendragon publi-
     cation is a limited edition, copies 1-1000 for Great
     Britain, 1001-2000 for the United States. Reviewed:
     <u>See</u> no. 1890.

47   "Memories of Cricket." <u>Daily Telegraph Magazine</u>, 16 May 1969.

48   "Pinter on Beckett." <u>New Theatre Magazine</u>, 11, No. 3 [May-
     June 1971], 3.

49   "Pinter on Pinter." <u>Cinebill</u>, 1, No. 2 (October 1973), 7.
          Remarks on the differences between writing for stage
     and for screen made on accepting the Shakespeare Prize at
     the University of Hamburg on June 4, 1970.

50   "Speech: Hamburg 1970." <u>Theatre Quarterly</u>, 1, No. 3 (July-
     September 1971), 3-4.

51   "Two People in a Room: Playwriting." <u>New Yorker</u>, 43 (25
     February 1967), 34-36.

Shorter Writings

52   "An Unpublished Speech." Theatre Quarterly, No. 3 (August-
        October 1974).
            Pinter comments on the pain of creation.

53   "Writing for Myself." Twentieth Century, 168 (February 1961),
        172-75.
            Pinter comments on the difficulties of writing stage
        drama, the influence of his acting career on his play-
        writing, the realistic/non-realistic qualities of his
        writing, and his refusal to write political drama.

54   "Writing for the Theatre." Evergreen Review, 8 (August-
        September 1964), 80-82. Reprinted in: Popkin, The New
        British Drama (See no. 1561), pp. 575-80; in: Goetsch,
        English Dramatic Theories IV: Twentieth Century (See
        no. 900), pp. 118-24.
            Contains much of the same material as in "Between the
        Lines" (See no. 43). Not actually written by Pinter but
        compiled by Findlater from the tape of an interview and
        reportedly considered unsatisfactory by Pinter.

SHORT STORIES

55   "The Black and White." The Spectator, 205 (1 July 1960),
        16. Reprinted in: Pinter, Complete Works: One. See no.
        25.
            Prose version.

56   "The Examination." Prospect, Summer 1959. Reprinted in:
        The Collection and The Lover. See no. 10.

57   "Tea Party." BBC Third Programme, 1964. See also nos. 14,
        15, 17, and 19.
            Read by Pinter.

58   "Tea Party." Playboy, January 1965, p. 124. See also nos.
        14, 15, 17, and 19.
            A prose version.

POETRY

59   "Afternoon." Twentieth Century, 169 (February 1961), 218.

60   "All of That." The Times Literary Supplement (London), 69
        (11 December 1970), 1436. Reprinted in: Vogue, 158
        (July 1971), 98.

61   "New Year in the Midlands" and "Chandeliers and Shadows."
        Poetry London, 19 (August 1950).
            Poems, concluding stanzas interchanged.

62   "New Year in the Midlands," "Rural Idyll," "European Revels."
        Poetry London, 20 (November 1950).
            Poems, by "Harold Pinta."

63   "One a Story, Two a Death." Poetry London, 22 (Summer 1951).
        A poem.

64   "poem." New York Times Magazine, 5 December 1971, p. 135.

65   Poems. London: Enitharmon, 1968.
            Includes most of Pinter's poems which have appeared in
        periodicals, with the exception of "Rural Idyll," "Euro-
        pean Revels," and "One a Story, Two a Death" which were
        published in Poetry London under the name of "Harold Pinta."
        Also includes "Kullus." The 18 poems were selected by Alan
        Clodd. Reviewed: See no. 1710. See also no. 66.

66   Poems. Revised edition. London: Enitharmon, 1971.
            The revised edition contains nine additional poems.
        See also no. 65.

CORRESPONDENCE

67   "Distressing." New York Times, 26 April 1970, p. 180.
            A letter to the editor in which Pinter rejects Clive
        Barnes' assessment (See no. 414) of the New York production
        of Landscape and Silence as being vastly inferior to the
        London production. Pinter replies that the Lincoln Cen-
        ter and director Peter Gill did not "betray" his inten-
        tions ("I totally reject this") and that the "emphasis of
        simplicity, economy and clarity" was "rewarding."

68   Letter to the Editor. The Sunday Times (London), 14 August
        1960, p. 21.
            Pinter's reply to Leonard Russell's criticism of the
        laughter evoked by The Caretaker: "The Caretaker is
        funny, up to a point. Beyond that point it ceases to be
        funny, and it was because of that point that I wrote it."
        (See no. 1656).

69   Letter to the Editor. The Times (London), 9 December 1970,
        p. 11.
            Cited in The Times Index (1970).

Shorter Writings

70   Letter to the Editor. The Times (London), 10 December 1973,
        p. 17.
           Pinter comments on the film industry.

71   Letter to the Editor. The Times (London), 22 March 1974,
        p. 17.
           Pinter comments on the imprisonment of Vladimir
        Bukovsky.

72   Letter to the Editor. The Times (London), 7 June 1975,
        p. 13.
           Cited in The Times Index (1975).

MISCELLANEOUS

73   The Homecoming manuscript notes and a page of the typescript.
        Reproduced in London Magazine, New Series No. 100 (July-
        August 1969), 153-54.
           The notes are just snips from here and there in the
        play; the typescript is the entrance of Ruth and Teddy.
        Another page of the original typescript, including Pin-
        ter's note, is also reproduced in Writers at Work: Third
        Series. New York: Viking, 1967, p. [348]. Part of the
        first exchange between Max and Lenny is reproduced. See
        no. 427.

JUVENILIA

74   "Blood Sports." Hackney Downs School Magazine, No. 163
        (Autumn 1947), 23-24.
           An essay.
75   "Dawn." Hackney Downs School Magazine, No. 161 (Spring
        1947), 27.
           A poem.

76   "James Joyce." Hackney Downs School Magazine, No. 160
        (Christmas 1946), 32-33.
           An essay expressing admiration for A Portrait of the
        Artist as a Young Man, Ulysses, and Finnegan's Wake.

77   "O beloved maiden." Hackney Downs School Magazine, No. 162
        (Summer 1947), 14.
           A poem.

78   "Speech: Realism and Post-Realism in the French Cinema."
        Hackney Downs School Magazine, No. 163 (Autumn 1947), 13.

79   "Speech: Supporting the Motion that 'In View of its Progress in the Last Decade, the Film is More Promising in its Future as an Art than the Theatre.'" Hackney Downs School Magazine, No. 164 (Spring 1948), 12.

80   "Speech: That a United Europe Would Be the Only Means of Preventing War." Hackney Downs School Magazine, No. 161 (Spring 1947), 14.

81   "Speech: That the War is Inevitable." Hackney Downs School Magazine, No. 162 (Summer 1947), 9.

COLLABORATIONS

82   Pinter, Harold and Clive Donner. "Filming 'The Caretaker.'" Transatlantic Review, No. 13 (Summer, 1963), 17-26. Reprinted in: McCrindle, Behind the Scenes (See no. 1366); in: Hurt, Focus on Film and Theatre (See no. 1092).
       An interview by Kenneth Cavander.

83   Pinter, Harold, John Fuller, and Peter Redgrove, eds. New Poems. 1967. Reprinted: London: Hutchinson, 1968. Reviewed: See no. 181.
       A P.E.N. anthology of contemporary poetry.

84   Pinter, Harold, Arnold Wesker, and George Steiner. "Harold Pinter, Arnold Wesker, and George Steiner appeal..." the Jewish Quarterly the only Anglo-Jewish literary magazine in Britain appeals to you.... London: Jewish Literary Trust, 1976, p. [2].
       An appeal for support of The Jewish Quarterly which appears over the signatures of Pinter, Wesker, and Steiner in a pamphlet printed for the Jewish Literary Trust.

MISCELLANEOUS INTERVIEWS WITH PINTER

85   Interview with John Sherwood. BBC European Service. In "The Rising Generation" series, 3 March 1960.**

86   Interview with Hallam Tennyson. BBC General Overseas Service. 7 August 1960.**

87   Interview with Kenneth Tynan. BBC Home Service. Recorded 19 August 1960, broadcast 28 October 1960.**

**Duplicated manuscript exists.

Miscellaneous Interviews

88 Interview with Carl Wildman and Donald McWhinnie. BBC Net-
    work Three. In the "Talking of Theatre" series, 7 March
    1961.**

89 Interview with Laurence Kitchin and Paul Mayersberg. BBC
    Third Programme. In "New Comment," 10 October 1963.

90 Interview with John Kershaw. ITV. 1964.

91 Interview in "The Actor," a CBS Television special, 1968.

92 Interview with Joan Bakewell. BBC 2 TV. 11 September 1969.

TRANSLATIONS OF PINTER'S PLAYS

CZECH

93 Norozeniny [The Birthday Party] and Navrat Domu [The Home-
    coming]. Translated by Milan Lukĕs. In Anglicke
    Absurdni Divaldo. Prague: Orbis, 1966. Navrat Domu
    reprinted in Svetlova Literatura, No. 4 (1966).

94 Správce [The Caretaker]. Translated by Milan Lukĕs. Prague:
    Orbis, 1966.

DANISH

95 En Tur i Byen [A Night Out]. Translated by Klaus Rifbjerg.
    "En Tur i Byen--Moderne Englesk Dramatik i TV og Radio."
    Fredensborg: Arena, 1962.

96 Vicevaerten [The Caretaker]. Translated by H. C. Branner.
    Fredensborg: Arena, 1961. Reprinted in: Udgivet au
    Dansklaererforeninged ved Th. Borup Jensen. Copenhagen:
    Gyldendal, 1972.
        Includes "Dramaturgisk analyse" and "Arbejdsspørgsmál"
    by Jensen (See no. 1111).

DUTCH

97 De Kamer, De Dienstlift, De Huisbewaarder, De Collectie,
    De Minnaar [The Room; The Dumb Waiter; The Caretaker;
    The Collection; The Lover]. Amsterdam: Uitgeverij De
    Bij, 1966.

FRENCH

98   L'Anniversaire [The Birthday Party]. Translated by Eric
       Kahane. Paris: Gallimard, 1968.

99   La Collection suivi de l'Amant et de Le Gardien [The Collec-
       tion; The Lover; The Caretaker]. Translated by Eric
       Kahane. Paris: Gallimard, 1967.

100   Le Retour [The Homecoming]. Translated by Eric Kahane.
       L'Avant-Scène, No. 378 (15 April 1967).

GERMAN

101   Dramen [Dramas]. Translated by Renate Esslin and Martin
       Esslin. Hamburg: Rowohlt, 1970.
          Includes Landschaft, Schweigen, Der Hausmeister, Eine
       Nacht ausser Haus, Abendkurs, and Ein leichter Schmerz
       [Landscape; Silence; The Caretaker; A Night Out; Night
       School; A Slight Ache].

102   Die Geburtstagsfeier, Der stumme Diener, Das Zimmer, Die
       Zwerge [The Birthday Party; The Dumb Waiter; The Room;
       The Dwarfs]. Translated by Willy H. Thiem. Revised
       edition. Hamburg: Rowohlt, 1969.

103   Der Hausmeister, Eine Nacht ausser Haus, Abendkurs, Ein
       leichter Schmerz [The Caretaker; A Night Out; Night
       School; A Slight Ache]. Translated by Willy H. Thiem.
       Revised edition. Hamburg: Rowohlt, 1969.

104   Die Heimkehr, Der Liebhaber, Die Kollektion, Teegesellschaft,
       Tiefparterre [The Homecoming; The Lover; The Collection;
       Tea Party; The Basement]. Translated by Willy H. Thiem.
       Hamburg: Rowohlt, 1967.

HUNGARIAN

105   A Gondnok [The Caretaker]. Translated by Tibor Bartos.
       In Mai Angol Drámák. Budapest: Europa, 1965.

ITALIAN

106   Il Gardiano e altri drammi [The Caretaker and Other Dramas].
       Translated by Elio Nissim. Milan: Bompiani, 1962.
          Includes La Stanza [The Room] and Il Calapranzi [The
       Dumb Waiter].

Translations

107 Un leggero malessere and Una serata fouori [A Slight Ache;
     A Night Out]. Translated by Laura del Bono and Elio
     Nissim. In Teatro Uno, edited by L. Codignola. Turin:
     Einaudi, 1962.

JAPANESE

108 Pintá Gikyoku Zenshu [Collected Plays of Harold Pinter].
     Edited by Tetsuo Kishi. Tokyo: Takeuchi Shotem, 1970.
     Includes Heya [The Room], translated by Tetsuo Kishi;
     Ryóri Shókot [The Dumb Waiter], translated by Kishi;
     Básudei Pátí [The Birthday Party], translated by Koji
     Numasswa; Kasuka na Itami [A Slight Ache], translated by
     Yushi Odashima; Yoasobi [A Night Out], translated by
     Yushi Odashima; Kanrinin [The Caretaker], translated by
     Tetsuo Kishi, revised edition; Naito Sukuru [Night School],
     translated by Koji Numasaw. Kanrinin was reprinted in:
     Gendai Sekai Engeki [Contemporary World Drama], Vol. 7.
     Tokyo: Hakusuisha, 1970.

109 Basudei Pati [The Birthday Party]. Translated by Koji
     Numasawa. In Pinta Gikyoku Zenshu. See no. 108.

110 Damu Weita [The Dumb Waiter]. Translated by Tetsuo Arakawa.
     Shingeki, September 1962.

111 Damu Witta [The Dumb Waiter]. Translated by Kobo Abe. Umi,
     February 1975.

112 Heya [The Room]. Translated by Tetsuo Kishi. In Pinta
     Gikyoku Senshu. See no. 108.

113 Kanrinin [The Caretaker]. Translated by Tetsuo Kishi.
     Shingeki, October 1968.

114 Kanrinin [The Caretaker]. Translated by Tetsuo Kishi.
     Revised edition. In Pinta Gikyoku Zenshu and Gendai
     Sekai Engeki. See no. 108.

115 Kasuka na Itami [A Slight Ache]. Translated by Yushi
     Odashima. In Pinta Gikyoku Zenshu. See no. 108.

116 Kikyo [The Homecoming]. Translated by Makoto Sugiyama. In
     Konnichi no Eibei Engeki [Contemporary English and Ameri-
     can Drama], Vol. 4. Tokyo: Hakusuisha, 1968.

117 Korekushon [The Collection]. Translated by Toshio Tamura.
     Gendai Engeki, No. 1, January 1967.

118 Mukashi no Hibi [Old Times]. Translated by Tetsuo Kishi. In
     Chikuma Sekai Bungaku Taikei [Chikuma Collection of World
     Literature]. Vol. 85. Tokyo: Chikuma Shobo, 1974.

119 Naito Sukuru [Night School]. Translated by Koji Numasawa.
     In Pinta Gikyoku Zenshu. See no. 108.

120 Ryori Shokoki [The Dumb Waiter]. Translated by Tetsuo
     Kishi. In Pinta Gikyoku Zenshu. See no. 108.

121 Yoasobi [A Night Out]. Translated by Yushi Odashima. In
     Pinta Gikyoku Zenshu. See no. 108.

POLISH

122 Dawne Czasy (Old Times]. Translated by B. Taborski. Dialog,
     No. 2, 1972.

122a Kochanek [The Lover]. Translated by B. Taborski. Dialog,
      No. 8 (1966).

123 Powrot do Dumo [The Homecoming]. Translated by Adam Tarn.
     Dialog, No. 12 (1965).

124 Urodziny Stanleys [The Birthday Party]. Translated by Adam
     Tarn. Dialog, No. 10 (1960).

PORTUGUESE

125 Feliz Aniversario [The Birthday Party]. Translated by
     Artur Ramos and Jaime Salazar Sempaio. Lisbon: Preto,
     1967.

126 O Monte Cargas [The Dumb Waiter]. Translated by Luis de
     Stau Moneiro. In Tempo de Teatro (Lisbon), No. 3 [n. d.].

SERBO-CROATIAN

127 Bez Pogovora [The Dumb Waiter]. In Avangardna Drama.
     Belgrade, 1964.

SPANISH

128 La Colleccion; El Amante [The Collection; The Lover].
     Translated by Luis Escobar. In Primero Acto, No. 83
     (1967).

129 El Conserje [The Caretaker]. Translated by Josefina Vidal
     and F. M. Lorda Alaiz. In Teatro inglés. Madrid:
     Aquilar, 1966.

Translations

130   El Cuidor, El Amante, El Montaplatas [The Caretaker; The
          Lover; The Dumb Waiter]. Translated by Manuel Barbera.
          Buenos Aires: Nueva Vision, 1965.

131   El Portero [The Caretaker]. Translated by T. R. Trives.
          In Primero Acto, January 1962.

SWEDISH

132   Mathissen [The Dumb Waiter]. Translated by Lars Göran
          Calsson. In I En Akt, edited by Ingvar Holm. Stockholm:
          Aldus, 1966.

TURKISH

133   Dodumgünü Partisi [The Birthday Party]. Translated by
          Memet Fuat. Published by De Yayinevi, 1965.

Writings about Harold Pinter
Literary Scholarship, Critical Articles, and Reviews

134   AARON, JULES L. "The Audience in the Mirror: the Role of Game Ritual in Contemporary Theatre." <u>Dissertation Abstracts International</u>, 31: 5563A. Ph.D. dissertation, New York University, 1970.

        Game-ritual functions as a shaping force in the dramas of Ionesco, Beckett, Albee, Genet, and Pinter. <u>The Caretaker</u> is used as a prime example.

135   ABIRACHED, ROBERT. "Le Jeune Théâtre Anglais." <u>Nouvelle Revue Francaise</u>, 29, No. 170 (February 1967), 314-21.

        Pinter, James Saunders, Osborne, Ann Jellicoe, and Arden have moved beyond avant-garde theatre to create a new kind of psychological drama. In French.

136   ABRAHAMS, WILLIAM. "Now and in England." <u>Atlantic</u>, February 1976, pp. 98, 102.

        Review of <u>No Man's Land</u>. Britain's current crises may foretell its coming doom in the not too distant future, and Pinter has "skillfully and disturbingly" evoked the atmosphere of depression and strident gaiety which symbolizes the times.

137   ADELMAN, IRVING and RITA DWORKIN. <u>Modern Drama: A Checklist of Critical Literature on Twentieth Century Plays</u>. Metuchen, N. J.: Scarecrow, 1967, pp. 241-42.

        A very short bibliography. Reviewed: <u>See</u> no. 555.

138   ADLER, THOMAS P. "Pinter's <u>Night</u>: A Stroll Down Memory Lane." <u>Modern Drama</u>, 17, No. 4 (December 1974), 461-65.

        A nice explication of <u>Night</u> as a poetic drama about time, including "an ongoing time of continual love and adoration." Surprisingly, Adler sees <u>Night</u> as the only play in Pinter's canon which portrays "a completely satisfactory and mutually satisfying relationship between a husband and wife."

*139   ABRENS, RUDIGER. "Das moderne englishe Drama: Möglichkeiten
       der Behandlung im Unterricht der gymnasialen Oberstufe."
       Der fremdsprachliche Unterricht, 4, No. 13 (February 1970),
       15-28.
           In German. Cited in Imhof (See no. 1098).

 140   ALEXANDER, NIGEL. "Past, Present, and Pinter." Essays and
       Studies, 27 (1974), 1-17.
           Pinter dramatizes the past and the present, leaving
       the future uncertain.

 141   ALLEN, BILL. "What The Tea Party Meant." London Daily
       Worker, 9 April 1965.
           Review of television production.

 142   ALLEN, ROBERT HADLEY. "The Language of Three Contemporary
       British Dramatists: John Osborne, Harold Pinter and John
       Arden." Ph.D. dissertation, University of Pennsylvania,
       1975.

*143   ALLGAIER, DIETER. "Die Dramen Harold Pinters: eine Unter-
       suchung von Form und Inhalt." Ph.D. dissertation, Uni-
       versity of Frankfurt, 1967.
           In German. Cited in Imhof (See no. 1098).

*144   _____. "Harold Pinter." Praxis des neusprachlichen Unter-
       richtes, 15 (1968), 403-07.
           In German. Cited in Imhof (See no. 1098).

 145   _____. "Harold Pinters 'The Caretaker' als Lese-und
       Diskussionsstoff in der gymnasialen Oberstufe." Neueren
       Sprachen, 19 (1970), 556-66.
           Details how the play was taught. In German.

 146   ALLISON, RALPH and CHARLES WELLBORN. "Rhapsody in an
       Anechoic Chamber: Pinter's Landscape." Educational
       Theatre Journal, 25 (May 1973), 215-25.
           Analyzes Landscape through a discussion of Pinter's use
       of silence in the play.

 147   ALPERT, HOLLIS. "Knock, Knock, Who's There?" Saturday
       Review, 14 March 1964, p. 17.
           A generally positive review of the film The Servant,
       which deals with the decay of the British upper classes
       in a way that shows director Losey's and Pinter's potential
       in its evocative qualities, but which does not realize that
       potential because it is too deliberately obscure.

148 _____. "The Losey Situation." Saturday Review, 14 August
1971, p. 42.
Film review of The Go-Between.

149 _____. "The Sour Smell of Failure." Saturday Review, 21
November 1964, p. 34.
Includes film review of The Pumpkin Eater which is seen
as failing because of an "unnecessarily obscure script."

150 _____. "Talkies." Saturday Review, 7 December 1968, p. 68.
Film review of The Birthday Party.

151 _____. "Where It's Happening." Saturday Review, 24 April
1967, p. 47. Reprinted in: Boyum and Scott, Film as
Film (See no. 473), pp. 26-28.
A review of the film Accident. Pinter's script con-
centrates on images rather than dialogue.

152 ALVAREZ, A. "Death in the Morning." New Statesman, 58 (12
December 1959), 836.
An examination of The Birthday Party as "a classic
paranoic set-up," with a discussion of Pinter's symbolism.

153 _____. "Olivier Among the Rhinos." New Statesman, 59 (7
May 1960), 666-67.
Review of original production of The Caretaker which
is seen as being too repetitive.

154 _____. "Wanted: A Language." New Statesman, 59 (30 January
1960), 150.
The violence and horror of The Room and The Dumb Waiter
grow out of Pinter's obsessions with time and the indif-
ference of society.

155 AMEND, VICTOR E. "Harold Pinter: Some Credits and Debits."
Modern Drama, 10, No. 2 (September 1967), 165-74.
Lists strenuous objections to Pinter: repetitious,
negative, ambiguous.

*156 AMETTE, JACQUES-PIERRE. "Osborne, Pinter, Saunders and Cie."
Nouvelle Revue Francaise, 18 (January 1970), 95-99.

157 ANDERSON, KARI. "Another Fine Play By Harold Pinter."
Stage, 1 April 1965, p. 12.
Review of television version of Tea Party.

Anderson

158 ANDERSON, MICHAEL. Anger and Detachment: A Study of Arden, Osborne and Pinter. London: Pitman, 1976, pp. 1-2, 6, 10-14, 88-[118].
    See especially Chapter 4: "Harold Pinter: journey to the interior." A "reassessment" of Pinter's work which traces his development through his imagery. Anderson concludes that Pinter is an innovator.

159 ANDERSON, PATRICK. "Pinter's Tea Party." Spectator, 2 April 1965, pp. 440, 442.
    Review of television production.

160 ANGUS, WILLIAM. "Modern Theatre Reflects the Times." Queens Quarterly, 70, No. 2 (Summer 1963), 155-63.
    Condemns the modern theatre for not holding the mirror up to nature in its portrayal of a sick society.

*161 ANON. Accident. Filmfacts, 10 (1967), 95.
    Film review. Cited in Reader's Guide to Periodical Literature (1967).

*162 ANON. Accident. Vogue, 49 (June 1967), 77.
    Film review. Cited in Reader's Guide to Periodical Literature (1967).

*163 ANON. Accident. Esquire, 68 (July 1967), 20.
    Film review. Cited in Reader's Guide to Periodical Literature (1967).

*164 ANON. Accident. International Film Guide, 5 (1968), 89-90.
    Film review. Cited in Reader's Guide to Periodical Literature (1968).

165 ANON. "Ambiguity." The Times Literary Supplement (London), 12 May 1961, p. 296.
    Review of British television production of The Collection. Notes the shift to middle-class characters--Pinter has been dealing with the concept of "modern man" all along. Ambiguity is the technique used to question the concept of truth.

166 ANON. "American Taste in British Plays of Today." The Times (London), 15 November 1961, p. 19.
    Discusses the reaction to the first American run of The Caretaker.

*167 ANON. Appointment. The Times (London), 14 March 1973, p. 19.
    Miscellaneous article concerning Pinter. Cited in The Times Index (1973).

168 ANON. "Autumn Plays for New Arts Theatre." The Times
       (London), 10 April 1963, p. 15.
         Review of The Lover.

169 ANON. Awarded Commander of the British Empire (C. B. E.).
       The Times (London), 11 June 1966, p. 1.

170 ANON. "Award for Pinter Play." The Times (London), 1 Octo-
       ber 1963, p. 15.
         Review of British television production of The Lover.

171 ANON. "Bad Times with a Bum in the House." Life, 51 (17
       November 1961), 195-96.
         Review of New York production of The Caretaker.

172 ANON. "BBC Radio." Microfiche. Cambridge, England: Chad-
       wyck-Healey; Teaneck, New Jersey: Somerset House [n.d.].
         Author and title catalogues of drama, poetry, and
       features transmitted over BBC Radio, 1923-1975.

173 ANON. "BBC Television." Microfiche. Cambridge, England:
       Chadwyck-Healey; Teaneck, New Jersey: Somerset House
       [n.d.].
         Author and title catalogues of dramas and features
       transmitted on BBC Television, 1936-1975, together with
       a "Chronological list of transmitted plays."

*174 ANON. The Birthday Party. The Times (London), 19 May 1958,
       p. 14.
         Miscellaneous article concerning Pinter. Cited in The
       Times Index (1958).

*175 ANON. The Birthday Party. Filmfacts, 11 (1968), 497.
         Film review. Cited in Reader's Guide to Periodical
       Literature (1968).

*176 ANON. The Birthday Party. Senior Scholastic, 94 (7 March
       1969), 7.
         Film review. Cited in Reader's Guide to Periodical
       Literature (1969).

*177 ANON. The Birthday Party. The Times (London), 9 January
       1975, p. 12.
         Miscellaneous article. Cited in The Times Index (1975).

*178 ANON. The Birthday Party. The Sunday Times (London), 12
       January 1975, p. 32.
         Miscellaneous article. Cited in The Times Index (1975).

Anon.

*179   ANON.   The Birthday Party: Diary Note.   The Times (London),
      7 August 1974, p. 14.
         Cited in The Times Index (1974).

180   ANON.   Book review of Five Screenplays.   The Times Literary
      Supplement (London).   18 June 1971, p. 695.
         (See no. 33).

181   ANON.   Book review of New Poems (edited by Pinter).   The Times
      Literary Supplement (London), 12 December 1968, p. 1407.
         (See no. 83).

182   ANON.   Book review of A Slight Ache and Other Plays.   The
      Times Literary Supplement (London), 30 June 1961, p. 400.
         (See no. 6).

183   ANON.   "British Theatre, 1956-1966."   Tulane Drama Review, 11,
      No. 2 (Winter 1966), 29-206.
         An issue of Tulane Drama Review devoted to subjects
      concerning the British theatre from 1956 to 1966, includ-
      ing Richard Schechner's "Puzzling Pinter" (See no. 1690)
      and Charles Marowitz's "Notes on the Theatre of Cruelty"
      (See no. 1401).

*184   ANON.   Butley.   New York Times, 7 April 1974, Sec. 9, p. 34.
         Film review.   Cited in Reader's Guide to Periodical
      Literature (1974).

*185   ANON.   Butley--Pinter to Direct S. Gray's Butley for Eli
      Landau and American Film Theatre.   New York Times, 4
      March 1973, Sec. 2, p. 13.
         Cited in The New York Times Index (1973).

186   ANON.   "The Caretaker."   Punch, 239 (3 August 1961), 177.
         Book review.

*187   ANON.   The Caretaker (The Guest).   Filmfacts, 8 (1964), 69.
         Film review.   Cited in Reader's Guide to Periodical
      Literature (1964).

*188   ANON.   The Caretaker (The Guest).   Films and Filming, Janu-
      ary 1964.
         Film review.   Cited in Reader's Guide to Periodical
      Literature (1964).

*189   ANON.   The Caretaker (The Guest).   The Sunday Times (London),
      15 March 1964.
         Film review.   Cited in Reader's Guide to Periodical
      Literature.

190 ANON. "The Caretaker: Harold Pinter and Donald Pleasence."
     Vogue, 15 January 1962, pp. 38-39.
         Brief comments on the film version of The Caretaker.

191 ANON. "Caretaker's Caretaker." Time, 78, No. 19 (10 Novem-
     ber 1961), 76.
         Biography.

192 ANON. "The Caretaker's New Home. Brilliant Production."
     The Times (London), 31 May 1960, p. 4.
         Review of The Caretaker.

193 ANON. Cartoon. The Sunday Times (London), 13 May 1973,
     p. 7.

*194 ANON. CBS Says That it Wants Pinter and Vidal Scripts.
     New York Times, 4 November 1967, p. 66.
         Cited in The New York Times Index (1967).

195 ANON. "Cheaper New York Prices for The Caretaker." The
     Times (London), 26 August 1961, p. 10.

196 ANON. "Comically Dreadful World." The Times (London), 2
     March 1960, p. 13.
         Review of radio production of A Night Out.

197 ANON. "Commonplace into Fantasy." The Times (London), 30
     July 1959, p. 8.
         Review of the radio version of A Slight Ache approving
     of the "ominous atmosphere" which Pinter creates by "man-
     handling commonplace utterance into fantasy." Compares
     the play to The Birthday Party.

198 ANON. "Complex Design of Marriage." The Times (London), 29
     March 1963, p. 15.
         Review of television production of The Lover.

199 ANON. "Destruction of a Tramp." The Times (London), 11
     February 1964, p. 13.
         Review of The Caretaker (Cambridge production).

*200 ANON. "Diary Note." The Times (London), 22 July 1968,
     p. 6.
         Miscellaneous article concerning Pinter. Cited in
     The Times Index (1968).

Anon.

*201   ANON. "Diary Note." The Times (London), 11 April 1969,
         p. 10.
              Miscellaneous article concerning Pinter. Cited in
         The Times Index (1969).

*202   ANON. "Diary Notes." The Times (London), 17 July 1970,
         p. 13.
              Plans for the screenplay of The Go-Between.

*203   ANON. Director of Butley. The Times (London), 15 July 1971,
         p. 13.
              Cited in The Times Index (1971).

*204   ANON. Director of Film on the Assassination of Trotsky.
         The Times (London), 13 October 1972, p. 15.
              Cited in The Times Index (1972).

 205   ANON. "Disturbing Television Play by Pinter." The Times
         (London), 26 March 1965, Sec. A, p. 15.
              Review of television production of Tea Party.

 206   ANON. Divorce Petition Published in List of Undefended
         Cases. The Times (London), 17 September 1974, p. 2.

 207   ANON. Divorce Proceedings Started by Sir Hugh Fraser
         against Lady Antonia Fraser. New York Times, 19 October
         1976, p. 23.
              Cited in New York Times Index (1976).

*208   ANON. Divorce Suit. New York Times, 30 July 1975, p. 29.
              Cited in The New York Times Index (1975).

 209   ANON. "Dreams of Reason." The Times Literary Supplement, 3
         August 1962, p. 556.
              Reference in Elliott (See no. 733), p. 549.

 210   ANON. "Dublin Theatre Festival Gets Off to a Good Start."
         The Times (London), 14 September 1961, p. 16.
              Review of A Night Out.

 211   ANON. "Eccentrics in the Attic." Newsweek, 58 (16 October
         1961), 101.
              Review of New York production of The Caretaker.

 212   ANON. "Empty." London Daily Mirror, 19 June 1962, p. 24.
              Review of The Collection.

*213   ANON. Englisches Theater unserer Zeit. Reinbeck, 1961.
         Introduced by Friedrich Luft.
              Cited in Imhof (See no. 1098), p. 10.

214   ANON. "Entertaining Triple Bill." The Times (London), 19
         January 1961, p. 16.

215   ANON. "Experimental Theatre Co. production of The Birthday
         Party." The Times (London), 28 November 1963, p. 17.
              Review of The Birthday Party (Oxford production).

216   ANON. "Experiment in TV: TV Program on Pinter." New York
         Times, 7 April 1969, p. 86.
              Concerns Pinter People.

*217   ANON. Filming of Plays. The Times (London), 9 January 1968,
         p. 6.
              Miscellaneous article concerning Pinter. Cited in The
         Times Index (1968).

*218   ANON. "Filming The Birthday Party." The Times (London),
         7 March 1968, p. 7.
              Notice that filming is to start.

*219   ANON. Filming The Homecoming. The Sunday Times (London),
         11 February 1973, p. 28.
              Cited in The Times Index (1973).

*220   ANON. Filming The Homecoming. The Times (London), 14
         March 1973, p. 19.
              Cited in The Times Index (1973).

221   ANON. "Film Script by Pinter." The Times (London), 2
         December 1965, p. 15.
              Plans for filming The Berlin Memorandum (The Quiller
         Memorandum).

222   ANON. "Finger Exercise in Dread." Time, 84 (18 December
         1964), 86.
              Review of A Slight Ache and The Room.

223   ANON. "First Play by Mr. Pinter. The Room Excusably
         Derivative." The Times (London), 9 March 1960, p. 4.
              Review of The Dumb Waiter and The Room, "strange and
         subtle" plays comparable to musical pieces.

Anon.

224 ANON. "Five Screenplays." Book World, 23 September 1973,
p. 15.
Book review. See no. 33.

225 ANON. "Five Screenplays." Choice, December 1973, p. 1559.
Book review. See no. 33.

*226 ANON. French Presentation of The Caretaker. The Times
(London), 26 January 1961, p. 3.
Cited in The Times Index (1961).

227 ANON. "From page to screen." The Times Literary Supplement
(London), 18 June 1971, p. 695.
Review of Five Screenplays. See no. 33.

*228 ANON. The Go-Between. Filmfacts, 14 (1971), 301.
Film review. Cited in Reader's Guide to Periodical
Literature.

*229 ANON. The Go-Between. Film Quarterly, 25 (Spring 1972),
37-41.
Film review. Cited in Reader's Guide to Periodical
Literature.

*230 ANON. The Go-Between Wins Award. The Times (London), 18
February 1972, p. 14.
Cited in The Times Index (1972).

*231 ANON. The Go-Between. New York Times, 30 July 1972, p. 21.
Film review. Cited in Reader's Guide to Periodical
Literature.

232 ANON. Gossip Columnist's Controversy. The Times (London),
5 August 1975, p. 5.
Miscellaneous article concerning Pinter. Cited in The
Times Index (1975).

233 ANON. "Guinness for Quiller Memorandum." Time and Tide,
7-13 April 1966, p. 16.
Reports on Alec Guinness' role in The Quiller Memorandum.

234 ANON. "Harold Pinter." Current Biography, 24 (November 1963),
41-44. Reprinted in Current Biography Yearbook 1963,
edited by Charles Marowitz. Bronx, N. Y.: H. W. Wilson,
1964, pp. 326-29.
Short biography.

235   ANON. "Harold Pinter." British Book Year, 1968, p. 157.
          Short biography.

236   ANON. "Harold Pinter." McGraw-Hill Encyclopedia of World
          Drama, Vol. 3. New York: McGraw-Hill, 1972, pp. 425-29.
          Short biography and critical overview.

237   ANON. "Harold Pinter, Director." Cinebill, 1, No. 7
          (January 1974), 8.
          Pinter discusses his work on the film Butley.

238   ANON. "High Praise for Mr. Pinter: New York Likes The Care-
          taker." The Times (London), 6 October 1961, p. 20.
          Review of The Caretaker.

239   ANON. "The Homecoming." The Listener, 24 June 1965, p. 936.
          Review.

240   ANON. The Homecoming. New York Times, 7 April 1974, Sec.
          2, p. 1.
          Film review.

241   ANON. The Homecoming Banned by Felixstowe Festival. The
          Times (London), 9 October 1968, p. 10.

242   ANON. "Interview with Harold Pinter." New York Times, 6
          November 1962, p. 39.

243   ANON. "Interview with Harold Pinter." London Daily Mirror,
          26 March 1965.

244   ANON. "Interview with Harold Pinter." New York Times, 10
          September 1967, Sec. 2, p. 3.

245   ANON. "Interview with Harold Pinter." New York Times, 27
          October 1967, Sec. 2, p. 3.

246   ANON. "Interview with Harold Pinter." New York Times, 27
          October 1968, Sec. 2, p. 3.

247   ANON. "Interview with Harold Pinter." New York Times, 18
          November 1971, p. 60.

248   ANON. "Interview with Harold Pinter." New York Times, 5
          December 1971, Sec. 6, p. 42.

Anon.

249   ANON. "Land of No Holds Barred." <u>Time</u>, 89 (13 January
        1967), 43.
            Review of <u>The Homecoming</u> (New York).

250   ANON. "<u>Landscape</u> and <u>Silence</u>." <u>The Stage</u>, 3 July 1969, p. 1.
        Review.

*251   ANON. <u>Landscape</u> Plans. <u>The Times</u> (London), 10 April 1968,
        p. 13.
            Cited in <u>The Times Index</u> (1968).

*252   ANON. <u>Langrishe, Go Down</u>. <u>New York Times</u>, 7 February 1971,
        Sec. 2, p. 13.
            Report that Pinter will direct film. Cited in <u>The
        New York Times Index</u> (1971).

253   ANON. "The Last Joke for the Phoenix Theatre." <u>The Times</u>
        (London), 12 September 1960, p. 3.
            Review of <u>The Birthday Party</u>.

*254   ANON. <u>Last Tycoon</u>. Pinter Script for Paramount Pictures
        Production. <u>New York Times</u>, 15 January 1975, p. 52.
            Cited in <u>The New York Times Index</u> (1975).

255   ANON. "Last Words on Pinter?" <u>New York Times</u>, 26 February
        1967, Sec. 2, p. 8.
            Review of <u>The Homecoming</u> (New York).

*256   ANON. Letters to the Editor of "Drama Mailbag." <u>New York
        Times</u>, 19 December 1971, Sec. 2, p. 6.
            Regarding <u>Old Times</u>: reference in Elliott (<u>See</u> no.
        733), p. 566.

257   ANON. "Life Can Be Ghastly." <u>Newsweek</u>, 63 (10 February
        1964), 84.
            Review of the film version of <u>The Caretaker</u> (<u>The Guest</u>)
        which successfully recreates the claustrophoebic effect
        which was so important in the stage version.

258   ANON. "Lightweight but Lively Pinter." <u>The Times</u> (London),
        12 May 1961, p. 19.
            Review of British television production of <u>The Collec-
        tion</u>.

259   ANON. "Loose Grip on Pinter Play." <u>The Times</u> (London), 11
        August 1961, p. 11.
            Review of British television production of <u>The Dumb
        Waiter</u>.

260   ANON. "Master of Silence." London <u>Observer</u>, 27 April 1975,
      p. 11.
          Updated profile of Pinter.

261   ANON. "Movies." <u>Playboy</u>, February 1977, p. 24.
          Includes a film review of <u>The Last Tycoon</u>.

262   ANON. "Mr. Harold Pinter: Avant-Garde Playwright and Inti-
      mate Revue." <u>The Times</u> (London), 16 November 1959, p. 4.
          Interview.

263   ANON. "Mr. Pinter at His Most Subtle." <u>The Times</u> (London),
      3 December 1960, p. 10.
          Review of radio version of <u>The Dwarfs</u> which is success-
      ful because it takes the audience into the mind of one of
      his characters. One of the few approving notices.

264   ANON. "Mr. Pinter Pursues an Elusive Reality." <u>The Times</u>
      (London), 19 September 1963, p. 16.
          Review of <u>The Lover</u> and <u>The Dwarfs</u>.

265   ANON. "Mr. Pinter Takes Over in <u>The Caretaker</u>." <u>The Times</u>
      (London), 21 February 1961, p. 15.
          Review. Pinter takes part as actor.

266   ANON. "Mr. Pinter's Concession." <u>The Times</u> (London), 22
      July 1960, p. 16.
          Review of television production of <u>Night School</u>.

267   ANON. "Mr. Pinter's Double Bill." <u>The Times</u> (London), 20
      June 1963, p. 16.
          Review of <u>The Lover</u> and <u>The Dwarfs</u>.

268   ANON. "Named British Order Commander." <u>New York Times</u>, 11
      June 1966, p. 11.
          Receives Commander of British Empire title.

269   ANON. "New Pinter Play." <u>The Times</u> (London), 22 March
      1969, p. 19.
          Review of <u>Landscape</u> and <u>Silence</u>.

270   ANON. "New Pinter Play for Aldwych." <u>The Times</u> (London), 27
      January 1965, p. 1.
          Concerned with plans for <u>The Homecoming</u>.

*271 ANON. New Play. <u>The Times</u> (London), 15 March 1969, p. 21.
          Concerns <u>Landscape</u>. Cited in <u>The Times Index</u> (1969).

Anon.

272   ANON. "New Plays. The Latest Pinters: Less is Less."
      Time, 18 July 1969, p. 67.
         Review of Landscape and Silence.

273   ANON. "New Plays: Translations from the Unconscious."
      Time, 25 October 1968, p. 69.
         Review of The Basement and Tea Party.

274   ANON. "New Plays: The Word as Weapon." Time, 90 (13
      October 1967), 71-72.
         Review of New York production of The Birthday Party.

275   ANON. "New York Picks Pinter Play." The Times (London), 10
      May 1967, p. 1.
         Discusses award for The Homecoming.

276   ANON. "News From the Universities." The Times (London), 8
      September 1970, p. 10.
         Pinter to receive honorary degree from the University
      of Reading.

*277 ANON. A Night Out. The Times (London), 17 June 1965, p. 17.
         Miscellaneous article concerning Pinter. Cited in
      The Times Index (1965).

278   ANON. No Man's Land. The Sunday Times (London), 20 April
      1975, p. 37.

279   ANON. No Man's Land. The Times (London), 24 April 1975,
      p. 10.

280   ANON. No Man's Land. The Times Higher Education Supplement
      (London), 9 May 1975, p. 7.

281   ANON. "Old Times." The Times Literary Supplement (London).
      29 December 1972, p. 1569.
         Book review.

282   ANON. "Old Times." Drama, No. 109 (Summer 1973), p. 45.
         Criticism.

283   ANON. "Old Times: Colin Blakely Talks to Plays and Players."
      Plays and Players, 18, No. 10 (July 1971), 22, 24.
         The actor talks about his understanding of Old Times.

284   ANON. Old Times--Rome Production. The Times (London), 11
      May 1973, p. 1.

*285 ANON. One to Another. The Times (London), 16 July 1959,
p. 8.
Miscellaneous article concerning Pinter. Cited in The
Times Index (1959).

286 ANON. "On the Fence between Farce and Tragedy." The Times
(London), 19 June 1962, p. 13.
Review of original stage production of The Collection.

287 ANON. "Pas de Trois--Twice." Time, 83 (17 January 1964), 64.
Review of The Lover (New York).

288 ANON. "People." Time, 106 (11 August 1975), 37.
Report of Pinter's affair with Lady Antonia Fraser.

289 ANON. "People." Time, 2 February 1976.
Pinter's affair with Lady Antonia and Vivien Merchant's
withdrawal of divorce papers mentioned.

290 ANON. "People." Time, 1 March 1976, p. 38.
Continued reportage of Pinter's affair with Lady
Antonia Fraser.

291 ANON. "People Are Talking about...." Vogue, 139 (15 January 1962), 38-39.
Review of New York production of The Caretaker.

292 ANON. "Personality of the Month." Plays and Players, 8,
No. 6 (March 1961), 3.

293 ANON. "Peter Hall on Pinter." Cinebill, 1, No. 2 (October
1973), 14-15.
Hall discusses his approaches to filming Pinter.

*294 ANON. Photo. The Times (London), 11 May 1973, p. 6.

*295 ANON. Photo. The Times (London), 27 July 1975, p. 27.

*296 ANON. Photo. The Times Higher Education Supplement (Lon-
don), 29 April 1977, p. 7.

297 ANON. "Pinter Gets His Eye In." London Evening News, 10
April 1969, p. 4.
Miscellaneous article concerning Pinter.

298 ANON. "Pinter Gives Evidence at Trial." The Times (London),
2 September 1967, p. 3.
Miscellaneous article concerning Pinter.

Anon.

299   ANON. "Pinter, Harold." In Crowell's Handbook of Contempo-
      rary Drama, edited by Michael Anderson, Jacques Guicharnard,
      Kristin Morrison, and Jack D. Zipes. New York: Crowell,
      1971, pp. 351-57.
          Brief biography, critical overview, plot summaries.

*300 ANON. "Pinter Has a Forthcoming Play." The Times (London),
      10 January 1968, p. 8.
          Cited in The Times Index (1968).

*301 ANON. Pinter Involved in Controversy over Parliamentary
      Requirement that Newspaper Editors Must Join National
      Union of Journalists. New York Times, 6 May 1975, p. 4.
          Cited in The New York Times Index (1975).

302   ANON. "Pinter Patter." Time, 80 (7 December 1962), 72-73.
          Review of The Dumb Waiter and The Collection, New York
      production. Approving. Pinter must break with his con-
      cern with the "sealed nursery--dungeon of fears" if he is
      to achieve true stature as a dramatic artist.

303   ANON. "Pinter Play Features Some Variations on Marital
      Theme." The Stage, 4 April 1963, p. 11.
          Review of television production of The Lover.

304   ANON. "Pinter Play on Television." The Times (London), 25
      April 1960, p. 16.
          Review of A Night Out.

305   ANON. "Pinter Pointers." The Times Literary Supplement, 1
      July 1965, p. 522.
          Book review of The Homecoming.

306   ANON. "The Pinter Puzzle." WNDT-TV, Channel 13, New York,
      1967.
          Interview.

307   ANON. "Pinter to Contribute to Book About Evacuated Child."
      The Times (London), 4 November 1967, p. 8.

*308 ANON. Pinter to Direct Exiles. The Times (London), 13
      November 1970, p. 13.
          Cited in The Times Index (1970).

309   ANON. "Pinter to Direct The Man in the Glass Booth." The
      Times (London), 1 June 1967, p. 10.

310   ANON. "Pinter Unperturbed." London <u>Daily Mail</u>, 28 November 1967, p. 4.

311   ANON. "Pinter Writes His Own Film Script." <u>The Times</u> (London), 10 March 1964, p. 15.
Review of film version of <u>The Caretaker</u>.

312   ANON. "Pinter's Demon Lover is a Husband." London <u>Evening News</u>, 19 September 1963, p. 4.
Review of <u>The Lover</u> and <u>The Dwarfs</u>.

313   ANON. "Pinter's Lovers." <u>The Stage</u>, 28 March 1963, p. 1.
Review of television production of <u>The Lover</u>.

314   ANON. <u>Pinter's Optics</u>: "Get Thee Glass Eyes." <u>Midwest Monographs</u>, Series 1, No. 1, University of Illinois, Urbans, Department of English, 1967, pp. 1-8.
Includes Daniel Curley's "A Night in the Fun House" (<u>See</u> no. 650), Niel Klineman's "Naming of Names" (<u>See</u> no. 1227), and Richard Wasson's "Mime and Dream" (<u>See</u> no. 1942).

315   ANON. "Pinterview." <u>Newsweek</u>, 38 (23 July 1962), 69.
An early interview with Pinter concerning his writing.

*316 ANON. Plans for <u>Tea Party</u>. <u>The Times</u> (London), 5 January 1965, p. 11.
Cited in <u>The Times Index</u> (1965).

*317 ANON. Plans for <u>The Room</u> and <u>The Dumb Waiter</u>. <u>The Times</u> (London), 18 February 1960, p. 5.
Cited in <u>The Times Index</u> (1960).

*318 ANON. Plans to Write Film Episode. <u>The Times</u> (London), 13 November 1963, p. 5.
Miscellaneous article concerning Pinter. Cited in <u>The Times Index</u> (1963).

319   ANON. "Playwrights in Apartheid Protest." <u>The Times</u> (London), 26 June 1963, p. 12.
Signatory to declaration against performance of plays at South African theatres with color bar.

*320 ANON. Poetry Reading. <u>The Times</u> (London), 22 June 1972, p. 10.
Cited in <u>The Times Index</u> (1972).

Anon.

321   ANON. "Profile: Playwright on His Own." <u>London Observer</u>,
    15 September 1963, p. 13.
       An early biographical sketch is included in this quick
    summary of Pinter's playwriting and screenwriting up to
    <u>The Lover</u> and <u>The Dwarfs</u>.

322   ANON. "Psychological Truth in Pinter's Play." <u>The Times</u>
    (London), 3 October 1961, p. 16.
       U. S. praise for <u>The Caretaker</u>.

*323   ANON. <u>The Pumpkin Eater</u>. <u>Filmfacts</u>, 7 (1964), 282.
       Film review. Cited in <u>Reader's Guide to Periodical
    Literature</u>.

324   ANON. "The Pumpkin Eater." <u>Films and Filming</u>, 10, No. 8
    (May 1964), 16–17.
       Film review.

*325   ANON. <u>The Pumpkin Eater</u>. <u>New Yorker</u>, 40 (14 November 1964),
    148.
       Film review. Cited in <u>Reader's Guide to Periodical
    Literature</u>.

*326   ANON. <u>The Pumpkin Eater</u>. <u>Vogue</u>, 45 (1 January 1965), 66.
       Film review. Cited in <u>Reader's Guide to Periodical
    Literature</u>.

327   ANON. "Puzzling Surrealism of the Birthday Party." <u>The Times</u>
    (London), 20 May 1958, p. 3.
       Review of the first run of <u>The Birthday Party</u> which is
    called unsuccessfully derivative of Ionesco.

*328   ANON. <u>The Quiller Memorandum</u>. <u>Filmfacts</u>, 9 (1966), 338.
       Film review. Cited in <u>Reader's Guide to Periodical
    Literature</u>.

329   ANON. "The Quiller Memorandum." <u>Films and Filming</u>, 13,
    No. 4 (January 1967), 12–13.
       Film review.

*330   ANON. Radio Program on Anew McMaster. <u>The Times</u> (London),
    6 July 1968, p. 19.
      Miscellaneous article concerning Pinter. Cited in
    <u>The Times Index</u> (1968).

331   ANON. "The Reaction Against Realism." The Times Literary
       Supplement (London), 30 June 1961, p. 400.
          Unlike other contemporary dramatists, Pinter is seen
       as consistently moving in the direction of realism.

332   ANON. "Rheum at the Top." Time, 83 (24 January 1964), 52.
          Film review of The Caretaker (The Guest), which is seen
       as flawed.

*333   ANON. The Servant. London Observer, 17 November 1963.
          Film review.

*334   ANON. The Servant. Films and Filming, 7 (1964), 98.
          Film review. Cited in Reader's Guide to Periodical
       Literature.

*335   ANON. The Servant. New York Times, 17 March 1964, p. 30.
          Film review. Cited in Reader's Guide to Periodical
       Literature.

*336   ANON. The Servant. New Yorker, 40 (21 March 1964), 172.
          Film review. Cited in Reader's Guide to Periodical
       Literature.

337   ANON. "Shorter Reviews: The Homecoming." Contemporary
       Review, 208 (February 1966), 112.
          Book review.

338   ANON. "Simon Gray's New Play." The Times (London), 31 May
       1975, p. 9d.
          Announcement about Otherwise Engaged, directed by
       Pinter.

339   ANON. "A Simple Play. The Birthday Party on Television."
       The Times (London), 23 March 1960, p. 16.
          Review of British television production of The Birth-
       day Party.

*340   ANON. Sketches Turned Into Cartoons. The Times (London),
       4 January 1969, p. 6.
          Concerns Pinter People. Cited in The Times Index
       (1969).

341   ANON. "A Slicker and Less Dangerous Pinter." The Times
       (London), 19 June 1964, p. 18.
          Review of The Birthday Party revival--uses stage
       clichés.

Anon.

342   ANON. "A Slight Case of Conversion." The Times (London),
         23 June 1962, p. 4.
             Review discussion of presentation of The Collection in
         three different media.

343   ANON. "A Slight Play that Pleases and Dazes." The Times
         (London), 28 April 1960, p. 6.
             Review of original production of The Caretaker.

344   ANON. "Spell Flawed in 'Birthday.'" Standard Star (New
         Rochelle, New York), 8 February 1971, p. 11.
             Review of The Birthday Party.

345   ANON. "Split." People, 4, No. 7 (18 August 1975), 28-29.
             Report of Pinter's affair with Lady Antonia Fraser.

346   ANON. "Split level." Newsweek, 60 (10 December 1962), 58.
             Review of The Dumb Waiter and The Collection, New York
         production.

*347   ANON. Stage Plans. The Times (London), 10 April 1965,
         p. 15.
             Miscellaneous article concerning Pinter. Cited in
         The Times Index (1965).

348   ANON. "Strange and Subtle Double Bill." The Times (London),
         22 January 1960, p. 6.
             Concerns New York production of The Dumb Waiter and
         The Room.

*349   ANON. Takes Legal Action over Butley. The Times (London),
         16 July 1971, p. 12.
             Cited in The Times Index (1971).

350   ANON. "Talk of the Town: Two People in a Room." New
         Yorker, 43 (25 February 1967), 34-36.
             An interview with Pinter.

351   ANON. "Tea Party, The Basement." For WCBS-2 Television, 15
         October 1968; in New York Theatre Critics' Reviews, 30
         December 1968, p. 141.
             Review.

*352   ANON. Television Award. The Times (London), 23 November
         1963, p. 5.
             Concerns The Lover. Cited in The Times Index (1963).

353   ANON. "Theatre der Sprache Bermerkungen zu Emigin Dramen der
       Gegenwart." Die Neuren Sprachen, No. 7 (July 1963), 302-
       13.
           In Pinter and other young British dramatists, dramatic
       conflict is initiated by the discrepency between language
       and meaning. In German.

354   ANON. "Theatre Without Adventure." The Times Literary
       Supplement (London), 29 December 1972, p. 1570.
       See also no. 1620. Discussion of Old Times.

*355   ANON. To Receive Honorary Degree at the University of
       Reading. The Times (London), 24 April 1970, p. 12.
       Cited in The Times Index (1970).

*356   ANON. To Receive Honorary Degree from Birmingham University.
       The Times (London), 18 January 1971, p. 14.
       Cited in The Times Index (1971).

357   ANON. "Translations from the Unconscious." Time, 92
       (25 October 1968), 69.
           Review of Tea Party and The Basement (New York).

*358   ANON. Two Hundred Fifty Seats in Second Balcony at Lyceum
       Theatre for Engagement of The Collection to Go on Sale
       for $1. New York Times, 24 August 1961, p. 24.
       Cited in The New York Times Index (1961).

359   ANON. "Two One-Act Plays by Harold Pinter." New York
       Morning Telegraph, 28 November 1962, p. 2.
           Review of The Dumb Waiter and The Collection, New York
       production.

360   ANON. "Two Pairs of Lovers." The Times (London), 28 Febru-
       ary 1964, p. 16.
           Review of The Collection (King's College, London).

361   ANON. "Two Pinter Plays for Broadway." The Times (London),
       12 August 1960, p. 5.
           Review of The Birthday Party; The Caretaker is mentioned.

362   ANON. "Unwrapping Mummies." Time, 78 (13 October 1961), 58.
           Review of New York production of The Caretaker.
       "Several levels of meaning are" suggested--isolation,
       failure, etc.

Anon.

363   ANON. "Vienna Prize for Harold Pinter." The Times (London),
       16 November 1973, p. 8.
            Pinter given award for contributions to European
       drama.

364   ANON. "Well's Despairing View of the Future." The Times
       (London), 26 October 1966, p. 14.
            Review of the film version of The Caretaker.

*365   ANON. West Berlin Film Festival Awards. New York Times,
       3 July 1974, p. 18.
            Cited in The New York Times Index (1974).

366   ANON. "What's Pinter Up To?" New York Times, 5 February
       1967, Sec. 2, p. 1.
            Review of The Homecoming (New York) in the form of
       queries to seven prominent figures ranging from writers
       to clergymen.

*367   ANON. Wife Sues for Divorce. The Times (London), 30 July
       1975, p. 3.

368   ANON. "A Wife's Tale." Time, 84 (13 November 1964), 125ff.
            Film review of The Pumpkin Eater, a successful movie.

369   ANON. "World Out of Orbit." The Times (London), 4 June
       1965, p. 15.
            Review of the original production of The Homecoming,
       which states that Pinter set out to show a "close family
       unit, but no such unit takes shape."

*370   ARAGONES, JUAN EMILO. "Dos hermeticas piezas breves de H.
       Pinter." La Estafeta Literaria, No. 31 (February 1967).
            In Spanish. Cited in Palmer (See no. 1530).

371   ARDEN, JOHN. "The Caretaker." New Theatre Magazine, 1,
       No. 4 (July 1960), 29-30.
            Review of the published text: a "study of the unex-
       pected strength of family ties against an intruder." A
       different kind of realism from that presented by Ibsen, in
       Arden's view.

372   ARMES, ROY. Film and Reality: An Historical Survey.
       Harmondsworth: Penguin, 1974.
            Even though "Pinter has been responsible for some of
       the most striking British films of the past ten years," he
       exemplifies the problem of relating experimental work in

other media to the cinema because his filmscripts are
"timid" when compared to his experimentation in the
theatre.

373 ARMSTRONG, MARION. "One Queen, Three Knaves." Christian
Century, 84 (7 June 1967), 754-55.
A film review of Accident.

374 ARMSTRONG, WILLIAM A., ed. Experimental Drama. London:
Bell, 1963.
A collection of lectures given at the University of
London, including those by Esslin (See no. 749) and
Welland (See no. 1964).

375 _____. "Tradition and Innovation in the London Theatre,
1960-1961." Modern Drama, 4, No. 2 (September 1961),
184-95.
"Like Beckett, whose influence he has acknowledged,
Pinter tries to put man and his dilemmas into a cosmic not
a social context, eschewing the social realism of Osborne,
Wesker, and Shelagh Delaney." The Caretaker is seen as
"an allegorical revelation of man's inability to find his
place and purpose in the scheme of things even when he
has the opportunity to do so."

376 ARONSON, STEVEN M. L. "Pinter's 'Family' and Blood Knowledge."
In Lahr, ed., A Casebook on Harold Pinter's The Homecoming
(See no. 1260), pp. 67-86.
The formal structure of The Homecoming is related to
the sense of the family as a unit.

377 ASHMORE, JEROME. "Interdisciplinary Roots of the Theatre
of the Absurd." Modern Drama, 14, No. 1 (May 1971),
72-83.
Pinter's three principal concerns are man's relationship to man, menace, and uncertainty.

378 ASHWORTH, ARTHUR. "New Theatre: Ionesco, Beckett, Pinter."
Southerly, 22, No. 3 (1962), 145-52.
A discussion of Pinter as a Kafkaesque compromise
between the Theatre of the Absurd and realistic theatre
in that his characters and situations are realistic but
become "twisted askew" during the course of their confrontations.

Auburn

379 AUBURN, MARK S. and KATHERINE H. BURKMAN. Drama Through
     Performance. Boston: Houghton Mifflin, 1977.
          Includes a reprint of A Slight Ache, pp. 709-36. An
     "Action analysis and performance suggestions" section
     follows which suggests ways in which the meaning of the
     play can be brought out through certain performance
     techniques. An "Instructor's Manual" is also available:
     pp. 66-71 deal with specific suggestions for teachers who
     are teaching A Slight Ache or who are staging the play.

380 AYLING, RONALD, ed. Blasts and Benedictions. New York:
     St. Martin's Press, 1967.
          Includes Sean O'Casey's "The Bald Primaqueera" (See
     no. 1499).

381 AYLWIN, TONY. "The Memory of All That: Pinter's Old Times."
     English, 22 (Autumn 1973), 99-102.
          Ambiguity is the keyword to understanding Old Times.

382 BAHRENBURG, BRUCE. "Birthday Party." Newark Evening News,
     10 December 1968, p. 58.
          Review.

383 BAILEY, PAUL. "Pinter Play." Listener, 79 (2 May 1968), 583.
          Disapproving review of the radio version of Landscape
     which is "Short and strange."

384 BAKER, PETER. "The Pumpkin Eater." Films and Filming, 10,
     No. 11 (August 1964), 20-21.
          Film review.

385 _____. "The Servant." Films and Filming, 10, No. 3 (Decem-
     ber 1963), 24-25.
          Film review.

386 BAKER, WILLIAM and STEPHEN E. TABACHNICK. Harold Pinter.
     Writers and Critics series. Edinburgh: Oliver and
     Boyd, 1973. Reprinted: New York: Barnes and Noble, 1973.
          In addition to examining Pinter's works through Old
     Times (emphasis on conflict--masculine versus feminine,
     etc.), this study contains a chapter discussing Pinter's
     background, the modern British Jew from Hackney. Re-
     viewed: See nos. 960 and 1103.

387 _____. "Reflections on Ethnicity in Anglo-Jewish writing."
     Jewish Quarterly, 21, No. 1-2 (1973), 94-97.
          Pinter universalizes his material; compares Pinter with
     Wesker and Kops.

388 BAKEWELL, JOAN. "In an Empty Bandstand: Harold Pinter in
     Conversation with Joan Bakewell." The Listener, 82,
     No. 2119 (November 1969), 630-31.
     Interview.

389 BANKS-SMITH, NANCY. "In my View." London Sun, 26 October
     1966, p. 16.
     Review of the film version of The Caretaker.

390 _____. "Television is not Only for Looking at." London Sun,
     21 February 1967, p. 12.
     Review of television version of The Basement.

391 BARBER, JOHN. "Brilliant Revival of The Caretaker." London
     Daily Telegraph, 3 March 1972, p. 11.
     Review.

392 _____. "Harold Pinter, Conscious Alien." London Daily
     Telegraph, 3 May 1975, p. 14.

393 _____. "Hushed Pinter Plays With Elusive Themes." London
     Daily Telegraph, 3 July 1969, p. 19.
     Review of original stage production of Landscape and
     Silence: objects that they are "almost too densely
     textured for immediate theatrical effect." Schroll (See
     no. 1700) records reprint 4 July 1969, p. 21.

394 _____. "Pinter Nightmares of Invaded Privacy." London Daily
     Telegraph, 19 September 1970, p. 9.
     Review of London production of Tea Party and The Base-
     ment.

395 _____. "Pinter's Old Times Static But Gripping." London
     Daily Telegraph, 2 June 1971, p. 12.
     Review.

396 _____. "Pinter The Incomplete." London Daily Telegraph, 16
     November 1970, p. 6.

397 _____. "Plays Show Wedlock At Its Worst." London Daily
     Telegraph, 10 April 1969, p. 19.
     Review of Night.

398 _____. "A Warning Perhaps, But a Bore!" London Daily Express,
     20 May 1958, p. 12.
     Review of the first run of The Birthday Party.

399 BARKER, FELIX. "The Critic Ventures Alone in Pinter-Land."
London Evening News, 4 June 1965, p. 8.
Review of The Homecoming.

400 _____. "He's a New Kind of Hero." London Evening News, 9
February 1967, p. 8.
Film review of Accident.

401 _____. "Mr. Pinter's Puzzles Leave Me Guessing." London
Evening News, 18 September 1970, p. 3.
Review of Tea Party and The Basement.

402 _____. "Pinter Comes Up With a Disaster." London Evening
News, 3 July 1969, p. 5.
Review of Landscape and Silence.

403 _____. "Pinter's Pregnant Pauses." London Evening News, 19
June 1962, p. 5.
Review of The Collection.

404 BARLOW, GRAHAM. "Plays and Players at Home: Manchester."
Plays and Players, 9, No. 2 (November 1961), 34.
Review of The Birthday Party.

405 BARNES, CLIVE. "Butley." New York Times, 28 August 1971,
p. 14.
Review noting Pinter's direction.

406 _____. "Harold Pinter's Debt to James Joyce." New York
Times, 25 July 1969, Sec. D, p. 8.
Review of original stage production of Landscape and
Silence.

407 _____. "A Mystery that Asks All the Questions." London
Daily Express, 9 March 1960, p. 17.
Review of The Dumb Waiter and The Room.

408 _____. "Pacino, Ice-Cold and Savage." New York Times, 4
November 1969, p. 55.
Review of revue sketches included.

409 _____. "Pinter Festival Bows at Lincoln Center." New York
Times, 7 February 1971, p. 80.
Review of The Birthday Party.

410 _____. "Pinter 'Homecoming' at CSC." New York Times, 18
September 1972, p. 22.
Review.

411   ____. "Pinter Play Looks at Man Searching for Place in
        Life." London Daily Express, 26 March 1965, p. 4.
        Review of television production of Tea Party.

412   ____. "Stage: Caught in the Sway of a Sea-Changed Pinter."
        New York Times, 18 October 1971, Sec. C, p. 8.
        An extremely laudatory review of Old Times as a memory
        play, mentioning similarities to James Joyce and Proust.

413   ____. "Stage: 'The Innocents' Stars Claire Bloom." New
        York Times, 22 October 1976, Sec. C, p. 3.
        Production review of William Archibald's The Innocents
        (based on Henry James's The Turn of the Screw), which
        was directed by Pinter.

414   ____. "Stage: Pinter's Small Talk of Reality." New York
        Times, 3 August 1971, p. 43.
        A review of the Lincoln Center production of Landscape
        and Silence which sees Pinter's greatness as an "ability
        to see the world as it exists." However, the critic
        feels that these poetic plays, perhaps the author's best,
        suffer from a poor production--an opinion which Pinter
        disputes (See no. 67).

415   ____. "The Theatre: Pinter's Birthday Party." New York
        Times, 4 October 1967, p. 40.
        A favorable article calling The Birthday Party the
        newest good thing on Broadway. It mentions that the
        influence is obviously from Samuel Beckett and comments
        on the dialogue.

416   ____. "Theatre: The Civilized Violence of Harold Pinter."
        New York Times, 16 October 1968, p. 40.
        Review of Tea Party and The Basement. Although "minor
        Pinter," these plays are "better than major almost any-
        one else."

417   BARRETT, GERALD R. "William Friedkin Interview." Literature/
        Film Quarterly, 3, No. 4 (Fall 1975), 334-62.
        Friedkin comments on his discussion with Pinter about
        filming The Birthday Party, pp. 354-55.

418   BARRETT, RONA. "Rona Barrett in Hollywood." "Good Morning
        America," ABC Television, 16 December 1976.
        Report on Warner Brothers' refusal to permit Steve
        McQueen to film Old Times because the movie company con-
        siders the play "unacceptable."

Barrett

419   ____. "Rona Reviews." "Good Morning America," ABC Tele-
        vision, 19 November 1976.
              Film review of The Last Tycoon: "Perfectly dreadful
        ....poor script."

420   BARTHEL, JOAN. "If You Didn't Know It Was By Pinter." New
        York Times, 1 October 1967, p. 2.
              Review of The Homecoming.

*421   BARTHOLOMEW, L. J. "Form in Modern Drama." Ph.D. disserta-
        tion, University of Edinburgh, 1967-68.
              Cited in Index to Theses (London: Aslib).

422   BECKERMAN, BERNARD. "The Artifice of 'Reality' in Chekhov
        and Pinter." Paper read at the Modern Language Association
        Convention, New York, 29 December 1976.

423   ____. Dynamics of Drama: Theory and Method of Analysis.
        New York: Knopf, 1970.
              Discusses Pinter, pp. 238-39.

*424   BECKMANN, HEINZ. "Harold Pinter." Zeitwende, 31 (1960),
        858-59.
              Cited in Imhof (See no. 1098).

425   BENDER, TODD K., NANCY ARMSTRONG, SUE M. BRIGGUM, FRANK A.
        KNOBLOCH. Modernism in Literature. New York: Holt,
        Rinehart and Winston, 1977.
              An anthology which includes Pinter in the section on
        "Expressionism." Reprints A Slight Ache.

426   BENEDICTUS, DAVID. "Pinter's Errors." Spectator, 214 (11
        June 1965), 775.
              Review of the original production of The Homecoming.

427   BENSKY, LAWRENCE M. "Harold Pinter: An Interview." Paris
        Review, 10, No. 20 (Fall 1966), 12-37. Reprinted in:
        Writers at Work: The Paris Review Interviews, edited by
        George Plimpton. Third series. New York: Viking, 1967,
        pp. 347-68; reprinted in: Wager, The Playwright Speaks;
        (See no. 1905); reprinted in: Ganz. Pinter: A Collection
        of Critical Essays (See no. 843), pp. 19-33: reprinted in:
        Marowitz and Trussler, Theatre at Work (See no. 1405),
        pp. 96-109; reprinted in: Writers at Work: Interviews
        from Paris Review, edited by Kay Dick. Harmondsworth;
        Penguin, 1972, pp. 296-314.
              A highly informative and interesting interview in which
        Pinter talks about his background, his writing career,

the influences on his writing, his concepts and techniques, and the writing process. The Writers at Work series includes a manuscript page from The Homecoming.

428   _____. "Pinter: Violence is Natural: Interview with Harold Pinter." New York Times, 1 January 1967, p. 7.
An interview about dramatic techniques.

429   BENTLEY, JACK. "The Week's New Shows." London Sunday Pictorial, 1 May 1960, p. 21.
Review of The Caretaker.

430   BEN-ZVI, LINDA. "The Devaluation of Language in Avant-Garde Drama." Dissertation Abstracts International, 33: 1158-59A. Ph.D. dissertation, Oklahoma University, 1972.
Silence as communication in Pinter is discussed.

431   BERGONZI, BERNARD, ed. The Twentieth Century. Sphere History of Literature in the English Language Series, Vol. 7. London: Barrie and Jenkins, 1970.
Includes Hunter's "English Drama, 1900-1960" (See no. 1089), pp. 310-33.

432   BERKOWITZ, GERALD M. "Pinter's Revision of The Caretaker." Journal of Modern Literature, 5, No. 1 (February 1976), 109-16.
Sees revisions as related to attempts of the characters "to establish ties to each other, and to define themselves in terms of such ties."

433   _____. "The Question of Identity in the Plays of Harold Pinter." M.A. Thesis, Columbia University, 1965.
Useful, though somewhat limited because of the date of its composition.

434   BERKVIST, ROBERT. "What Does Pinter Mean? Don't Ask!" New York Times, 7 November 1976, Sec. D, pp. 1, 22.
A review of the Washington, D. C. production of No Man's Land (1976) which is largely an interview with Sir John Guilgud and Sir Ralph Richardson regarding whether the play has to have a meaning.

435   BERMEL, ALBERT. Contradictory Characters: An Interpretation of the Modern Theatre. New York: Dutton, 1973.
Looks at the artistry in contemporary theatre--A Slight Ache used as an example. Interesting.

Bermel

436   _____. "The Father as Fate." New Leader, 50 (23 October
       1967), 27-28.
           Review of The Birthday Party (New York).

437   _____. "Pinter's Nightmare." New Leader, 50 (30 January
       1967), 30-31.
           Review of the New York production of The Homecoming.

438   BERNHARD, F. J. "Beyond Realism: The Plays of Harold Pinter."
       Modern Drama, 8, No. 2 (September 1965), 185-91.
           The poetic quality of Pinter's language and the
       techniques which make it suprarealistic are examined.

439   _____. "English Theater 1963: In the Wake of the New Wave."
       Books Abroad, 38 (Spring 1964), 143-44.
           The Caretaker is seen as one of the landmarks in a
       revolution in the English theatre because it manages to
       break the conventions of form, yet does not descend to the
       inane. Also considers The Dwarfs and The Lover.

440   BIGSBY, C. W. E. "Pinter." In Vinson, Contemporary Drama-
       tists (See no. 1900), pp. 608-13.
           A brief overview.

441   BILL, JACK. "A Too-Sexy Pinter?" London Daily Mirror, 28
       March 1963, p. 18.
           Review of television production of The Lover.

442   BILLINGTON, MICHAEL. "The Caretaker." Manchester Guardian,
       3 March 1972, p. 8.
           Review.

443   _____. "Losey's Go-Between." Illustrated London News, July
       1971, p. 63.
           Film review.

444   _____. "Our Theatre in the Sixties." In Theatre 71,
       edited by Sheridan Morley (See no. 1447), pp. 208-33.
           Overview.

445   _____. "Persecution on the Plane." The Times (London), 3
       July 1969, p. 13.
           Review of Landscape and Silence.

446   BISHOP, GEORGE W. "Mr. Pinter Won't Answer." London Daily
       Telegraph, 25 April 1960, p. 15.
           Review of The Caretaker.

447 _____. "Zena Dare Says Farewell." London Daily Telegraph, 28 April 1958, p. 11.
Review of The Birthday Party.

448 BLACK, PETER. "Mr. Pinter Again--But Not So Obscure." London Daily Mail, 25 April 1960, p. 16.
Review of television version of A Night Out.

449 _____. "Peter Black's Teleview." London Daily Mail, 23 March 1960, p. 16.
Review of the British television production of The Birthday Party.

450 _____. "Teleview." London Daily Mail, 12 May 1961, p. 3.
Review of British television production of The Collection, "an almost painfully explicit study of jealousy."

451 _____. "TV." London Daily Mail, 26 March 1965, p. 3.
Review of television production of Tea Party.

452 BLACK, SUSAN M. "Play Reviews." Theatre Arts, 45 (December 1961), 8-13.
Includes a critical review of New York production of The Caretaker, p. 12.

453 BLAU, HERBERT. The Impossible Theatre: A Manifesto. New York: Macmillan, 1964, pp. 254-56.
Pinter is essentially pessimistic, as in The Birthday Party.

454 _____. "Politics and the Theatre." Wascana Review, 2, No. 2 (1967), 5-23.
Discussion of how Pinter (The Homecoming), Beckett, and Genet exploit present social and political conditions.

455 BLEICH, DAVID. "Emotional Origins of Literary Meaning." College English, 31, No. 1 (October 1969), 30-40.
Literary criticism is emotionally based, according to Bleich, and The Caretaker is used as an example to prove his point.

456 BOGART, TRAVIS MILLER and WILLIAM I. OLIVER, eds. Modern Drama: Essays in Criticism. New York: Oxford University Press, 1965, pp. 3-19.
Includes Oliver's "Between Absurdity and the Playwright" (See no. 1515).

457 BOLTON, WHITNEY. "Brilliant the Word for Two Pinter Plays."
     New York Morning Telegraph, 23 October 1968, p. 3.
          Review of Tea Party and The Basement (New York). The
     battle of the sexes is seen as the main theme of these
     plays.

458 _____. "'Caretaker' is Vivid, Intensely Satisfying." New
     York Morning Telegraph, 6 October 1961, p. 2.
          Review of New York production of The Caretaker.

459 _____. "'Caretaker' Still Exerts Fascination." New York
     Morning Telegraph, 1 February 1964, p. 2.
          Review of the film version of The Caretaker.

460 _____. "Harold Pinter Play: 'The Homecoming.'" New York
     Morning Telegraph, 7 January 1967, p. 3.
          Review of The Homecoming (New York), dealing with
     Teddy's dream/reality, in which the play is seen as being
     long and tedious.

461 _____. "Harold Pinter's 'The Birthday Party.'" New York
     Morning Telegraph, 5 October 1967, p. 3.
          Review of The Birthday Party (New York).

462 _____. "Pinter Plays Heady, But Foggy, too." New York
     Morning Telegraph, 11 December 1964, p. 2.
          Review of New York production of A Slight Ache and The
     Room.

463 _____. "Two Off-Beat Plays by Beckett, Pinter." New York
     Morning Telegraph, 7 January 1964, p. 2.
          Review of The Lover (New York).

464 BOOTHROYD, BASIL. "At the Play." Punch, 234 (28 May 1958),
     721.
          Review of the first run of The Birthday Party, "a
     masterpiece of meaningless significance."

465 _____. "At the Play." Punch, 245 (25 September 1963), 467.
          Review of The Dwarfs and The Lover.

466 BOSWORTH, PATRICIA. "Why Doesn't He Write More?" New York
     Times, 27 October 1968, Sec. D, p. 3.
          Interview.

467 BOULTON, JAMES T. "Harold Pinter: The Caretaker and Other
     Plays." Modern Drama, 6, No. 2 (September 1963), 131-40;

reprinted in: Ganz, Pinter: A Collection of Critical
Essays (See no. 843), pp. 93-104.
    An examination of themes (especially the terror of
man's loneliness) and poetic methods of Pinter's work up
to and including The Caretaker, with a comparison to
Kafka.

468   BOURNE, RICHARD. "New Pinter on Television." Manchester
      Guardian, 29 March 1963, p. 9.
          Review of The Lover.

*469 BOURQUE, JOSEPH H. "Theatre of the Absurd: A New Approach
      to Audience Reaction." Research Studies, Washington State
      University, 36 (1968), 311-24.

470   BOVIE, PALMER. "Seduction: The Amphitryon Theme from
      Plautus to Pinter." Minnesota Review, 7, No. 3-4 (1967),
      304-13.
          The Lover is placed in this tradition.

471   BOWEN, JOHN. "Accepting the Illusion." Twentieth Century,
      169 (February 1961), 153-65.
          Classifies Pinter as a realist on the basis of his
      dialogue.

*472 _____. "Changing Fashions in the English Theatre." Listener,
      60 (1958), 269.

473   BOYUM, JOY GOULD, and ADRIENNE SCOTT, eds. Film as Film:
      Critical Responses to Film Art. Boston: Allyn and Bacon,
      1971.
          Includes reprints of six reviews of Accident by Alpert
      (See no. 151), Crist (See no. 639), Gill (See no. 871),
      Milne (See no. 1428) and Sarris (See nos. 1677 and 1686).

474   BRADBROOK, MURIEL C. English Dramatic Form: A History of
      its Development. New York: Barnes and Noble, 1965, pp.
      188-90; London: 1965.
          Feels Pinter is limited because the individual in his
      plays is unable to feel "true responsibility, and there-
      fore little genuine guilt."

475   BRAHMS, CARYL. "Share My Fall-Out." Plays and Players, 6,
      No. 12 (September 1959), 11.
          Revue sketches reviewed.

Brahms

476 ____. "The Silence of the Pope." Time and Tide, 3-9
     October 1963, p. 33.
          Review of The Lover and The Dwarfs.

477 BRANIGAN, ALAN. "Impressive. Pinter Plays Puzzle and
     Enchant in Village." Newark Evening News, 27 November
     1962, p. 62.
          Review of The Dumb Waiter and The Collection, New York
     production.

478 BRATER, ENOCH. "Pinter's Homecoming on Celluloid." Modern
     Drama, 17, No. 4 (December 1974), 443-48.
          Discusses the transformation of The Homecoming to the
     screen and how the play is opened out--"deliberately
     violates the claustrophobic atmosphere of his original
     one-room set."

478a BRAUNMULLER, ALBERT R. "Film and Narrative in Pinter's Old
     Times." Paper read at the Modern Language Association
     Convention, Chicago, 30 December 1977.
          A discussion of "links between the speaker and the
     narrated past," sexuality, and the function of filmic
     references, in particular Odd Man Out, in Old Times.

479 BRAY, J. J. "The Ham Funeral." Meanjin, 21 (March 1962),
     32-34.
          Traces the influence of the Australian Patrick White
     in Pinter's work.

*480 BREDELLA, LOTHAR. "Die Intention und Wirkung literarischer
     Texte: Arnold Weskers Chips With Everything und Harold
     Pinters The Birthday Party." Der fremdsprachliche Unter-
     richt, 7, No. 25 (February 1973), 34-49.
          In German.

481 BRIEN, ALAN. "Chelsea Beaujolais." Spectator, 209 (6 May
     1960), 661.
          The Caretaker presents a realistic picture of man in
     Hitchcockian terms.

482 ____. "Communications." Spectator, 200 (30 May 1958), 687.
          Again compares Pinter to Hitchcock, but this time sees
     The Birthday Party as a failure because of its overuse
     of reversed clichés and lack of humor (!).

483 ____. "The Guilty Seam." Spectator, 204 (29 January 1960),
     137-38.
          An ambivalent review of The Room and The Dumb Waiter,
     approving of the plays, but suggesting that Pinter "must

now start to answer his own questions." Somewhere between Brecht and Chayefsky, Pinter's dramas of ritualism and manipulation remain "obstinately a-plicit (as opposed to 'explicit')."

484 ____. "In London: The Homecoming, 'an unnerving horror-comic skill.'" Vogue, 146 (15 September 1965), 75.
Review of the original production of The Homecoming. The play has no relationship to modern England and remains unexplained, as though the last reel of a Hitchcock film is missing. Pinter does "see in the lower depths the only reserves of vitality and energy, however perverted and violent, to be found in a declining society."

485 ____. "Pinter's first Play." London Sunday Telegraph, 21 June 1964, p. 10.
Review of The Birthday Party revival.

486 ____. "A Pinter Week." London Sunday Telegraph, 8 October 1961, p. 10.
Review of A Night Out.

487 ____. "Something Blue." Spectator, 204 (10 June 1960), 835-36.
Review of the original production of The Caretaker. With its assertions about the nature of communication (lack of communication stifles, but actually communicating can lead to something worse), The Caretaker is a change from the earlier plays. Brien sees the drama as non-symbolic.

488 BRIGG, PETER A. "The Understanding and Uses of Time in the Plays of John Boynton Priestley, Samuel Beckett and Harold Pinter." Dissertation Abstracts International, 32: 6964A. Ph.D. dissertation, University of Toronto, 1971.
Pinter is only peripherally aware of time as a problem in the construction of his plays, according to Brigg.

489 BRINE, ADRIAN. "In Search of a Hero." Spectator, 26 February 1965, p. 264.
Because of the functional non-functioning of dialogue in Pinter's plays, a new type of actor is needed to fulfill the demands of the roles. A brief look at many modern playwrights, including N. F. Simpson and John Arden.

490 ____. "MacDavies Is No Clochard." Drama, 61 (Summer 1961), 35-37.

Brockett

> Davies in The Caretaker is portrayed as a peculiarly
> English character, thus allowing only an inadequate
> transfer of the drama to other countries. Using the
> failure of the French production of The Caretaker as a
> starting point, Brine discusses modern drama and the
> differences in national character, as well as the need
> of the audience to grow accustomed to some playwrights.

491 BROCKETT, OSCAR G. The Essential Theatre. New York: Holt,
Rinehart and Winston, 1976, pp. 232-33.
Includes a brief discussion of Pinter as the "most
admired" of all contemporary English dramatists.

492 _____. History of the Theatre. Boston: Allyn and Bacon,
1974. Third edition, 1977.

493 _____. Perspectives on Contemporary Theatre. Baton Rouge,
Louisiana: Louisiana State University Press, 1971.

494 _____ and ROBERT R. FINDLAY. A Century of Innovation:
A History of European and American Theatre and Drama
1870-1970. Englewood Cliffs, New Jersey: Prentice-Hall,
1973, pp. 584, 626-30, 683, 694, 697, 700.
Includes overview of Pinter's major plays through
Old Times.

495 BRODY, ALAN. "The Gift of Realism: Hitchcock and Pinter."
Journal of Modern Literature, 3 (1973), 149-72.
Hitchcock and Pinter alternately influence each other
--Pinter uses Hitchcock's conventions to structure his
plays, which prepare for Hitchcock's later films.

496 BROOK, PETER, PETER HALL, MICHEL ST. DENIS, and PETER SHAFFER.
"Artaud for Artaud's Sake." Encore, 11, No. 3 (May-June
1964), 20-31.

497 BROOKE, NICHOLAS. "The Characters of Drama." Critical
Quarterly, 6 (1964), 78-82.
Passing references to Pinter.

498 BROOKS, MARY ELLEN. "The British Theatre of Metaphysical
Despair." Literature and Ideology, No. 12 (1972), pp.
49-58.
The Birthday Party expresses and promotes helplessness.
Brooks also considers Waiting for Godot.

499 BROWN, JOHN RUSSELL. "Dialogue in Pinter and Others."
Critical Quarterly, 7, No. 3 (Autumn 1965), 225-43; reprinted in: Brown, Modern British Dramatists (See no.
501), pp. 122-44.

Pinter's dialogue, influenced by Beckett and Chekhov, lies behind his success. A study of the texture of that dialogue.

500 _____. "Mr. Pinter's Shakespeare." Critical Quarterly, 5, No. 3 (Autumn 1963), 251-65; reprinted in: Freedman, Essays in the Modern Drama (See no. 799), pp. 352-66.
With Beckett, Ionesco, and Shakespeare, Pinter shares the slow exposure of character and motivation through seemingly meaningless repetitions, silences, insistences, and denials which imply the underlying context of the character's actions (See also no. 1772).

501 _____, ed. Modern British Dramatists: A Collection of Critical Essays. London: Heinemann, 1968; reprinted in Twentieth Century Views series, Englewood Cliffs, New Jersey: Prentice Hall/Spectrum, 1968.
A discussion of Pinter's work is included as part of this brief survey. Includes: Brown (See no. 499), Brustein (See no. 512), Esslin (See no. 749); Milne (See no. 1430), Nelson (See no. 1481), Worsley (See no. 2002).

502 _____. Theatre Language: A Study of Arden, Osborne, Pinter and Wesker. London: Penguin, 1972; New York: Taplinger, 1972.
Includes: "Harold Pinter: Action and Control; The Homecoming and Other Plays," pp. 93-117; "Harold Pinter: Gestures, Spectacle and Performance; The Caretaker, The Dwarfs and Other Plays," pp. 55-92; and "Harold Pinter: The Birthday Party and Other Plays," pp. 15-54.

503 _____ and BERNARD HARRIS, eds. Contemporary Theater. Stratford-on-Avon Studies, No. 4. London: Edward Arnold, 1962.
Nine essays, including Kenneth Muir (See no. 1457), R. D. Smith (See no. 1757), and J. L. Styan (See no. 1790).

504 BROWNE, E. MARTIN. "A First Look Round the English Theatre, 1965." Drama Survey, 4 (Summer 1965), 177.
Review of the original production of The Homecoming.

505 _____. "A Look Round the English Theatre, 1961." Drama Survey, 1 (1961), 227-31.
Review of The Caretaker included.

506 _____. "A Peep at the English Theatre, Fall 1963." Drama Survey, 3 (February 1964), 413-16.
Review of The Dwarfs and The Lover.

Browne

507 _____. "Theatre Survey: A Look Round the English Theatre, 1962." Drama Survey, 2 (1962), 182-83.
Includes a review of The Collection.

508 BROWNE, TERRY. Playwright's Theatre: The English Stage Company at the Royal Court. London: Pitman, 1975.
A history. Reviewed: 1032.

509 BRUDNOY, DAVID. "Film." National Review, 3 December 1971, p. 1368.
Film review of The Go-Between.

*510 B[RULEZ], R[AYMOND]. "Nieuwe Dramatick?" Nieuwe Vlaams Tijdschrift, 18 (1965), 835-36.

511 BRUNIUS, JOSEPH. "Pinter in Paris." Plays and Players, 8, No. 9 (June 1961), 3.
Review of The Caretaker.

512 BRUSTEIN, ROBERT. "The English Stage." New Statesman, 70, No. 1795 (6 August 1965), 193-94. Reprinted in Brown, Modern British Dramatists (See no. 501).
Brief survey. Brustein feels that Pinter "excludes statement from his work altogether."

513 _____. "Mid-Season Gleanings." New Republic, 150 (1 February 1964), 28, 30.
Review of The Lover (New York): "a feeble anecdote."

514 _____. "A Naturalism of the Grotesque." New Republic, 145 (23 October 1961), 29-30. Reprinted in: Brustein Seasons of Discontent (See no. 516). See also no. 1620.
The Caretaker is about the "spiritual vacancy of modern life" and lack of communication.

515 _____. "Saturn Eats His Children." New Republic, 156 (28 January 1967), 34-36.
Review of The Homecoming (New York). Brustein finds Pinter too "bizarre" and "vulgar."

516 _____. Seasons of Discontent: Dramatic Opinions, 1959-1965. New York: Simon and Schuster, 1965.
Includes "A Naturalism of the Grotesque" (See no 514).

517 _____. The Theater of Revolt: An Approach to the Modern Drama. Boston: Atlantic/Little, Brown, 1962. Reprinted: London and Toronto: Methuen, 1965.
A study of rebellion in the theatre in existential terms; Pinter's debt to Pirandello is cited.

518 _____. The Third Theatre. New York: Knopf, 1969. Reprinted: New York: Simon and Schuster/Clarion, 1970.
In his section on "The Thoughts from Abroad" Brustein
says he does not like The Homecoming, which he clearly
did not understand.

519 _____. "Thoughts from Home and Abroad." New Republic, 152
(26 June 1965), 29-30.
Review of the original production of The Homecoming.

520 BRYDEN, RONALD. "Atavism." New Statesman, 66 (27 September
1963), 420.
Review of The Dwarfs and The Lover. Bryden sees The
Lover as a criticism of the "contradictory liberal axioms
of sex by which we moderns try to operate."

521 _____. "Fulfillments." New Statesman, 31 December 1965,
pp. 1037-38.
Review of The Homecoming.

522 _____. "Pared to Privacy, Melting Into Silence." London
Observer, 6 July 1969, p. 22.
Beckett's influence can be seen in Landscape and Silence.

523 _____. "Pinter." London Observer, 19 February 1967, p. 11.
A portrait.

524 _____. "Pinter's New Pacemaker." London Observer, 6 June
1971, p. 27.
Review of Old Times.

525 _____. "A Stink of Pinter." New Statesman, 69 (11 June
1965), 928.
About Pinter's imagery in the original production of
The Homecoming.

526 _____. "Three Men in a Room." New Statesman, 67 (26 June
1964), 1004. Reprinted in: Bryden, The Unfinished Hero,
pp. 86-90 (See no. 527).
The underlying theme of domination runs through Pinter's work. The plays present a self-contained world in
which nothing important is said but everything reflects
a battle for control over others.

527 _____. The Unfinished Hero. London: Faber, 1969.
Includes "Three Men in a Room" (See no. 526). Reviewed: See no. 1486.

528   BURGHARDT, LORRAINE HALL. "Game Playing in Three by Pinter."
      Modern Drama, 17, No. 4 (December 1974), 377-88.
            "Games people play" is seen as the frame for under-
      standing The Dumb Waiter, The Birthday Party, and Tea
      Party.

529   BURKMAN, KATHARINE H. The Dramatic World of Harold Pinter:
      Its Basis in Ritual. Columbus: Ohio State University
      Press, 1971.
            Two kinds of ritual--everyday meaningless and meaning-
      ful sacrificial--are counterpointed. Draws upon Frazier's
      The Golden Bough. Interesting and valid to a point, but
      lacks unity. Reviewed: See no. 825.

530   _____. "Pinter's A Slight Ache as Ritual." Modern Drama,
      11 (December 1968), 326-35.
            The fertility ritual pattern is traced: Edward is the
      winter god-king sacrificed for the resurrection of the
      spring god (the Matchseller); Flora is the earth-mother
      fertility goddess.

531   BUSCH, LLOYD. "The Plot-Within-the-Plot: Harold Pinter's
      The Caretaker." Paper given at an S.A.A. Convention, 8
      December 1967, Los Angeles, Calif.

532   BUTCHER, MARYVONNE. "Achtung!" Tablet, 218 (14 March 1964),
      301-2.
            Review of the film version of The Caretaker.

533   _____. "Modern Love." Tablet, 218 (July 1964), 809-10.
            Film review of The Pumpkin Eater.

534   _____. "Outrageous Fortunes." Tablet, 221 (11 February
      1967), 159.
            Film review of Accident.

535   CAIN, ALEX MATHESON. "Critics' Column." Tablet, 214 (16
      March 1960), 272.
            Review of The Room and The Dumb Waiter.

536   _____. "Strange Menages." Tablet, 216 (30 June 1962), 624.
            Review of original stage production of The Collection.

537   _____. "Worlds of Fantasy." Tablet, 215 (25 February 1961),
      178.
            Review of original stage production of A Slight Ache.

538 CAIN, CINDY S. A. M. "Structure in the One-Act Play."
        Modern Drama, 12, No. 4 (February 1970), 390-98.
            Today's one-act plays fall into two categories accord-
        ing to the emphasis on one of two major components: "the
        tension line and individual sections." The Dumb Waiter
        is placed in the "tension line" category.

539 CAIRNS, D. A. "Batting for Pinter." The Times (London), 7
        June 1975, p. 13.
            Correspondence regarding the names of the characters
        in No Man's Land--former cricket players.

540 CALAS, ANDRE. "Plays and Players Abroad: Paris." Plays
        and Players, 8, No. 6 (March 1961), 31.
            Review of The Caretaker.

541 CALLEN, ANTHONY. "Comedy and Passion in the Plays of Harold
        Pinter." Forum for Modern Language Studies, 4, No. 3
        (1968), 297-306.
            A semi-answer to Richard Schechner (See no. 1690).
        Callen uses The Caretaker and The Homecoming to show that
        rather than mystifying us, Pinter clarifies for us.

542 _____. "Stoppard's Godot: Some French Influences on Post-
        War English Drama." New Theatre Magazine, 10, No. 1
        (Winter 1969), 22-30.
            Callen calls Pinter "the major English playwright to
        have felt the influence of the French." The Caretaker
        is discussed briefly, as are Beckett, Stoppard, Ionesco,
        Simpson, and Osborne.

543 CALLENBACK, ERNEST. "The Servant." Film Quarterly, 18,
        No. 1 (Fall 1964), 36-38.
            Film review.

544 CANADAY, NICHOLAS, JR. "Harold Pinter's 'Tea Party': Seeing
        and Not Seeing." Studies in Short Fiction, 6 (1969), 580-85.
            The short story version of "Tea Party" is examined;
        the victory of violence by an "enemy-usurper" is traced.

545 CANBY, VINCENT. "The Homecoming." New York Times, 13 Novem-
        ber 1973, p. 53.
            A review with high praise for the film--which opens
        out, as when Ruth leaves the house: "...but even the
        street we see her walk down is as sealed off from humanity
        as the interior of the house. It's not that we sense that
        other lives are not being lived elsewhere in Pinter's world,
        but rather that those lives are simply reflections and ex-
        tensions of those Pinter has chosen to show us."

Canby

546 _____. "In Films, Acting Is Behavior." New York Times, 12
     December 1976, Sec. 2, pp. 1, 13.
         Includes film review of The Last Tycoon.

547 _____. "Screen: Unsettling World of 'The Birthday Party.'"
     New York Times, 10 December 1968, p. 54.
         Review of film version of The Birthday Party which is
     seen as a "good recording of an extraordinary play."

548 CANNY, MILDRED ROSEMARY. "Patterns of Human Interaction
     in the Drama of Harold Pinter." Dissertation Abstracts
     International, 31: 6204A. Ph.D. dissertation, University
     of Wisconsin, 1970.
         Imagery and structure in Pinter's drama create a fusion
     of realistic and poetic qualities.

*549 CAPONE, GIOVANNA. Drammi per voci: Dylan Thomas, Samuel
     Beckett, Harold Pinter. Bologna, 1967.
         In Italian. Cited in Palmer (See no. 1530).

*550 CARAT, J. "Harold Pinter et W. Gombrowicz." Preuves, No.
     177 (November 1965), pp. 75-77.
         In French. Cited in 1965 M. L. A. International
     Bibliography.

551 CAREY, GARY. "No Man's Land." Library Journal, 15 October
     1975, p. 1945.
         Book review: "typical, but not first-rate Pinter....it's
     time to move on to new territory."

552 CARPENTER, CHARLES A. "The Absurdity of Dread: Pinter's The
     Dumb Waiter." Modern Drama, 16, No. 3 (December 1973),
     279-85.
         The play is called "a mock melodramatic farce."

553 _____. "Harold Pinter." In Insight IV: Analyses of Modern
     British and American Drama. Frankfurt: Hirschgraben, 1975,
     pp. 102-27.
         Includes an analysis of The Caretaker.

554 _____. Modern British Drama. Northbrook, Ill.: AHM
     Publishing Corp., 1975. Reprinted: 1977. In the "Golden-
     tree Bibliographies in Language and Literature Series."
         A bibliography which includes a section on Pinter.

555 _____. "The New Bibliography of Modern Drama Studies."
     Modern Drama, 12 (1969), 49-56.
         Book review of Adelman and Dworkin, Modern Drama:
     A Checklist (See no. 137).

556   _____. "'What Have I Seen, the Scum or the Essence?'
        Symbolic Fallout in Pinter's Birthday Party." Modern
        Drama, 17 (December 1974), 389-402.
            Carpenter finds that certain symbols (e.g., news-
        papers) function in clusters in The Birthday Party.

557   CARTHEW, ANTHONY. "This is the Best Play in London." Lon-
        don Daily Herald, 28 April 1960, p. 3.
            Review of original production of The Caretaker.

558   CARTHEW, PETER. "Three." Plays and Players, 8, No. 6
        (March 1961), 11.
            Review of A Slight Ache.

559   CASE, L. L. "A Parody on Harold Pinter's Style of Drama."
        New York Times, 16 May 1965, Sec. 2, p. 6.

560   CAVANAUGH, ARTHUR. "Stage." Sign, 46 (March 1967), 31.
            Review of The Homecoming (New York) which is seen as
        "sordid" and lacking significance.

561   _____. "Stage." Sign, 47 (December 1967), 46.
            Review of The Birthday Party (New York).

562   C. B. "Unhappy With the World." Jewish Chronicle, 2 April
        1965, p. 54.
            Review of television production of Tea Party.

563   CECIL, NORMAN. "The Go-Between." Films in Review, 22, No.
        8 (October 1971), 509-10.
            Film review; essentially a synopsis.

564   C. H. "Harold Pinter's Old Times." London Sunday Express,
        6 June 1971, p. 23.
            Review.

565   CHAPMAN, JOHN. "'The Birthday Party' A Whatsit by Pinter."
        New York Daily News, 4 October 1967, p. 86. Reprinted in:
        New York Theatre Critics' Reviews, 9 October 1967, p. 248.
            Review of New York production of The Birthday Party.

566   _____. "Donald Pleasence Superb Actor and 'Caretaker'
        Splendid Play." New York Daily News, 5 October 1961,
        p. 73. Reprinted New York Theatre Critics' Reviews, 9
        October 1961, p. 280.
            Review of The Caretaker.

Chapman

567 _____. "Pinter's 'Homecoming' a Weirdy." New York Daily
News, 6 January 1967, p. 68. Reprinted in: New York
Theatre Critics' Reviews, 16 January 1967, p. 394.
Review of The Homecoming (New York).

568 CHIARI, JOSEPH. Landmarks of Contemporary Drama. London:
Herbert Jenkins, 1965.
Expresses a high opinion of Pinter's ability to create
jigsaw puzzle plays as excellent as The Caretaker, though
Chiari feels that the plays have no cosmic significance.

*569 CHRISTOPHORY, JULES. "Artaud and Pinter." Nouvelle Revue
Luxembourgeoise Academia, 1971, pp. 197-204.

570 C. L. "The Birthday Party." Jewish Chronicle, 23 May 1958,
p. 26.
Review.

571 _____. "Double Bill." Jewish Chronicle, 18 March 1960,
p. 39.
Review of The Room and The Dumb Waiter.

572 _____. "Pinter's Humour." Jewish Chronicle, 22 June 1962,
p. 30.
Review of The Collection.

573 CLAYTON, SYLVIA. "'Basement' Is Ornate with No Magic."
London Daily Telegraph, 21 February 1967, p. 17.
Review of television version of The Basement which for
Clayton provides no tension in its depiction of a battle
for territory.

574 _____. "Close-Ups Aid 'Caretaker' Hypnotism." London Daily
Telegraph, 26 October 1966, p. 17.
Review of the film version of The Caretaker.

575 CLURMAN, HAROLD. All People are Famous: Instead of an Auto-
biography. New York: Harcourt, 1974.

576 _____. The Divine Pastime. New York: Macmillan, 1974.
The Homecoming, The Caretaker, and Old Times discussed.

577 _____. "Films." Nation, 6 January 1969, pp. 29-30.
Review of the film version of The Birthday Party.
While the review is generally favorable, Clurman feels
that the essence of the work has been changed: "On the

screen The Birthday Party becomes a suspense and horror
story--albeit a very special one...on the stage The
Birthday Party, less obviously ominous, is an inescapably
living experience, life itself!"

578   . The Naked Image: Observations on the Modern Theatre.
    New York: Macmillan, 1966, pp. 105-14.
        Includes discussion of The Caretaker, The Collection,
The Dumb Waiter, The Lover, The Room, and A Slight Ache.

579   . Seven Plays of the Modern Theatre. New York: Grove,
    1967.
        Includes a reprint of The Birthday Party.

580   . "Theatre." Nation, 193 (21 October 1961), 276.
        A favorable review of the New York production of The
Caretaker which suggests "ideological patterns": Mick
is godhead (both angel and devil); Aston is Christ figure;
Davies represents mankind.

581   . "Theatre." Nation, 195 (15 December 1962), 429-30.
        Negative review of The Dumb Waiter and The Collection,
New York production. The Collection is a "protest, albeit
a hopeless one, against the pressure of our industrial
civilization" which has no "feeling."

582   . "Theatre." Nation, 198 (27 January 1964), 106.
        Review of The Lover (New York).

583   . "Theatre." Nation, 199 (28 December 1964), 522-24.
        Review of A Slight Ache and The Room.

584   . "Theatre." Nation, 204 (23 January 1967), 122-23.
        Review of The Homecoming (New York).

585   . "Theatre." Nation, 205 (23 October 1967), 412-14.
        Positive review of New York production of The Birthday
Party which is "not obscure."

586   . "Theatre." Nation, 207 (4 November 1968), 477.
        Review of Tea Party and The Basement (New York).

587   . "Theatre." Nation, 20 April 1970, pp. 473-74, 476.
        Review of Landscape and Silence (New York).

588   . "Theatre." Nation, 212 (7 June 1971), 732-33.
        Clurman finds The Homecoming "a powerful statement
wrought by a master hand."

Clurman

589   ____. "Theatre." Nation, 213 (6 December 1971), 603.
         Review of Old Times, Pinter's "most poetic" work,
         which is filled with masterly craftsmanship.

590   ____. "Theatre." Nation, 16 August 1975, pp. 123-24.
         Pinter, Orton, and Stoppard are compared, with special
         emphasis on No Man's Land--while fascinating, it is "an
         utterance which has its source in a society at a dead
         end."

591   ____. "Theatre." Nation, 233 (27 November 1976), 572-73.
         A production review of No Man's Land, which Clurman
         likes, although he admits that he does not know what it
         is about.

592   COCKS, JAY. "Babylon Revisited." Time, 108 (6 December
         1976), 87-88.
         Film review of The Last Tycoon.

593   ____. "Fire and Ice." Time, No. 25 (17 December 1973),
         pp. 80-81. See also no. 1620.
         An extremely flattering review of the film version of
         The Homecoming, especially of Pinter's writing, "probably
         the best scenario writing now being done in English."

594   ____. "Two by Losey." Time, 9 August 1971, p. 63.
         A favorable film review of The Go-Between.

595   COE, RICHARD M. "Logic, Paradox, and Pinter's Homecoming."
         Educational Theatre Journal, 27 (1975), 488-97.
         The Homecoming is a successful piece of theatre be-
         cause it mystifies by excluding contextual information in
         ways similar to the audiences' real world experiences,
         though it makes no attempt to resolve those fears which
         it reflects.

596   COHEN, MARK. "The Plays of Harold Pinter." Jewish Quarterly,
         8 (Summer 1961), 21-22.
         Pinter's cliché-filled, repetitious dialogue and themes
         of domination, menace, security, and the malignant orga-
         nization are mentioned in this book review of A Slight
         Ache and Other Plays.

597   COHEN, MARSHALL. "Theater 67." Partisan Review, 34, No. 3
         (Summer 1967), 436-44.
         Review of The Homecoming, New York production.

598   COHN, RUBY. "The Absurdly Absurd: Avatars of Godot." <u>Com-</u>
<u>parative Literature Studies</u>, 2 (1965), 233-40.
     As examples of the Absurd, both <u>Waiting for Godot</u> and
<u>The Dumb Waiter</u> exemplify the Absurd doctrine of man's
awareness of his place in the universe through the
absurdity of the play's form.

599   _____. <u>Currents in Contemporary Drama</u>. Bloomington, Indiana:
Indiana University Press, 1969, pp. 15-17, 78-81, 177-81.
     Includes an evaluation of Pinter. <u>See</u> especially
Chapter Five, "The Role and the Real."

600   _____. "Latter Day Pinter." <u>Drama Survey</u>, 3, No. 3
(Winter 1964), 366-77.
     Pinter's career to this point displays a concern with
appearance vs. reality, but it also shows technical
progress.

601   _____. "The World of Harold Pinter." <u>Tulane Drama Review</u>,
6 (March 1962), 55-68. Reprinted in: Ganz, <u>Pinter: A</u>
<u>Collection of Critical Essays</u> (<u>See</u> no. 843), pp. 78-92.
     "Man vs. the System" with a "central victim-villain"
conflict is proposed as Pinter's main theme as revealed
through the cumulative use of symbols and dialogue.

602   _____, and BERNARD DUKORE. <u>Twentieth Century Drama: England,</u>
<u>Ireland, the United States</u>. New York: Random House,
1966.
     Includes reprint of <u>The Dumb Waiter</u>.

603   COLEMAN, ARTHUR and GARY TAYLER. <u>Drama Criticism: Vol. 1:</u>
<u>A Checklist of Interpretations Since 1940 of English and</u>
<u>American Plays</u>. Denver: Alan Swallow, 1966.
     Bibliography.

604   COLEMAN, JOHN. "Malice Domestic." <u>New Statesman</u>, 15 Novem-
ber 1963, p. 718.
     Film review of <u>The Servant</u>.

605   _____. "No Accident." <u>New Statesman</u>, 10 February 1967,
p. 198.
     Film review of <u>Accident</u>.

606   _____. "Pinter's Party Pictured." <u>New Statesman</u>, 20 Febru-
ary 1970, p. 267.
     Review of film version of <u>The Birthday Party</u>.

Coleman

607 _____. "Pumpkin Pie." New Statesman, 17 July 1964, p. 97.
Film review of The Pumpkin Eater.

608 _____. "The Road to Sidcup." New Statesman, 13 March 1964,
p. 423.
A very favorable review of the film version of The
Caretaker which discusses some of the differences between
the play and the film. Comments on Pinter's ability to
reproduce everyday language and man's propensity to de-
grade others in order to upgrade himself as seen in The
Caretaker.

609 COLEMAN, ROBERT. "'Caretaker' Cheered; Oh Well!" New York
Mirror, 5 October 1961, p. 28. Reprinted in: New York
Theatre Critics' Reviews, 9 October 1961, p. 250.
Disapproving review of New York production of The Care-
taker. Coleman is disturbed by the "maladjusted" char-
acters.

610 COLIN, SAUL. "Plays and Players in New York." Plays and
Players, 9, No. 3 (December 1961), 19.
Review of The Caretaker.

611 COMERFORD, ADELAIDE. "The Quiller Memorandum." Films in
Review, 18, No. 1 (January 1967), 54.
Film review; essentially a synopsis.

612 CONLON, PATRICK O[WEN]. "Social Commentary in Contemporary
Great Britain as Reflected in the Plays of John Osborne,
Harold Pinter, and Arnold Wesker." Dissertation Abstracts,
29: 3713-14A, Northwestern University, 1969.
Conlon finds that Pinter's works "portray the contemporary Briton's pitiful defenses against a suffocating
world of violence and frustration."

613 COOK, ALTON. "'The Guest' Lacks Stage Version's Force."
New York World Telegram and Sun, 21 January 1964, p. 12.
Disparaging review of film version of The Caretaker.

614 COOK, DAVID. "Of the Strong Breed." Transition, 3 (1964),
38-40.
Wole Soyinka's portrayal of Nigeria is in part influenced by Pinter.

615 _____, and HAROLD F. BROOKS. "A Room with Three Views:
Harold Pinter's The Caretaker." Kosmos, 1 (June 1967),
62-69.
The Caretaker is a "tragic farce" about the fear of
being known.

616 COOKE, FRED. "Mystery." London Reynolds News, 27 March
1960, p. 11.
Review of British television production of The Birthday
Party.

617 _____. "Pinter." London Sunday Citizen, 28 March 1965,
p. 23.
Review of television production of Tea Party.

618 COOKE, RICHARD P. "Beckett and Pinter." Wall Street Journal,
7 January 1964, p. 18.
Review of The Lover (New York).

619 _____. "A Pair from Pinter." Wall Street Journal, 17 October 1968, p. 20. Reprinted in: New York Theatre Critics'
Reviews, 30 December 1968, pp. 138-39.
Review of Tea Party and The Basement (New York) stating
that these plays attract attention only because they are
written by Pinter.

620 _____. "Pinter Party." Wall Street Journal, 5 October 1967,
p. 16. Reprinted in: New York Theatre Critics' Reviews,
9 October 1967, p. 279.
Review of New York production of The Birthday Party.

621 _____. "Pinter's Mysteries." Wall Street Journal, 11 December 1964, p. 16.
Review of A Slight Ache and The Room.

622 _____. "Pinter's Technique." Wall Street Journal, 28 November 1962, p. 12.
Review of The Dumb Waiter and The Collection, New York
production: "there are times when the author seems to
become the prisoner of his own technique."

623 _____. "Strange Family Album." Wall Street Journal, 9 Janu-
ary 1967, p. 12. Reprinted in: New York Theatre Critics'
Review, 16 January 1967, pp. 395-96.
Review of The Homecoming (New York).

624 COOPER, ARTHUR. "Sunburn." Newsweek, 16 August 1971, p. 76.
Film review of The Go-Between.

625 COOPER, R. W. "Mr. Pinter is a Conspiracy of Silence." The
Times (London), 21 February 1967, p. 8.
Review of television version of The Basement.

Corey

626 COREY, STEPHEN. "Correspondence." The American Poetry Re-
     view, March/April 1976.
          An answer to Charles Fair (See no. 765) which contends
     that Fair fails to see Pinter within the context of his
     time and, therefore, does not recognize that Pinter is
     producing a picture of the modern world, a world in flux.

627 CORRIE, TIM. "The Homecoming." New Theatre Magazine, 6,
     No. 2 (1965), 31-32.
          Review.

628 CORRIGAN, ROBERT W. The Theatre in Search of a Fix. New
     York: Delacorte, 1973. Reprinted: New York: Delta,
     1974.
          Discusses Pinter's work. Pinter is compared to Chekhov:
     both use trival remarks, gestures, and inuendoes to ulti-
     mately reveal the truth about people. Concentrates on
     The Homecoming, in which the characters tell the truth
     from the beginning. Jungian archetypes are also discussed.

629 COTON, A. V. "What was the Matter with Stanley?" London
     Daily Telegraph, 23 March 1960, p. 14.
          Review of British television production of The Birthday
     Party.

630 COTTER, JERRY. "The New Plays." Sign, 41 (December 1961),
     48.
          Review of New York production of The Caretaker.

631 COVENEY, M. "No Man's Land." Plays and Players, 22 (July
     1975), 22-23.
          Production review.

632 COWAN, MARGARET. "The World of Harold Pinter." Stage, 5
     May 1960, p. 19.

*633 COWARD, NOËL. "These Old-Fashioned Revolutionaries." Lon-
     don Daily Herald, 28 April 1960, p. 3.
          Review of The Caretaker. Cited in Imhof (See no. 1098).
     Elliott (See no. 733) cites in The Sunday Times Magazine
     (London), 15 January 1961, p. 23.

634 _____. "These Old-Fashioned Revolutionaries." London
     Sunday Times Magazine, 15 January 1961, p. 23.
          Deals with The Caretaker. Possibly a reprint: See
     also no. 633.

*635 COWELL, RAYMOND. <u>Twelve Modern Dramas</u>. Oxford: Pergamon, 1967, pp. 134-35.

636 CRAIG, H. A. L. "Poetry in the Theatre." <u>New Statesman</u>, 59 (12 November 1960), 734, 736.
A discussion about the lack of verse drama in the contemporary theatre which comes to the conclusion that Pinter is skillful at <u>continuo</u> phrasing. Compared to Donald Duncan, Beckett, Arden, and Whiting, with mention of Yeats, Eliot, and Ibsen. Pinter is one of the few artists who can still create a "mood, a pervasion of poetry."

637 _____. "The Sound of the Words." <u>New Statesman</u>, 61 (27 January 1961), 152-53.
Review of original stage production of <u>A Slight Ache</u>.

638 CRINKLEY, RICHMOND. "The Development of Edward Albee." <u>National Review</u>, 23, No. 21 (1 June 1971), 602-04.
Albee is seen as resembling Pinter.

639 CRIST, JUDITH. "The Agony Beneath the Skin Revealed with Surgical Skill." <u>New York World Journal Tribune</u>, 18 April 1967. Reprinted in: Boyum and Scott, <u>Film as Film</u> (<u>See</u> no. 473), pp. 29-31.
A review of the film <u>Accident</u>, mentioning Pinter's use of language and the excellence and importance of the dialogue.

640 _____. "'Caretaker'--New House Not Enough." <u>New York Herald Tribune</u>, 31 January 1964, p. 8.
Review of the film version of <u>The Caretaker</u>. The claustrophobic effect of the stage play has been lost in the transfer to the screen, in Crist's opinion. Content similar to no. 641.

641 _____. "Movie Dims Stage's Magic." <u>New York Herald Tribune</u>, 21 January 1964, p. 12.
Review of the film version of <u>The Caretaker</u>. The claustrophobic effect of the stage play has been lost in the transfer to the screen, in Crist's opinion.

642 _____. "Murder in the Reverential Degree: Fumbling Fitzgerald." <u>Saturday Review</u>, 4, No. 6 (11 December 1976), 77-78.
Film review of <u>The Last Tycoon</u>.

Crist

643 _____. "A Mystery: Pinter on Pinter." Look, 24 December
1968, p. 77.
Partly a character sketch/biography of Pinter, the
article also discusses both the stage and film versions
of The Birthday Party.

644 CROCE, ARLENE. "Invisible to the Naked Eye." National Review, 2 May 1967, pp. 482-85.
Review of The Homecoming (New York).

645 CROWTHER, BOSLEY. "Screen: Unruly and Irritating Visitor."
New York Times, 21 January 1964, p. 25.
Review of the film version of The Caretaker (The Guest).

646 CROYDEN, MARGARET. "Pinter." New York Times, 14 November
1971, Sec. 2, p. 1.
Pinter and his plays are discussed.

647 _____. "Pinter's Hideous Comedy." In Lahr, A Casebook on
Harold Pinter's The Homecoming (See no. 1260), pp. 45-56.
The Homecoming is a combination of sexual ritual and
comedy of manners in a modern form.

648 CROZIER, MARY. "Pinter's Tea Party on BBC Television."
London Guardian, 26 March 1965, p. 13.
Review.

649 CULKIN, JOHN M., S. J. "'Ruthless Ruth.'" New York Times,
5 February 1967, Sec. 2, p. 3.
Discusses The Homecoming.

650 CURLEY, DANIEL. "A Night in the Fun House." In Pinter's
Optics (See no. 311), pp. 1-2.
Discusses the "intruder-woman complex."

651 CURTIS, ANTHONY. "Among Men." London Sunday Telegraph, 6
June 1965, p. 10.
Review of the original production of The Homecoming
which fails because of the conclusion, according to
Curtis.

652 CUSHMAN, ROBERT. "A Case of Mixed Feelings." Plays and
Players, 16, No. 9 (June 1969), 22-25.
Review of Night.

653 _____. "Evidence and Verdict." Plays and Players, 16, No.
11 (August 1969), 27.

Review of the original stage production of <u>Landscape</u> and <u>Silence</u>. Pinter has lost his skill for creating the "crushing, inevitable symbol."

654 _____. "Mr Pinter's Spoonerism's." <u>Observer Review</u>, 27 April 1975, p. 32.
Review of <u>No Man's Land</u> which compares Spooner to Davies in <u>The Caretaker</u> and comments on the language of the play.

655 _____. "Pinter's Mixed Double." London <u>Observer</u>, 21 October 1973, p. 38.
Review of <u>Landscape</u> and <u>Silence</u>.

656 _____. "True Love Conquers All--as Usual." London <u>Observer</u>, 19 January 1975, p. 29.
Review of <u>The Birthday Party</u>.

657 CUTTS, JOHN. "The Caretaker." <u>Films and Filming</u>, 10, No. 4 (January 1964), 24-25.
Review of the film version.

657a DAICHES, DAVID. <u>The Present Age in British Literature</u>. Bloomington, Indiana: Indiana University Press, 1958.
An encyclopedia of modern British writers.

658 DARLINGTON, W. A. "Actibility of Harold Pinter. The Caretaker." London <u>Daily Telegraph</u>, 31 May 1960, p. 14.
Review of original production of <u>The Caretaker</u>.

659 _____. "Cross-Talk Good, Point Unknown." London <u>Daily Telegraph</u>, 22 January 1960, p. 14.
Review of <u>The Room</u> and <u>The Dumb Waiter</u>.

660 _____. "Enjoyable Pinter." London <u>Daily Telegraph</u>, 19 June 1964, p. 18.
Review of <u>The Birthday Party</u> revival.

661 _____. "Jekyll-Hyde Pinter." London <u>Daily Telegraph</u>, 3 October 1961, p. 14.
Review of <u>A Night Out</u>.

662 _____. "Mad Meg and Lodger. Play Revels in Obscurity." London <u>Daily Telegraph</u>, 20 May 1958, p. 10.
Review of the first run of <u>The Birthday Party</u> which Darlington finds "most determinedly obscure."

Darlington

663   _____. "Mr. Pinter's Might-Have-Beens." London Daily Tele-
       graph, 19 June 1962, p. 14.
           Review of original stage production of The Collection.
       As the audience becomes more familiar with Pinter's idiom,
       "the flavour of his subtle sense of comedy grows less
       tantalizing."

664   _____. "Pinter at his most Pinteresque." London Daily Tele-
       graph, 19 September 1963, p. 16.
           Review of The Dwarfs and The Lover showing frustration
       with the loss of meaning in Pinter's words.

665   _____. "Pinter's Play's Obscurity." London Daily Telegraph,
       19 January 1961, p. 14.
           Castigating review of original stage production of A
       Slight Ache.

666   DASH, THOMAS R. "Prize Play From London Gets No Garlands
       Here." Women's Wear Daily, 5 October 1961, p. 44.
           Critical review of New York production of The Caretaker
       which should have been "compacted into a one-act."

667   _____. "Two Ironic Pinter Plays are Vivid and Engrossing."
       Women's Wear Daily, 105 (27 November 1962), 28.
           Review of The Dumb Waiter and The Collection, New York
       production.

668   DAVENPORT, JOHN. "Plays. Pinter and Brecht." Queen, 422
       (1 July 1964), 8.
           Review of The Birthday Party revival.

669   DAVIS, CLIFFORD. "Last Night's TV." London Daily Mirror,
       11 August 1961, p. 14.
           Review of British television production of The Dumb
       Waiter.

670   _____. "Provocative Pinter." London Daily Mirror, 26 March
       1965, p. 18.
           Review of television production of Tea Party.

671   DAVIES, JAMES. "A Good Pinter Drama." New York Daily News,
       10 December 1964, p. 92.
           Review of New York production of A Slight Ache and The
       Room.

672   _____. "Two Fine Pinter Plays." New York Daily News, 16
       October 1968, p. 101.
           Review of Tea Party and The Basement (New York).

673 DAVISON, PETER. "Contemporary Drama and Popular Dramatic
     Forms." The Kathleen Robinson lecture delivered at the
     University of Sydney, 6 November 1963; published in Aspects
     of Drama and the Theatre. Sydney: Sydney University
     Press, 1965, pp. 143-97.
         Includes a discussion of language in The Birthday Party,
     The Caretaker, and The Dumb Waiter. Examines the use of
     techniques from the music hall, pantomime, radio, and
     television in the work of Pinter and Beckett.

674 DAWICK, JOHN D. "Punctuation and Patterning in The Homecom-
     ing." Modern Drama, 14 (May 1971), 37-46.
         Punctuation is a clue to meaning and the communication
     of that meaning as it cues the actors.

675 DAWSON, HELEN. "Fledglings in a Limbo." London Observer, 20
     September 1970, p. 25.
         Review of Tea Party and The Basement (London).

676 DAY-LEWIS, SEAN. "Pinter's TV Plays." Drama, 98 (Autumn
     1970), 76.
         Review of Tea Party.

677 _____. Book review of Tea Party and Other Plays. Drama,
     Autumn 1970, p. 76.

678 DEAN, MICHAEL. "Late Night Line-Up. Harold Pinter talks to
     Michael Dean." Listener, 81 (6 March 1969), 312.
         Brief interview from "Late Night Line-Up" (BBC-2) in
     which Pinter talks about acting, Landscape, and The Home-
     coming.

679 DELAHAYE, MICHEL. "The Guest." Cahiers du Cinema in English,
     No. 6 (December 1966), pp. 52-53.
         Review of the film version of The Caretaker.

680 DELPECH, B. POROT. "'Le Gardien,' adapté de Harold Pinter
     par Eric Kahane." Le Monde, 19 September 1969, Special
     Supplement, p. v.
         Discussion of French production of The Caretaker.

681 DE NITTO, DENNIS, and WILLIAM HERMAN. Film and The Critical
     Eye. Riverside, New Jersey: Macmillan, 1975.
         Includes notes on the films The Servant and The Care-
     taker.

Dennis

682   DENNIS, NIGEL. Book review of Landscape and Silence. New
      York Review of Books, 17 December 1970, p. 21. (See
      no. 21).

683   _____. "Optical Delusions." Encounter, 15 (July 1960),
      63-66.
            Review of original production of The Caretaker which
      is seen as an "inadequate imitation" of Beckett.

684   _____. "Pintermania." New York Review of Books, 17 December
      1970, pp. 21-22.
            Book review of The Peopled Wound: The Work of Harold
      Pinter by Martin Esslin (See no. 755); Harold Pinter: The
      Poetics of Silence by James R. Hollis (See no. 1055); and
      Landscape and Silence by Harold Pinter (See no. 21).

685   DENT, ALAN. "The Case of Non-Involvement." Illustrated
      London News, August 1964, p. 170.
            Film review of The Pumpkin Eater.

686   _____. "He Gets His Effect by Silence." London News
      Chronicle, 9 March 1960, p. 5.
            Negative review of The Room and The Dumb Waiter which
      baffle the critic.

687   _____. "Love Among the Dons." Illustrated London News, 25
      February 1967, p. 34.
            Film review of Accident.

688   _____. "Mr. Pinter Misses his Target." London News Chronicle,
      20 May 1958, p. 5.
            Review of the first run of The Birthday Party.

689   _____. "Tragedy of a Tramp Alarms Me." London News Chronicle,
      31 May 1960, p. 3.
            Review of original production of The Caretaker. Sug-
      gests that Davies is already dead, symbolically, when the
      curtain rises.

690   _____. "Two Grisly Experiences." Illustrated London News,
      28 March 1964, p. 502.
            Review of the film version of The Caretaker.

*691 DEURBERQUE, JEAN. "Sujet, personnage, parole dans The Care-
      taker de Harold Pinter." Recherches Anglaises et Améri-
      caines (Strasbourg), 5 (1972), 47-62.

692   DIACK, PHIL. "Here's One Pinter Too Many." London <u>Daily</u>
       <u>Herald</u>, 12 May 1961, p. 4.
            Totally negative review of British television pro-
       duction of <u>The Collection</u>--Pinter has exhausted his talent.

693   _____. "Oh, the Irony of Pinter!" London <u>Daily Herald</u>, 11
       August 1961, p. 5.
            Review of British television production of <u>The Dumb</u>
       <u>Waiter</u>.

694   _____. "A Stage Flop is Big Hit." London <u>Daily Herald</u>,
       23 March 1960, p. 5.
            Review of British television production of <u>The Birthday</u>
       <u>Party</u>.

695   DIAS, EARL J. "The Enigmatic World of Harold Pinter." <u>Drama</u>
       <u>Critique</u>, 11 (1968), 119-24.
            In examining <u>The Birthday Party</u>, <u>The Caretaker</u>, and
       <u>The Homecoming</u>, Dias determines that dominance and
       society's "fundamental hypocrisy" are recurring themes
       and that Pinter is a "serious craftsman."

696   DIBB, FRANK. "Plays and Players at Home: Birmingham."
       <u>Plays and Players</u>, 9, No. 2 (November 1961), 35.
            Review of <u>The Caretaker</u>.

697   _____. "Plays and Players at Home: Oxford." <u>Plays and</u>
       <u>Players</u>, 9, No. 4 (January 1962), 27.
            Review of <u>The Caretaker</u>.

698   DICK, KAY. "Mr. Pinter and the Fearful Matter." <u>Texas</u>
       <u>Quarterly</u>, 4 (Autumn 1961), 257-65.
            Stresses Pinter's concern with communication.

699   DIDION, JOAN. "The Guest 'narcoleptic dialogue.'" <u>Vogue</u>,
       143 (1 March 1964), 57.
            Review of the film version of <u>The Caretaker</u>.

700   DILLON, PERRY C. "The Characteristics of the French Theater
       of the Absurd in the Plays of Edward Albee and Harold
       Pinter." <u>Dissertation Abstracts International</u>, 29:
       257-58A, University of Arkansas, 1968.
            Dillon examines the characteristics of the Theatre of
       the Absurd (as defined by Esslin) and finds Pinter's work
       closer to the definition than Albee's.

701 DOHMEN, WILLIAM F. "Possession of People on the Past: Competition for Dominance in Pinter's Recent Drama." Dissertation Abstracts International, 34: 5165A, Ph.D. dissertation, University of Virginia, 1973.
There is a return to the "battle for positions" in Old Times.

702 DONNER, CLIVE. "The Caretaker." Sight and Sound, 33, No. 2 (Spring 1964), 64-65.
Discusses the film version of The Caretaker.

703 DONOGHUE, DENIS. "The Human Image in Modern Drama." Lugano Review, 1, No. 3-4 (1965), 155-68.
An unfavorable assessment of Pinter, in contrast to Beckett, O'Neill, and Miller.

704 _____. "London Letter: Moral West End." Hudson Review, 14 (Spring 1961), 93-103.
Emphasizes the triangular relationships between characters in The Room, The Dumb Waiter, The Birthday Party, and The Caretaker. The general conclusion is not flattering.

705 DONOVAN, J. "The Plays of Harold Pinter, 1957-1961: Victims and Victimization." Recherches Anglaises et Américaines (Strasbourg), 5 (1972).

706 DORFMAN, ARIEL. El absurdo entre cuatro paredes: el teatro de Harold Pinter. Santiago, Chile: Editorial Universitaria, S.A., 1968.
Mainly a summary of other critics. Several pages are missing because of an error in the printing. In Spanish.

707 DOUGLAS, REID. "The Failure of English Realism." Tulane Drama Review, 7, No. 2 (Winter 1962), 180-83.
In the new English theatre, such as in The Caretaker, it is the actor, not the author, who "saves the play."

708 DOWNER, ALAN S. "The Doctor's Dilemma: Notes on the New York Theatre 1966-67." Quarterly Journal of Speech, 53 (October 1967), 213-23.
Includes review of The Homecoming (New York) which is "pure theatre" that "invites the audience to make of it what they will." The play is successful and exciting.

709 _____. "Experience of Heroes: Notes on the New York Theatre, 1961-62." Quarterly Journal of Speech, 48, No. 3 (October 1962), 261-70.

Each of the three men in The Caretaker deserves sympathy
as an example of the character "sustained by a dream that
stands between him and despair." The Caretaker illustrates
the "gap between the traditional function of the hero and
his place in the contemporary theatre."

710 ____. "Old, New, Borrowed, and (a Trifle) Blue: Notes on
the New York Theatre 1967-68." Quarterly Journal of
Speech, 54 (October 1968), 199-211.
Review of the New York production of The Birthday Party.

711 DRAKE, CAROL DIXON. "Harold Pinter and the Problem of
Verification." M.A. thesis, University of Southern
California, 1964.
A short study of Pinter's concept of verification, as
delineated in the Royal Court program notes for the
performance of The Room and The Dumb Waiter and expressed
in his dramas to this date.

*712 DRESCHER, HORST W. "Die englische Literatur." In Modern
Weltliteratur: die Gegenwartsliteratur Europas und
Amerikas, edited by Gero von Wilpert and Ivar Ivask.
Stuttgart, 1972, pp. 323-26.
In German.

*713 ____. "Einleitung." In Englische Literatur der Gegenwart
in Einzeldarstellung, edited by Horst W. Drescher.
Stuttgart, 1970, pp. 17 ff.

714 DRIVER, TOM F. "On the Way to Madness." Christian Century,
78 (22 November 1961), 1403-06.
A discussion of nihilism in The Caretaker.

715 DUBERMAN, MARTIN. "Theater 69." Partisan Review, 36, No.
3 (1969), 483-500.
Review of Tea Party and The Basement (New York).

716 DUKORE, BERNARD F. "The Pinter Collection." Educational
Theatre Journal, 26 (March 1974), 81-85.
An explication of The Collection which stresses the
visual aspects and sees the shifting relationships between the characters as shaping the scenes. Pinter's
refusal to place Bill and Stella together on stage is a
dramatic strategem for dealing with the question of
domination and control.

716a ____. "Pinter's Staged Monologue." Paper read at the
Modern Language Association Convention, Chicago, 30
December 1977.

Dukore

        Dukore stresses the importance of seeing Monologue
staged (as opposed to hearing the radio version) in
determining the play's meaning.

717   ____. "The Royal Shakespeare Company." Educational Theatre
       Journal, 22 (December 1970), 412-14.
       Review of Landscape and Silence.

718   ____. "The Theater of Harold Pinter." Tulane Drama Review,
       6, No. 3 (March 1962), 43-54.
       Pinter's theatre is seen as "a picture of contemporary
man beaten down by the social forces around him," partly
based on "man's failure to communicate with other men"
and partly based on avoidance of communication.

719   ____. Where Laughter Stops: Pinter's Tragicomedy. Columbia,
       Missouri: University of Missouri Press, 1976.
       Analyzes Pinter's plays in terms of modern tragicomic
structure.

720   ____. "A Woman's Place." Quarterly Journal of Speech, 52,
       No. 3 (1967), 237-41. Reprinted in: Lahr, A Casebook on
       Harold Pinter's The Homecoming (See no. 1260), pp. 109-16.
       Ruth's role in The Homecoming is described as a catalyst
which brings out the animal instincts for a mating ritual
among the members of the family.

721   DUMUR, GUY. "Une Misogynie atroce." "La Critique: Le
       Retour." L'Avant-Scène, 15 April 1967, p. 29.
       Discusses The Homecoming.

722   DUNNE, J. G. "Hauntingly Simple Denial." National Review,
       23 December 1961, p. 424.
       Dunne states that Pinter is "a master of vernacular"
and the power of The Caretaker comes from its disturbing
and hauntingly simple denial of John Donne's line, "no
man is an island."

723   DURBACH, ERROL. "The Caretaker: Text and Subtext." English
       Studies in Africa (Johannesburg), 18, No. 1 (1975), 23-29.
       An analysis of the unspoken subtext which establishes
the relationship between Mick and Aston in The Caretaker.

724   DURGNAT, RAYMOND. "Losey: Puritan Maids." Films and Film-
       ing, 12, No. 7 (April 1966), 28-33.
       Includes an analysis of The Servant film.

725   ____. Sexual Alienation in the Cinema. London: Studio
       Vista, 1972, pp. 103-08, 118-21.

Includes discussion of The Pumpkin Eater, which is seen
as an examination of the moral destruction of Jo (parent-
hood versus adult and civilized preoccupations), and The
Servant, which illustrates the destruction of Tony's ego
(his conscience has become defective). Based on Durgnat's
Films and Filming material. Lack of an index is a major
inconvenience.

726   EASTAUGH, KENNETH. "A Pinter Below Par Still Has That Sure
Touch of Genius." London Daily Mirror, 21 February 1967,
p. 14.
        Review of television version of The Basement which is
simple to understand by "Pinter standards."

727   _____. "A Sorry Version of Pinter's Play." London Daily
Mirror, 26 October 1966, p. 18.
        Review of the film version of The Caretaker.

728   EDER, RICHARD. "A Critic's Jottings: On Being Gripped
Versus Being Touched." New York Times, 28 November 1976,
Sec. 2, p. 17.
        Includes film review of The Last Tycoon.

729   _____. "Losey to Film 'Remembrance.'" New York Times, 14
February 1973, p. 24.
        Director Joseph Losey, who has worked with Pinter on
several films, discusses Pinter's problems in transform-
ing Proust's A la recherche du temps perdu from novel
into screenplay, his own problems in preparing to film the
work, and the keys to understanding the piece.

730   EIGO, JAMES. "Pinter's Landscape." Modern Drama, 16
(September 1973), 179-83.
        Very short discussion of language in Landscape. Too
limited. Beth and Duff's speech patterns are keys to
their personalities.

731   EILENBERG, LAWRENCE I. "Rehersal as Critical Method: Pinter's Old Times." Modern Drama, 18 (December 1975),
385-92.
        Eilenberg stresses theatrical rather than literary
methods of arriving at a critical understanding of Old
Times.

*732   EKBOM, TORSTON. "Pa jackt efter en identitet: Harold
Pinter och den absurda traditionen." Bonniers Literara
Magasin, 31 (1962), 809-14.

Elliott

733 ELLIOTT, SUSAN MERRITT. "Fantasy Behind Play: A Study of
Emotional Responses to Harold Pinter's 'The Birthday
Party,' 'The Caretaker,' and 'The Homecoming.'" <u>Dis-
sertation Abstracts International</u>, 34: 5963A, Ph.D. dissertation, Indiana University, 1973.
Dealing with the "psychological dynamics of the Pinter
experience," Elliott also examines various critical
approaches to Pinter to uncover the subjective bases of
the interpretations of the plays. A "free association
response" to the dramas is offered in balance. Bibliography, pp. 545-567.

734 _____. "Harold Pinter: His Works and His Critics. An Essay
in Bibliography and Critical Response."
In preparation.

735 _____. Review of Quigley's <u>The Pinter Problem</u> (See no. 1595)
and Gabbard's <u>The Dream Structure of Pinter's Plays</u> (See
no. 815). <u>Hartford Studies in Literature</u> [1976].

736 _____. "You Say It's Your Birthday." <u>Spectator</u> (Bloomington,
Indiana), 11 March 1969.
On <u>The Birthday Party</u>.

737 ELSOM, JOHN. "The End of the Absurd." <u>London Magazine</u>, 4,
No. 3 (June 1964), 62-66.
Davies in <u>The Caretaker</u> is mentioned as a typical
Absurd character.

738 _____. <u>Erotic Theatre</u>. New York: Taplinger, 1974.
Discusses Pinter.

739 _____. <u>Post-War British Theatre</u>. Boston: Routledge and
Kegan Paul, 1976.

740 ENGLER, BALZ. "Shakespeare und das moderne Theater--Eine
Konfrontation auf der Bühne: Bericht über Aufführung
und Diskussion." In <u>Deutsche Shakespeare Gesellschaft
West</u>, edited by Heuer Hermann. Heidelburg, 1971, pp.
18-22.
Uses <u>The Birthday Party</u> to show the modernity of
Shakespeare. In German.

741 ENGLISH, ALAN C. "A Descriptive Analysis of Harold Pinter's
Use of Comic Elements in His Stage Plays." <u>Dissertation
Abstracts International</u>, 30: 4596-98A. Ph.D. dissertation,
University of Missouri, Columbia, 1969.
The elements of situation, character, and dialogue are
examined.

*742 _____. "Feeling Pinter's World." Ball State University
Forum, 14, No. 1 (1973), 70-75.
Review of original stage production of A Slight Ache
which the reviewer considers unimportant.

743 ESSLIN, MARTIN. Absurd Drama. London: Penguin, 1965.
Revised 1969.
Discusses Pinter's plays and techniques on an individual
basis and places the dramatist in the tradition of the
Theatre of the Absurd. Basically a shorter version of
The Theatre of the Absurd.

744 _____. "The Absurdity of the Absurd." Kenyon Review, 22
(Autumn 1960), 670-73.

745 _____. "Alienation in Brecht, Beckett, and Pinter." Perspectives on Contemporary Literature, 1, No. 1 (1975), 3-21.
Esslin distinguishes between various kinds of alienation, as represented in the work of Brecht, Beckett, and
Pinter.

746 _____. "Brecht, the Absurd, and the Future." Tulane Drama
Review, 7, No. 4 (Summer 1963), 43-54.
Pinter and Albee are called Absurdists as opposed to
Brechtians.

747 _____. Brief Chronicles: Essays on the Modern Theatre.
London: Temple Smith, 1969. Reprinted as Reflections
(See no 760).
Includes occasional references to Pinter in overall
view of modern theatre.

*748 _____. "Der Commonsense der Nonsense." In Sinn oder Unsinn:
Theater unserer Zeit, Bd. III. Stuttgart, Basel, 1962.

749 _____. "Godot and His Children: The Theater of Samuel
Beckett and Harold Pinter." In Armstrong, Experimental
Drama (See no. 374), pp. 128-46. Reprinted in: Brown,
Modern British Dramatists (See no 501), pp. 58-70.
Compares Beckett and Pinter, especially in the area of
language, which he finds most realistic in the latter.
Decides that Pinter does not belong to the "kitchen
sink" school of dramatists in his almost allegorical
presentation of the human condition.

Esslin

750 _____. *Harold Pinter*. Friedrichs Dramatiker des Welt-
theaters, No. 38. Velber bei Hannover: Friedrich
Verlag, 1967.
In German. Essentially *The Peopled Wound*.

751 _____. "Harold Pinter, un dramaturge anglais de l'absurde."
Preuves, No. 151 (1964), pp. 45-54.
Examines *The Room*, *The Birthday Party*, *The Caretaker*,
and Pinter's techniques. In French.

752 _____. "The Homecoming: An Interpretation." In Lahr, *A
Casebook on Harold Pinter's The Homecoming* (See no.
1260), pp. 1-8.
Repeats Esslin's earlier conclusions about *The Homecoming*.

753 _____. "Language and Silence." In Ganz, *Pinter: A Collection of Critical Essays* (See no 843), pp. 34-59.
An excerpt from *The Peopled Wound*.

754 _____. "Orgien und Exzesse." *Theater Heute*, August 1965,
pp. 40-42.
In German. Discusses *The Homecoming*.

755 _____. *The Peopled Wound: The Work of Harold Pinter*. New
York: Doubleday/Anchor, 1970. Published under the title
The Peopled Wound: The Plays of Harold Pinter in Great
Britain, London: Methuen, 1970. Reprinted as *Pinter: A
Study of His Plays* (See no. 757).
Information (some from Pinter) and background material
not available elsewhere make this book both interesting
and important, although the mixture of psychological and
existential interpretations of the plays is not always
satisfactory. Contains an excellent section on Pinter's
use of language and silence. Reviewed: See nos. 684,
835, 888, 1079, 1103, 1140, 1261, 1653.

756 _____. "Pinter and the Absurd." *Twentieth Century*, 169
(February 1961), 176-85.
Pinter's poetic use of dialogue is the factor which
successfully creates an Absurd realism. Pinter and
Simpson are called English exponents of the Absurd.

757 _____. *Pinter: A Study of His Plays*. London: Eyre
Methuen, 1973. Modern Theatre Profiles series. Reprinted: New York: W. W. Norton, 1976.
A revision of *The Peopled Wound* (See no 755), expanded
to cover Pinter's plays through *No Man's Land*.

758 ____. "Pinter Translated." Encounter, 30, No. 3 (March 1968), 45-47.
    Esslin feels that the German translations of Pinter's works are so bad that they lead to a misunderstanding of his plays and a devaluation of his talents.

759 ____. "Radio Drama." Theatre Quarterly, No. 3 (August-October 1974).

760 ____. Reflections: Essays on Modern Theatre. New York: Anchor, 1971.
    American reprint of Brief Chronicles (See no. 747).

761 ____. The Theatre of the Absurd. New York: Doubleday/Anchor, 1961. Revised 1969. Reprinted: London: Eyre and Spottiswoode, 1965. Revised: London, Pelican, 1968; New York: Doubleday/Anchor, 1968. See also no. 1620.
    Summarizes plays and deals with themes (menace) and techniques in general. Reviewed: See no. 1102.

762 ____. "The Theatre of the Absurd Revisited." University of Florida (Gainesville) College of Fine Arts, Dean's Lecture Series, 10 March 1976.
    Discussion of the Theatre of the Absurd after twenty years: its effect on drama in general; current users of Absurdist techniques. Pinter is no longer considered an Absurdist, but is "the acknowledged master of the poetic theatre," though he still uses some Absurdist techniques. Pinter's effective use of language alluded to. Note: There is also a chapter under this title in Esslin's Reflections, pp. 183-91 (See no 760).

763 ____. "Violence in Drama." Encounter, 11, No. 3 (May-June 1964), 6-15.

764 EVANS, GARETH LLOYD. "Pinter's Black Magic." Guardian, 30 September 1965, p. 8. Reprinted in: Dick Richards, The Curtain Rises (See no. 1604), pp. 69-73.
    Suggests that The Homecoming is too limited in meaning because Pinter is not working with universally applicable themes.

765 FAIR, CHARLES M. "The Poet as Specialist." The American Poetry Review, 4, No. 6 (November/December 1975), 19-20.
    A cursory examination of the limited nature of modern poetry which mentions Pinter as an author who, "as with much psychoanalysis...is all just talk." Answered by Stephen Corey. (See no. 626).

Farber

766   FARBER, STEPHEN. "Film Notes: How Do You Find a New Clark
        Gable?" New York Times, 16 February 1975, Sec. D, p. 15.
            Elia Kazan to direct The Last Tycoon from Pinter's
        script.

767   _____. "Hollywood Takes On 'The Last Tycoon.'" New York
        Times, 21 March 1976, Sec. D, p. 15.
            Discussion of the up-coming film of Fitzgerald's novel
        and Pinter's role in writing the screenplay.

768   _____. "The Quiller Memorandum." Film Quarterly, 20, No.
        3 (Spring 1967), 62-63.
            Film review.

769   FARRINGTON, CONOR. "The Language of Drama." Tulane Drama
        Review, 5 (December 1960), 65-72.

770   FAY, STEPHEN. "Will Tamburlaine arrive in time?" London
        Sunday Times, 27 April 1975, p. 3.
            Explains that the opening of No Man's Land, originally
        set for 1974, was delayed nine times.

771   FEIFFER, JULES. "Threat of Sex." New York Times, 5 Febru-
        ary 1967, Sec. II, p. 3.
            The "seemingly innocent Teddy" is proposed as the
        "prime manipulator" in The Homecoming.

*772   FELDMANN, HEINZ. "Harold Pinter." In Englische Literatur
        der Gegenwart in Einzeldarstellung, edited by Horst W.
        Drescher. Stuttgart, 1970; pp. 431-57.

773   FELDSTEIN, ELAYNE PHYLISS. "The Evolution of the Character-
        istics of Harold Pinter." Dissertation Abstracts Inter-
        national, 34:7748-A. Ph.D. dissertation, New York Univer-
        sity, 1973.
            The Birthday Party, The Caretaker, The Homecoming, and
        Old Times show the movement from victim or victimized to
        victim/victimized, etc.

773a   _____. "From Novel to Film: The Impact of Harold Pinter on
        Robert Maugham's The Servant." Studies in the Humanities,
        5, No. 2 (October 1976), 9-14.

774   _____, FERRIS, PAUL. "Fresh and Bloody." London Observer,
        6 March 1960.
            Review of radio production of A Night Out.

775   _____. "Pop Press Intimations." London Observer, 28 April
       1968, p. 32.
          Review of the radio version of Landscape.

776   _____. "Radio Notes." London Observer, 2 August 1959, p. 12.
          Review of the radio version of A Slight Ache: "identity
       and personality aren't as stable as we think, but this
       isn't really much to discover after an hour of intricate
       dialogue."

777   _____. "Radio Notes." London Observer, 11 December 1960,
       p. 26.
          Review of radio version of The Dwarfs. The hero is
       "tedious and unimportant" because he is in fashion.

778   FEYNMAN, ALBERTA E. "The Fetal Quality of 'Character' in
       Plays of the Absurd." Modern Drama, 9 (May 1966), 18-25.
          The characters in Pinter's plays are regarded as too
       nebulous to be true characters.

779   F. G. "Innocuous Revue." Jewish Chronicle, 6 May 1960,
       p. 34.
          Review of The Caretaker.

780   FIELDS, SUZANNE. "Levels of Meaning in Structural Patterns
       of Allegory and Realism in Selected Plays of Harold
       Pinter." Dissertation Abstracts International, 32:
       2087-88A. Ph.D. dissertation, Catholic University, 1971.
          In The Room, The Birthday Party, The Caretaker, and
       A Slight Ache, "levels of meaning are supported by formal
       principles of organization," as opposed to the more
       recent poetic dramas Pinter has been writing.

781   FINDLATER, RICHARD. "Doubling the Pleasure." Time and Tide,
       12 October 1961, p. 1701.
          Review of A Night Out.

782   _____. "In the Deep Freeze." Time and Tide, 27 January
       1961, p. 130.
          Review of A Slight Ache.

783   _____. "Theatre." Time and Tide, 19 March 1960, p. 314.
          Review of The Room and The Dumb Waiter.

784   _____. "Theatre." Time and Tide, 7 May 1960, p. 509.
          Review of The Caretaker.

Fischer

*785 FISCHER, PETER. "Versuch uber das scheinbar absurde Theater."
Merkur, 19, No. 2 (1965), 151-63.
Cited in Imhof (See no 1098), p. 10.

786 FITZGERALD, MARION. "Playwriting Is Agony, Says Hugh
Leonard." Irish Digest, 79 (January 1964), 34-36.
Pinter is Leonard's favorite playwright.

787 FJELDE, ROLF. "Plotting Pinter's Progress." In Lahr, A
Casebook on Harold Pinter's The Homecoming (See no.
1260), pp. 87-108.
Tries to detail The Birthday Party, The Caretaker, and
The Homecoming as steps in Pinter's development as seen
through his imagery.

788 FLAKES, NANETTE S. B. "Aesthetics of Modern Play Direction:
Non-Realistic Drama from Pirandello to Pinter." Disserta-
tion Abstracts International, 34: 896-A. University of
Minnesota, 1973.
Includes discussion of Pirandello, Brecht, Sartre,
Camus, Beckett, Pinter. Pinter is used as an example in
an exploration of the aesthetics of modern play production.

789 FLETCHER, JOHN. "Confrontations: I. Harold Pinter, Rolland
Dubillard and Eugene Ionesco." Caliban, 3, No. 2 (1967),
149-52. Cited in Imhof (See no. 1098), p. 11; cited in
PMLA Bibliography (1968) as 4 (1968), 149-59.

790 FORD, BORIS, ed. The Pelican Guide to English Literature,
Vol. 7: The Modern Age. Harmondsworth: Pelican, 1964.
Includes Raymond Williams's "Recent English Drama"
(See no. 1986), pp. 496-508.

791 FOREMAN, CARL. "Majors and Minors." New Statesman, 22
June 1962, p. 917.
Review of original stage production of The Collection.

792 FORSTER, PETER. "Back to the Saltmines." London Sunday
Telegraph, 22 September 1963, p. 12.
Review of The Dwarfs and The Lover which claims that
Pinter fails to communicate with his audience.

793 _____. "Inconsequences." Spectator, 29 July 1960, p. 186.
Review of television production of Night School.

794 FRAME, COLIN. "The Caretaker." London Evening News, 3 March
1972, p. 3.
Review.

795 _____. "Old Times." London <u>Evening News</u>, 2 June 1971, p. 3.
Review.

796 FRANZBLAU, ABRAHAM N. "A Psychiatrist Looks at The Homecoming."
<u>Saturday Review</u>, 50 (8 September 1967), 58.
A psychological interpretation of <u>The Homecoming</u> (as
a <u>ménage à trois</u>) which does not seem to be based on
either the characters or the action of the drama.

797 FRASER, GEORGE SUTHERLAND. <u>The Modern Writer and His World</u>.
Baltimore: Penguin. Revised, 1964. Reprinted: New York:
Praeger, 1965; Harmondsworth, 1970.
See pp. 238-43 for discussion of Pinter's work (includ-
ing <u>The Caretaker</u>) recognizing Pinter's debt to Beckett
and Ionesco and praising his "literary quality."

798 FREE, WILLIAM J. "Treatment of Character in Harold Pinter's
<u>The Homecoming</u>." <u>South Atlantic Bulletin</u>, 34, No. 4
(1969), 1-5.
Character takes precedence over language in <u>The Home-</u>
<u>coming</u>.

799 FREEDMAN, MORRIS, ed. <u>Essays in Modern Drama</u>. Boston:
D. C. Heath, 1964.
Includes John Russell Brown's "Mr. Pinter's Shakespeare"
(<u>See</u> no 500).

800 _____. <u>The Moral Impulse: Modern Drama from Ibsen to the</u>
<u>Present</u>. Carbondale and Edwardsville: Southern Illinois
University Press, 1967, pp. 124-26.
Mentions Pinter.

*801 FRICKER, ROBERT. <u>Das moderne englische Drama</u>. Göttingen,
1964.
In German. Cited in Esslin, <u>The Peopled Wound</u> (<u>See</u>
no. 755).

802 FRISCH, JACK E. "Ironic Theater: Techniques of Irony in
the Plays of Samuel Beckett, Eugene Ionesco, Harold Pinter
and Jean Genet." <u>Dissertation Abstracts</u>, 25: 6114-15A.
Ph.D. dissertation, University of Wisconsin, 1965.
Irony in the modern theatre is directed at the audience.

803 FRYE, CLARENCE. "Guaranteed." <u>The Times</u> (London), 9 December 1970, p. 7.
Review of <u>Landscape</u> and <u>Silence</u>.

F. S.

804   F. S. "The Birthday Party." Theatre World, 60, No. 475
(August 1964), 13.
Review.

805   _____. "The Dumb Waiter and The Room." Theatre World, 56,
No. 423 (April 1960), 8.
Review.

806   _____. "The Homecoming." Theatre World, 61, No. 486 (July
1965), 19.
Review of The Homecoming.

807   _____. "The Lover and The Dwarfs." Theatre World, 59, No.
465 (October 1963), 10-11.
Review.

808   _____. "Three." Theatre World, 57, No. 433 (February 1961),
16.
Review of A Slight Ache.

*809   FUJII, TAKEO. "Naked Primitiveness in the World of Harold
Pinter." Bulletin of Kansai University of Foreign Lan-
guages, No. 17.
Reference: Tetsuo Kishi in private correspondence.

*810   FUKAKI, KAZUTOSHI. "Two Men in a Room: An Essay on Harold
Pinter." Essays on Modern Literature and Language, No. 3.
In Japanese. Reference: Tetsuo Kishi.

811   FULLER, PETER. "Pinter's Enigmas." London City Press, 24
September 1970, p. 12.
Review of Tea Party and The Basement (London).

812   FUNKE, LEWIS. "Theater: 'The Caretaker.'" New York Times,
31 January 1964, p. 16.
Review of the film version of The Caretaker.

813   FURBANK, P. N. "A Bad Dream." Listener, 7 May 1964, p. 772.
Revue sketches reviewed.

814   GABBARD, LUCINA PAQUET. "The Dream Structure of Pinter's
Plays: A Psychoanalytic Approach." Dissertation Abstracts
International, 35: 3914A. Ph.D. dissertation, Univ-
ersity of Illinois (Urbana), 1974.
Gabbard's approach is used to expand existing interpret-
ations of Pinter's work, rather than to deny them.

815 ____. The Dream Structure of Pinter's Plays: A Psychoanalytic Approach. Rutherford, New Jersey: Fairleigh
Dickinson University Press, 1976. Reviewed: See no.
735.

816 GALE, JOHN. "Taking Pains With Pinter." Observer, 10 June
1962, p. 19.

817 GALE, STEVEN H. "Austin Quigley's The Pinter Problem."
Journal of Modern Literature, 5, No. 4 (February 1977),
784-86.
Book review of Quigley's linguistic study of Pinter
(See no. 1595).

818 ____. "Book Reviews." Modern Drama, February 1972, pp.
478-79.
Book reviews of Harold Pinter by Ronald Hayman (See
no. 983), Harold Pinter by John Russell Taylor (See no.
1818), and A Casebook on Harold Pinter's The Homecoming,
edited by John Lahr (See no. 1260).

819 ____. "The Breakers of Illusion: George in Edward Albee's
Who's Afraid of Virginia Woolf? and Richard in Harold
Pinter's The Lover." In preperation.
Albee and Pinter deal with illusion in marriage in
remarkably similar ways, yet come to opposite conclusions
about its necessity.

820 ____. Butter's Going Up: A Critical Analysis of Harold
Pinter's Work. Durham, North Carolina: Duke University
Press, 1977.
The most complete study of all of Pinter's work
available. Traces thematic and stylistic developments.

821 ____. "The Films of Harold Pinter." Paper delivered at a
meeting of the College English Association, San Juan,
Puerto Rico, April 1973.
A discussion of Pinter's techniques, with special
attention to the differences between written versions
and his screen adaptations.

822 ____. The Films of Harold Pinter. In preparation.

823 ____. "Game Playing in Harold Pinter and Edward Albee."
Paper read at the Modern Language Association, Chicago,
29 December 1977.
Discusses the types of games and game playing in Pinter's dramas, and their functions, with comparative
emphasis on The Lover and Who's Afraid of Virginia Woolf?.

Gale

824   _____. "Harold Pinter." Speech in the College of Humanities
       Lecture Series, University of Puerto Rico, Spring 1971.

825   _____. "Harold Pinter." Journal of Modern Literature, 3,
       No. 3 (February 1974), 746-47.
          Book review of Katherine Burkman's The Dramatic World
       of Harold Pinter (See no. 529) and Arlene Sykes's Harold
       Pinter (See no. 1798).

826   _____. "Harold Pinter: A Filmography." In preparation.

827   _____. "Harold Pinter: An Annotated Bibliography 1957-
       1971." Bulletin of Bibliography, 29, No. 2 (April-June
       1972), 43-65.
          The most comprehensive bibliography published up to
       this time.

828   _____. "Harold Pinter: dramatico moderno." Rio Piedras,
       [1978].
          An overview of Pinter's place in the modern theatre,
       stating that Pinter cannot be categorized, as he borrows
       techniques from the Theatre of the Absurd and other
       contemporary schools of writing which best fit his talents
       and dramatic needs. In Spanish.

829   _____. "Harold Pinter's A Slight Ache." Paper delivered at
       the Modern Language Association, Chicago, 29 December 1977.
          A discussion of Pinter's development with emphasis on
       A Slight Ache as a major turning point in his writing.

830   _____. Harold Pinter's The Birthday Party and Other Works.
       New York: Simon and Schuster's Monarch Notes, 1972.
          An in-depth study guide to The Birthday Party, pro-
       viding background material and an analysis of the play,
       as well as placing it in Pinter's canon.

831   _____. "Harold Pinter's The Homecoming: A Question of Need."
       In preparation.
          Discusses the characters' motivations in The Homecoming.

832   _____. Harold Pinter's The Homecoming and Other Works. New
       York: Simon and Schuster's Monarch Notes, 1971.
          An in-depth study guide to The Homecoming, providing
       background material and an analysis of the play, as well
       as placing it in Pinter's canon.

833   _____. "Harold Pinter's No Man's Land: Life at a Stand-
       still." Jewish Quarterly, 24, No. 4 (Winter 1976/1977),
       13-18, 20.

Hirst and Spooner represent two approaches to life in time; literary allusions reinforce the expression of these approaches.

834   ____. "McCann's Political and Religious Allusions in Harold Pinter's The Birthday Party." Notes on Contemporary Literature, 7, No. 3 (May 1977), 5-6.
Much of what McCann says has references in Irish history or religion or both.

835   ____. "The Peopled Wound: The Work of Harold Pinter." Chicago Review, 25, No. 1 (Fall 1972), 177-80.
Book review of Martin Esslin's The Peopled Wound (See no. 755).

836   ____. "Screening Pinter." Literature/Film Quarterly, 5, No. 1 (Winter 1977), 94-95.
Book review of Five Screenplays (See no. 33).

837   ____. "Thematic Change in the Stage Plays of Harold Pinter, 1957-1967." Dissertation Abstracts International, 31: 3546A. University of Southern California, 1970.
A study of Pinter's first ten years of playwriting, tracing the movement from the simple exposure of the existence of menace and its disintegrating effect on the individual in the "comedies of menace" to the later plays which examine the source of menace (individual psychological needs) and the desperate attempts of the characters to fulfill their needs.

838   ____. "The Weasel Under the Cocktail Cabinet." Paper given at the College English Association, San Juan, Puerto Rico, 18 April 1971.
An examination of Pinter's techniques and thematic and artistic development.

839   ____. "The Writing of Harold Pinter: An Overview." Literary Half-Yearly, January 1976.
An examination of thematic and stylistic developments in Pinter's writing from 1957 through No Man's Land.

840 GALLAGHER, KENT G. "Harold Pinter's Dramaturgy." Quarterly Journal of Speech, 52, No. 3 (October 1966), 242-48.
The language of The Caretaker is an excellent example of Pinter's influence and position in the Theatre of the Absurd.

841 GANZ, ARTHUR. "A Clue to the Pinter Puzzle: The Triple
Self in The Homecoming." Educational Theatre Journal, 21
(May 1969), 180-87.

842 _____. "Mixing Memory and Desire: Pinter's Vision in Landscape, Silence, and Old Times." In Ganz, Pinter: A
Collection of Critical Essays (See no. 843), pp. 161-78.
An attempt to read the later plays in terms character-
istic of the early plays.

843 _____, ed. Pinter: A Collection of Critical Essays.
Englewood Cliffs, N.J.: Prentice-Hall, 1972.
A collection of critical essays by Lawrence Bensky,
"Harold Pinter: An Interview" (See no 427); Martin
Esslin, "Language and Silence" (See no. 753); John Lahr,
"Pinter and Chekhov: The Bond of Naturalism" (See no.
1265); Valerie Minogue, "Taking Care of the Caretaker"
(See no. 1434); Ruby Cohn, "The World of Harold Pinter"
(See no. 601); James T. Boulton, "Harold Pinter: The
Caretaker and Other Plays" (See no. 467); John Russell
Taylor, "A Room and Some Views: Harold Pinter" (See no.
1826); John Pesta, "Pinter's Usurpers" (See no. 1544); R.
F. Storch, "Harold Pinter's Happy Families" (See no. 1780);
and Bert O. States, "Pinter's Homecoming: The Shock of
Nonrecognition" (See no. 1774). Introduced by Ganz, this
volume is in the Twentieth Century Views series. All of
the essays are available elsewhere, with the exception of
Ganz's "Mixing Memory and Desire: Pinter's Vision in
Landscape, Silence, and Old Times" (See no. 842).

844 GARBER, STEPHEN M. "Open and Closed Sequences in the Plays
of Harold Pinter." Dissertation Abstracts International,
34: 312-13A. Ph.D. dissertation, University of Illinois,
Urbana-Champaign, 1973.
The relationships between the plays as works of art
and the viewer are examined.

845 GASCOIGNE, BAMBER. "Cult of Personality." Spectator, 208
(29 June 1962), 857-58.
A review of The Collection which considers Strindberg's
influence on Pinter.

846 _____. "Love in the Afternoon." London Observer, 22 September 1963, p. 26.
Review of The Dwarfs and The Lover.

847   ____. "Pinter Makes It all too Plain." London Observer, 21
        June 1964, p. 24.
            Disapproving review of The Birthday Party revival and
        Pinter's direction.

848   ____. "Pulling the Wool." Spectator, 206 (27 January 1961),
        106.
            Review of original stage production of A Slight Ache
        which, according to Gascoigne, keeps hinting at deeper
        meanings which are not there.

*849   ____. Twentieth Century Drama. London: Hutchinson, 1962.
            Cited in Cummulative Book Index.

850   GASSNER, JOHN. "Broadway in Review." Educational Theatre
        Journal, 13 (December 1961), 289-97. Reprinted in:
        Dramatic Soundings (See no. 852).
            Discussion of the use of allegory and symbol in The
        Caretaker.

*851   ____. Directions in Modern Theatre and Drama. Toronto:
        Holt, 1965.
            An expanded version of Form and Idea in the Modern
        Theatre (See no. 853). Cited in Cummulative Book Index
        1965-1966).

852   ____. Dramatic Soundings. New York: Crown, 1968.
            Includes "Foray Into the Absurd," pp. 503-07, which
        deals with The Caretaker. (See nos. 850 and 1620).

*853   ____. Form and Idea in the Modern Theatre.
            Cited in Cummulative Book Index (1965-1966) as part of
        notation for Directions in Modern Theatre and Drama (See
        no. 851).

854   ____. "Osborne and Pinter." In Gassner, The World of
        Contemporary Drama (See no. 855), pp. 21-23.

855   ____. The World of Contemporary Drama. New York: American
        Library Association, 1965.
            Includes "Osborne and Pinter," pp. 21-23.

856   GAUTIER, JEAN-JACQUES. "Au Théâtre de Lutèce 'Le Gardien.'"
        Le Figaro, 27 January 1961, p. 12.
            Concerns The Caretaker.

857   GEDULD, HARRY M. "The Trapped Heroes of Harold Pinter."
        Humanist, 28 (March-April 1968), 24, 31.
            Concerned with The Birthday Party.

Gellert

858   GELLERT, ROGER. "Religion and Sex." New Statesman, 13
          October 1961, p. 529 f.
             Review of A Night Out.

859   GHOSE, ZULFIKAR. "Ghose's London: A Valediction." Hudson
          Review, 22 (Autumn 1969), 378, 380.
             Includes a review of Landscape and Silence.

860   GIANNETTI, LOUIS D. "The Drama of the Welfare State."
          Dissertation Abstracts International, 28: 229-30A.
          Ph.D. dissertation, University of Iowa, 1967.
             Pinter's plays (The Room, The Birthday Party, The Care-
          taker, and The Dumb Waiter) deal symbolically with the
          impersonality of contemporary society.

861   _____. "Henry Livings: A Neglected Voice in the New Drama."
          Modern Drama, 12, No. 1 (May 1969), 38-48.
             Livings resembles Pinter, Osborne, and Wesker.

862   GIBBS, PATRICK. "'The Caretaker' in Close-up." London Daily
          Telegraph, 13 March 1964, p. 13.
             Review of the film version of The Caretaker.

863   _____. "Mr. Pinter Returns to Enigma." London Daily Tele-
          graph, 28 April 1960, p. 14.
             Review of original production of The Caretaker as a
          pessimistic "criticism of life."

864   _____. "People Shut in Private Worlds. Symbolic Plays."
          London Daily Telegraph, 9 March 1970, p. 14.
             Review of New York production of The Dumb Waiter and
          The Room which show a preoccupation with death and the
          purposelessness of life following the lines of Waiting
          for Godot.

865   _____. "The Softer Side of Oxford." London Daily Telegraph,
          10 February 1967, p. 19.
             Review of Accident.

866   GILBERT, W. STEPHEN. "A Slight Ache, Landscape." Plays and
          Players, 21, No. 3 (December 1973), 52-53.
             Review.

867   GILDERDALE, MICHAEL. "Spellbinder Made of Three Men."
          London News Chronicle, 28 April 1960, p. 3.
             Review of original production of The Caretaker.

868 GILL, BRENDAN. "The Cry." <u>New Yorker</u>, 47 (27 November 1971), 89.
    Review of <u>Old Times</u> in which Pinter is equated with Faulkner and Beckett.

869 _____. "Drawback of Domesticity." <u>New Yorker</u>, 14 November 1964, pp. 148-49.
    Film review of <u>The Pumpkin Eater</u>.

870 _____. "Going Mad." <u>New Yorker</u>, 52 (1 November 1976), 99-100.
    Production review of William Archibald's <u>The Innocents</u> (based on Henry James's <u>The Turn of the Screw</u>), which was directed by Pinter.

871 _____. "Inside the Redoubt." <u>New Yorker</u>, 15 April 1967. Reprinted in: Boyum and Scott, <u>Film as Film</u>, pp. 36-37 (<u>See</u> no. 473).
    A review of the film <u>Accident</u> and Pinter's belief that "evil is an entity and that man is capable of being invaded and possessed by it."

872 _____. "Nightcap and After." <u>New Yorker</u>, 52 (22 November 1976), 109.
    A highly laudatory review of <u>No Man's Land</u> (New York production).

873 GILLEN, FRANCIS. "'All These Bits and Pieces': Fragmentation and Choice in Pinter's Plays." <u>Modern Drama</u>, 17, No. 4 (December 1974), 477-87.
    Using <u>The Caretaker</u> to shed light on <u>Silence</u> and <u>Old Times</u>, Gillen sees Pinter's characters as being fragmented (the concrete, physical, or material <u>versus</u> the incomprehensible, the spiritual, or the untouchable) and the plays concerned with the metaphysical question of the nature of man--"doomed to desire a completeness he can never possess and to make choices which constantly frustrate that desire." Conclusion is convincing.

874 _____. "'...Apart from the Known and the Unknown': The Unreconciled World of Harold Pinter's Characters." <u>Arizona Quarterly</u>, 26 (1970), 17-24.
    The major characters in <u>Tea Party</u> and <u>The Homecoming</u> are involved in the "known," physical world which they can touch, and threatened by the "unknown" world of abstractions which they can neither understand nor control.

Gilliatt

875 GILLIATT, PENELOPE. "Accumulating a Calamity." London
     Observer, 12 February 1967, p. 24.
        Film review of Accident.

876 _____. "Achievement from a Tight-Rope." London Observer,
     6 June 1965, p. 25.
        Review of The Homecoming which sees the play as a
     territorial struggle.

877 _____. "Away From Home." New Yorker, 47 (31 July 1971),
     55-56.
        Film review of The Go-Between in which the auteur theory
     is discussed.

878 _____. "Beefing About Opera." Queen, 1 February 1961, p. 15.
        Review of A Slight Ache.

879 _____. "The Caretaker." London Observer, 1 October 1963.
        Review.

880 _____. "The Caretaker." London Observer, 14 March 1964.
        Review.

881 _____. "Comedy of Menace." Queen, 216 (25 May 1960), 21-22.
        Review of The Caretaker.

882 _____. "The Conversion of a Tramp." London Observer, 15
     March 1964, p. 24.
        Review of the film version of The Caretaker.

883 _____. "Interview With a Marathon Critic Nearing Wit's
     End." Queen, 30 March 1960, p. 18.
        Review of The Room and The Dumb Waiter.

884 _____. "The Masterful Silence." London Observer, 17 Novem-
     ber 1963, p. 27.
        Film review of The Servant.

885 _____. "The Pinter Mouse is the Menace." Life, 62 (21
     April 1967), 12.
        Film review of Accident.

886 _____. Unholy Fools: Wits, Comics, Disturbers of the Peace.
     New York: Viking, 1973.
        Discusses Pinter, pp. 109-12.

887 GILMAN, RICHARD. "The Absurd and the Foolish." <u>Commonweal</u>,
76, No. 2 (6 April 1962), 40-41.
Very brief, Gilman gives his own definition of absurd.

888 _____. Book review of <u>The Peopled Wound: The Work of Harold
Pinter</u> by Martin Esslin (<u>See</u> no. 755). <u>New York Times
Book Review</u>, 13 September 1970, pp. 34, 36.

889 _____. <u>Common and Uncommon Masks</u>. New York: Random House,
1971.
Includes discussions of <u>The Birthday Party</u>, <u>The Care-
taker</u>, <u>The Collection</u>, <u>The Dumb Waiter</u>, <u>The Homecoming</u>
and <u>The Lover</u>, pp. 93-113.

890 _____. "The Homecoming." <u>New York Times</u>, 22 January 1967,
Sec. 2, p. 1.
Review. Probably "The Pinter Puzzle" (<u>See</u> no. 893),
cited in Imhof (<u>See</u> no. 1098), p. 31.

891 _____. "Mortal Combat." <u>Newsweek</u>, 69 (16 January 1967), 93.
Review of <u>The Homecoming</u> (New York) as a movement
toward a ritualistic and mythic confrontation between
the characters' fantasies.

892 _____. "Patience Rewarded." <u>Commonweal</u>, 79 (24 January
1964), 484-85.
Review of <u>The Lover</u> (New York) comparing Pinter to
Beckett. <u>The Lover</u> is so shallow that it is clearly
inferior and "too schematic--Pinter's periodic curse."

893 _____. "The Pinter Puzzle." <u>New York Times</u>, 22 January
1967, Sec. 2, p. 1.
Review of <u>The Homecoming</u>.

894 _____. "Pinter's Hits--and Misses." <u>Commonweal</u>, 77 (28
December 1962), 366-67.
Review of <u>The Dumb Waiter</u> and <u>The Collection</u>, New York
production. Pinter's images "are skeletal and unfinished."

895 _____. "Pre-Vintage Pinter." <u>New Republic</u>, 157 (21 October
1967), 36-38.
Review of New York production of <u>The Birthday Party</u>:
"so much manner and so little style."

896 _____. "Reflections at Midterm." <u>Commonweal</u>, 75 (22 December 1961), 339-40.
Generally critical review of New York production of
<u>The Caretaker</u>.

Gilman

897 _____. "Straightforward Mystification." Commonweal, 75
      (27 October 1961), 122-23.
         Review of New York production of The Caretaker, which
      is straightforward drama.

898 GLOVER, WILLIAM. "Busy Playwright Lost in Creative Desert."
      Durham (N.C.) Herald, 21 October 1973.
         An Associated Press interview in which Pinter discusses
      his feelings about his writing, at the age of 43: "my
      juices...seem to have dried up." Perhaps he has become
      "arid" because "I feel when writing...that I'm freeing
      myself from what I've written before. That I'm getting
      freer. You just end up in another trap afterwards."
      Though he is fond of what he has written, he would be
      "more economic" and "spare" if he were rewriting his plays.

*899 GOETSCH, PAUL. "Das englische Drama seit Shaw." In Das
      englische Drama, edited by Josefa Nünning (See no. 1495),
      pp. 404, 406, 430, 444-48, 492.
         In German. Cited in Imhof (See no. 1098), p. 11.

900 _____. English Dramatic Theories, IV: Twentieth Century.
      Tubingen, 1972, pp. 118-24.
         Includes reprint of Pinter's "Writing for the Theatre"
      (See no. 54).

901 _____. "Harold Pinter: Old Times." In Das Englische Drama
      der Gegenwart, edited by Horst Oppel. Berlin: Schmidt,
      1975, pp. 206-21.

902 GOLDMAN, WILLIAM. The Season: A Candid Look at Broadway.
      New York: Bantam, 1970.
         A brilliant display of reverse snobbery. Rejects Pinter,
      Miller, Albee, Williams, Osborne, Arden, and Inge as being
      less valuable than Neil Simon because there have been more
      Broadway performances of Simon plays than of all these
      other playwrights combined (which tells us something about
      Broadway, too). Pinter is singled out, partly because he
      is English, as both representative and epitome of dramatists
      who write meaningfully, and anti-intellectual Goldman in-
      cludes amusing parodies of Pinter and Kenneth Tynan to
      prove his point. Unsatisfactory.

903 GOLDSTEIN, RUTH M. A Discussion Guide for the Film Pinter
      People. New York: Grove, (no date).
         A twenty-three-page pamphlet which is obviously meant
      to advertise Grove Press products, though the guide proposes

some interesting questions to be used in connection with the film (some of the questions relate techniques and concepts from the sketches to other works).

904   GOLDSTONE, HERBERT. "Not so Puzzling Pinter: The Homecoming." Theatre Annual, 25 (1969), 20-27.
      The Homecoming contrasts male and female attitudes toward sexuality.

905   GOODLAD, J. S. R. "A Sociology of Popular Drama: An Analysis of the Social Content of Popular Drama 1955-1965." Ph.D. dissertation, London School of Economics.

906   _____. A Sociology of Popular Drama. London: Heinemann, 1971. Reprinted: Totowa, N. J.: Rowman and Littlefield, 1972.
      Sees the function of drama as "reassurance," brought about by helping the audience understand and accept society as it is. Pinter's work is regarded in this light, though some of the definitions of "popular" drama are not clear.

907   GOODMAN, FLORENCE. "Pinter's The Caretaker: The Lower Depths Descended." Midwest Quarterly, 5, No. 1 (Winter 1964), 117-26.
      Pinter as an Absurdist stresses that man's hellish condition is a result of his own humanity. Contrasts The Caretaker with Gorky's The Lower Depths and O'Neill's The Iceman Cometh.

908   GORDON, LOIS G. "The Birthday Party." Deland, Florida: Everett/Edwards, 1975.
      Tape (#302) discussion of the play.

909   _____. "Harold Pinter: Past and Present." Kansas Quarterly, 3, No. 2 (Spring 1971), 89-99.
      Pinter's characters cope with "the ordeal of ordinary experience" by attempting "the games that people play" or by abandoning themselves "to the world of fantasy and silence."

910   _____. "Pigeonholing Pinter: A Bibliography." Theatre Documentation, 1, No. 1 (1968), 3-20.
      A fairly thorough annotated bibliography through mid-1967.

Gordon

911 _____. Stratagems to Uncover Nakedness: The Dramas of Harold
Pinter. Columbia: University of Missouri Press, 1968.
Role playing, sex, etc., in Pinter's work are viewed
from a Freudian viewpoint. Reviewed: See no. 1018.

912 GOTTFRIED, MARTIN. "'The Birthday Party.'" Women's Wear
Daily, 115 (4 October 1967), 44. Reprinted in: New York
Theatre Critics' Reviews, 9 October, 1967, p. 280.
Review of New York production of The Birthday Party
which sees the play as proof of Pinter's "status as an
artist valid beyond time."

913 _____. "The Caretaker." Women's Wear Daily, 108 (31 January
1964), 24.
Review of the film version of The Caretaker (The Guest).

914 _____. "Harold Pinter Cracks His Cool in His First Major Play
Since 1965." Vogue, 158 (1 August 1971), 71.
Review of Old Times, which Gottfried mistakenly sees
as being "about a woman who comes to visit a former room-
mate and takes her away from her husband." In spite of
being "almost self-satirical Pinter," the play succeeds
because Pinter has rejected the style of Landscape and
Silence, but has retained the content ("the undependable
and self-serving nature of memory") and the dramatist's
work now shows sympathy for the losers as the surrealism
has been altered sufficiently to allow them to wonder
aloud about what is happening.

915 _____. "'The Homecoming.'" Women's Wear Daily, 114 (6 Janu-
ary 1967), 101. Reprinted in: New York Theatre Critics'
Reviews, 16 January 1967, p. 397.
Review of New York production of The Homecoming.

916 _____. "'The Homecoming': '...perhaps the most fascinating
play of our time.'" Women's Wear Daily, 19 May 1971.
Reprinted in: New York Theatre Critics' Reviews, 14 June
1971, pp. 262-63.
Review.

917 _____. "'The Lover' and 'Play.'" Women's Wear Daily, 108
(6 January 1964), 18.
Review.

918 _____. "New Pinter Plays." Women's Wear Daily, 117 (16
October 1968), 67, 71. Reprinted in: New York Theatre
Critics' Reviews, 30 December 1968, p. 139.
Review of Tea Party and The Basement (New York).

919 _____. Opening Nights. New York: Putnam, 1969.
Includes a discussion of Beckett's influence on Pinter.

920 _____. "'The Room'--'A Slight Ache.'" Women's Wear Daily,
109 (10 December 1964), 48.
Review.

921 _____. A Theatre Divided: The Postwar American Stage.
Boston: Little, Brown, 1969.
Examines the American theatre as a contrast between
the "left" (new, innovative, not seeking answers) and
the "right" (establishment, demanding answers). Includes
a section on Pinter as an international writer with "left"
ideas expressed through acceptable "right" modes.

922 _____. "Two New Pinter Plays." Women's Wear Daily, 120 (3
April 1970), 12. Reprinted in: New York Theatre Critics'
Reviews, 1 June 1970, p. 246.
Review of Landscape and Silence (New York).

923 GOUGH-YATES, KEVIN. "Harold Pinter." In Twentieth Century
Writers, edited by Kenneth Richardson. London: Newnes,
1969, pp. 490-91.
Short biography.

924 GOULD, JACK. "TV: Harold Pinter's Baffling Dwarfs." New
York Times, 29 January 1968, p. 63.
Review of American television presentation of The
Dwarfs.

925 GOW, GORDON. "The Birthday Party." Films and Filming, 16,
No. 7 (April 1970), 41.
Review of film version of The Birthday Party.

926 _____. "The Quiller Memorandum." Films and Filming, 13,
No. 4 (January 1967), 29-30.
Film review.

927 _____. "Weapons: Joseph Losey in an Interview." Films and
Filming, 18, No. 1 (October 1971), 36-41.

928   GOWERS, MICHAEL. "Freud, no doubt, had the Word." London
       Daily Mail, 29 March 1963, p. 18.
            Review of British television production of The Lover.

929   _____. "This was Vintage Pinter." London Daily Mail, 11
       August 1961, p. 3.
            Review of British television production of The Dumb
       Waiter.

930   G. R. "Pinter's First Play Revived." Time and Tide, 28
       July 1964, p. 28.
            Review of The Birthday Party.

931   GRAHAM, PETER. "The Pumpkin Eater." International Film
       Guide, 2 (1965), 86.
            Film review.

932   GRANGER, DEREK. "The Birthday Party." London Financial Times,
       20 May 1958, p. 5.
            Review.

933   GRAY, WALLACE. "The Uses of Incongruity." Commonweal, 15
       (December 1963), 343-47.
            Characteristic of the Absurdists, Pinter utilizes the
       three kinds of incongruity ("rational and meaningful,
       irrational and meaningless, and irrational and apparently
       meaningless") to develop both the meaning and humor in
       his plays.

934   GREEN, HARRIS. "Less is More, Nothing is Everything." New
       Leader, 27 April 1970, pp. 32-33.
            Review of Landscape and Silence (New York).

935   GRENIER, CYNTHIA. "Americans Sweep Prizes at Cannes Festival."
       New York Times, 28 May 1971, p. 20.
            Discusses best picture award for The Go-Between.

936   GRIFFITHS, GARETH. "New Lines: English Theatre in the
       Sixties and After." Kansas Quarterly, 3, No. 2 (1971), 77-78.

*937   GROENE, HORST. "The Caretaker--Interpretionsprobleme bei
       Pinter." Literatur in Wissenschaft und Unterricht, 8
       (April 1975), 18-29.
            Cited in 1975 MLA International Bibliography, 1,
       p. 126.

938   GROSS, BEN. "Homosexual Play." New York Daily News, 29
      January 1968, p. 22.
         Review of American television presentation of The
      Dwarfs. Gross is one of the first to recognize homo-
      sexuality as an element in the play.

939   GROSS, JOHN. "Amazing Reductions." Encounter, 23 (Septem-
      ber 1964), 50-52.
         Pinter's poetic drama is revitalizing the English
      theatre. Discusses The Birthday Party.

940   GUARINO, ANN. "Few Happy Returns in Enigmatic 'Party.'"
      New York Daily News, 10 December 1968, p. 81.
         Review of film version of The Birthday Party.

941   GUERNSEY, OTIS L., JR. The Best Plays of 1964-1965. New
      York: Dodd, 1965.
         Pinter's plays on Broadway.

942   _____. The Best Plays of 1966-1967. New York: Dodd, 1967.
         Pinter's plays on Broadway. Guernsey sees The Home-
      coming as a simultaneous dramatization of the conscious
      and the subconscious.

943   GUSSOW, MEL. "Casting Around; Who Else Could Play Pinter?"
      New York Times, 5 December 1976, Leisure section, p. 5.
         Discusses who might replace Sir Ralph Richardson and
      Sir John Gielgud in No Man's Land.

944   _____. "A Conversation (Pause) with Harold Pinter." New
      York Times Magazine, 5 December 1971, pp. 42-43+.
         An interview of interest as it deals with Pinter's
      latest period of creativity, beginning with a focus on
      Old Times and involving some insights into the dramatist's
      creative process (partially as related to his personal
      interests, etc.).

945   _____. "'Old Times' Ushers in New Pinter Era." New York
      Times, 18 November 1971, p. 60.

946   GUPTA, MANJU DUTTA. "Recent Experimental Drama." Bulletin
      of the Department of English (Calcutta University), 4
      (NS), No. 1 (1968-1969), 13-32.
         Beckett, Pinter, and Ionesco share a world view which
      is dominated by angst.

947 GUTHKE, KARL S. "Die metaphysische Farce im Theater der
Gegenwart." In Deutsche Shakespeare-Gesellschaft West.
Heidelburg, 1970, pp. 46-76.
Man as a victim of absurd tragedy is seen in King Lear,
Salacrou, Stoppard, Bridie, Ionesco, Beckett, Albee, Mac-
Leish, and Pinter. In German.

948 HABICHT, WERNER. "Der Dialog und das Schweigen im 'Theater
des Absurden.'" Die Neueren Sprachen, 16 (NS), No. 1
(January 1967), 53-66.
Discusses the relationship between dialogue and silence
in Pinter, Ionesco, and Beckett. In German.

949 _____. "Theater der Sprache: Bemerkungen zu einigen
englischen Dramen der Gegenwart." Die Neueren Sprachen,
No. 7 (July 1963), 303-13.
Pinter, Simpson, and Wesker use language to show the
impossibility of human contact in the modern world. In
German.

950 HAFFENDEN, JOHN. Letter to the Editor. American Poetry
Review, 4, No. 2, p. 47.
A reply to Stanley Kauffmann's "Pinter and Sexuality:
Notes, Mostly on Old Times" (See no. 1157).

951 HAFLEY, JAMES. "The Human Image in Contemporary Art."
Kerygma, 3 (Summer 1963), 23-24.
A comparison of themes in the Theatre of the Absurd
and Abstract Expressionism in art.

*952 HALBRITTER, RUDOLF. Konzeptionsformen des modernen angloamer-
ikanischen Kurzdramas: Dargestellt an Stücken von W. B.
Yeats, Th. Wilder und H. Pinter. Göttingen: Vandenhoeck
und Ruprecht, 1975.
Cited in Modern Drama, 20, No. 2 (June 1977), 182.

953 HALE, WANDA. "Pleasence Perfect in 'The Guest.'" New York
Daily News, 21 January 1964, p. 39.
Review of the film version of The Caretaker.

954 HALL, PETER. "Directing Pinter." Theatre Quarterly, 14,
No. 16 (November 1974-January 1975), 4-17.
An interview conducted by Catherine Itzin and Simon
Trussler in which Hall discusses all aspects of directing
Pinter's work. Very comprehensive.

955 _____. "Is the Beginning the Word?" Theatre Quarterly, 2,
No. 7 (July-September 1972), 5-11.

956   HALL, RODNEY. "Theater in London." <u>Westerly</u>, No. 3 (October 1963), pp. 57-60.
        <u>The Birthday Party</u> is found to contain both the strengths and the weaknesses of serious English drama.

957   HALL, STUART. "Home Sweet Home." <u>Encore</u>, 12 (July-August 1965), 30-34.
        Review of <u>The Homecoming</u> which sees the play as Teddy's, i.e., a struggle between Teddy and his family for possession of Ruth.

958   _____. "<u>The Lover</u> and <u>The Dwarfs</u>." <u>Encore</u>, 10 (November-December 1963), 47-49.
        Review of <u>The Dwarfs</u> and <u>The Lover</u>. Ultimately, <u>The Lover</u> is "profoundly, deeply optimistic," <u>The Dwarfs</u> lacks conviction.

959   HALTON, KATHLEEN. "Pinter." <u>Vogue</u>, 150 (1 October 1967), 194-95+.
        Includes useful background material and quotations by Pinter.

960   HAMMOND, GERALDINE. "Something for the 'Nothings' of Beckett and Pinter." <u>The CEA Critic</u>, 39, No. 2 (January 1977), 40-47.
        Book review of William Baker and Stephen Tabachnick's <u>Harold Pinter</u> (See no 386), Andrew Kennedy's <u>Six Dramatists in Search of a Language</u> (See no. 1176), and Austin Quigley's <u>The Pinter Problem</u> (See no. 1595).

961   HANCOCK, JIM ROB. "The Use of Time by Absurdist Playwrights: Beckett, Ionesco, Genet, and Pinter." <u>Dissertation Abstracts International</u>, 33: 5876A. Ph.D. dissertation, University of Minnesota, 1972.
        Hancock determines that "the use of time <u>is</u> a valid mode of analysis in absurdist drama, for time is the essential of life, of character, and situation."

962   HARE, CARL. "Creativity and Commitment in the Contemporary British Theatre." <u>Humanities Association Bulletin</u>, 16, No. 1 (Spring 1965), 21-28.
        Pinter, Osborne, Wesker, and Arden are concerned with "exposing the bases of human relationships."

963   HARE, NORMAN. "Miss Withers saves the Show." London <u>News Chronicle</u>, 22 March 1960, p. 5.
        Review of British television production of <u>The Birthday Party</u>.

Harrington

964   HARRINGTON, DONALD S. "'The Real Horror.'" New York Times,
      5 February 1967, Sec. 2, pp. 1, 3.
          Review of The Homecoming.

965   HARRIS, LEONARD. "Grandly Absurd, That's Pinter." New York
      World Telegram and Sun, 31 January 1964, p. 15.
          Review of the film version of The Caretaker (The Guest).

966   _____. "The Homecoming." For WCBS-2 television, 18 May
      1971; in New York Theatre Critics' Reviews, 14 June 1971,
      p. 263.
          Review.

967   HART, HENRY. "The Birthday Party." Films in Review, 20,
      No. 1 (January 1969), 55-56.
          Review of the film version of The Birthday Party.

968   _____. "The Guest." Films in Review, 15, No. 2 (February
      1964), 114-15.
          Review of the film version of The Caretaker; essentially
      a synopsis.

969   HARTE, BARBARA, and CAROLYN RILEY, eds. 200 Contemporary
      Authors. Detroit: Gale, 1969, pp. 211-14.
          Very brief survey.

970   HARTUNG, P. T. "Checking Chekhov." Commonweal, 7 February
      1969, p. 591.
          Review of the film version of The Birthday Party.

971   _____. "Flow Gently Sweet Aston." Commonweal, 79 (7 Febru-
      ary 1964), 571.
          Brief film review of The Caretaker (The Guest): the
      film is called as fascinating as the play.

972   _____. "Had a Wife." Commonweal, 27 November 1964, p. 331.
          Film review of The Pumpkin Eater.

973   _____. "How Grey was our Dorian." Commonweal, 20 March
      1964, p. 751-52.
          Film review of The Servant. Although The Servant is a
      good film, it is not great because it is too long, "lacks
      the humor, mystery, and warmth" of The Caretaker, and
      presents no sympathy-eliciting characters.

974   _____. "I Spy." Commonweal, 3 February 1967, p. 489.
          Film review of The Quiller Memorandum.

975 _____. "The Screen." Commonweal, 94 (17 September 1971),
480-81.
Film review of The Go-Between which is fairly lavish
in praise of Pinter and Losey, though some fault is found
with the movie.

976 _____. "A Successful Accident." Commonweal, 28 April 1967,
p. 177.
Film review of Accident.

977 HASLER, JORG. "Bühnenanweisung und Spiegeltechnik bei
Shakespeare und im modernen Drama." In Deutsche
Shakespeare Gesellschaft West. Heidelburg, 1970, pp.
99-117.
Pinter and Beckett use stage directions to replace or
contrast with dialogue. In German.

978 HATCH, ROBERT. "Films: Accident." Nation, 204 (15 May
1967), 638.
Film review of Accident.

979 _____. "Films: The Go-Between." Nation, 4 October 1971,
pp. 316-17.
Film review of The Go-Between, which Hatch dislikes,
saying there is nothing there in spite of the big name
talent employed.

980 _____. "Films: The Last Tycoon." Nation, 223 (11 December
1976), 637.
Film review of The Last Tycoon.

981 _____. "Films: The Servant." Nation, 6 April 1964, pp.
354-55.
Film review of The Servant.

982 HAYMAN, RONALD. "Gray, Pinter and Bates: a triangular
alliance." The Times (London), 26 July 1975, p. 9.
Comments revolving around Otherwise Engaged which
say very little about Pinter.

983 _____. Harold Pinter. Contemporary Playwrights series.
London: Heinemann Educational Books, 1968. Reprinted in:
World Dramatists Series, New York: Ungar, 1973.
Very limited; serves only as a brief introduction.
Reviewed: See no. 818.

Hayman

983a ___. How to Read a Play. New York: Evergreen/Grove Press, 1977, pp. 74-76.
Includes a very brief mention of Pinter's use of silence in A Slight Ache and The Birthday Party.

984 ___. "Landscape Without Pictures: Pinter, Beckett, and Radio." London Magazine, 8, No. 4 (July 1968), 72-77.

985 ___. "Tragedy in the Holiday Camp." London Magazine, 9, No. 6 (September 1969), 83-92.
Whiting prepared the ground for Beckett and Pinter, in Hayman's opinion.

986 HAYS, H. R. "Transcending Naturalism." Modern Drama, 4 (May 1962), 27-36.
The realism of Pinter's work covers the chaos which exists underneath.

987 HEILMAN, ROBERT B. "Demonic Strategies: The Birthday Party and The Firebugs." In Sense and Sensibility in Twentieth-Century Writing: A Gathering in Memory of William Van O'Connor, edited by Brom Weber (See no. 1961), pp. 57-74. See also no. 1620.

988 ___. The Iceman, The Arsonist, and The Troubled Agent. Seattle: University of Washington Press, 1973.
A discussion of tragedy and melodrama on the modern stage which mentions Pinter in passing (The Birthday Party and The Caretaker are referred to).

989 ___. Tragedy and Melodrama: Versions of Experience. Seattle: University of Washington Press, 1968.
Includes passing mentions of Pinter (The Birthday Party).

990 HENKLE, ROGER B. "From Pooter to Pinter: Domestic Comedy and Vulnerability." Critical Quarterly, 16, No. 2 (Summer 1974), 174-89.
Compares elements in Pinter's comedies with those in nineteenth century comedies, using George and Weedon Grossmith's The Diary of a Nobody as a prime example.

991 HENRY, PATRICK. "Acting the Absurd." Drama Critique, 6 (Winter 1963), 9-19.
The actor's approach to performing a piece by Pinter.

992 HERIN, MIRIAM M. "An Analysis of Harold Pinter's Use of Language as Seen in The Birthday Party, The Caretaker, The Homecoming, and Old Times." Dissertation Abstracts

International, 34: 1913A. Ph.D. dissertation, University
of South Carolina, 1973.
"At the center of our modern crisis lies a failure of
language." Pinter is seen as using a multi-faceted poetic
image instead of a linear plot.

993 HEWES, HENRY, ed. The Best Plays of 1961-62. New York
and Toronto: Dodd, 1962.
Includes reprint of The Caretaker.

994 _____. The Best Plays of 1962-63. New York and Toronto:
Dodd, 1963.
Includes reprint of The Collection.

995 _____. "Best of the 1966-67 Theatre Season." Saturday
Review, 50 (10 June 1967), 18-22.
Includes review of The Homecoming (New York).

996 _____. "The British Bundle." Saturday Review, 54, No. 37
(11 September 1971), 20, 54.
Includes a review of Old Times.

997 _____. "The Company It's Kept." Saturday Review, 52 (15
November 1969), 20.
Review of The Homecoming (Minneapolis).

998 _____. "Disobedience, Civil and Uncivil." Saturday Review,
50 (28 October 1967), 46-47.
Review of the New York production of The Birthday Party.

999 _____. "The Frisco Kids." Saturday Review, 44 (26 August
1961), 26.
Review of The Birthday Party (San Francisco).

1000 _____. "Intramural Sport." Saturday Review, 47 (25 January
1964), 25.
Review of The Lover, New York production.

1001 _____. "Like Birth Warmed Over." Saturday Review, 50 (21
October 1967), 50.
Review of the New York production of The Birthday Party.

1002 _____. "Matched Pairs." Saturday Review, 48 (26 December
1964), 33.
Review of A Slight Ache and The Room.

Hewes

1003 _____. "Nothing Up the Sleeve." Saturday Review, 44 (21 October 1961), 34.
   Hewes feels that there is no hidden meaning to be found in The Caretaker and that the play lives in the "absolute urgency of the stage action."

1004 _____. "Odd Husband Out." Saturday Review, 54 (4 December 1971), 20, 22.
   Review of Old Times. Anna and Kate shut Deeley out of their past, according to Hewes.

1005 _____. "Pinter's Hilarious Depth Charge." Saturday Review, 50 (21 January 1967), 51.
   Review of The Homecoming (New York) highly praising the play's achievements.

1006 _____. "Probing Pinter's Play." Saturday Review, 50 (8 April 1967), 56.
   An invaluable look at The Homecoming with comments by Pinter which are extremely important in understanding the play.

1007 _____. "Thought Games." Saturday Review, 53 (25 April 1970), 16, 20.
   Review of Landscape and Silence (New York).

1008 _____. "Winter Pinter." Saturday Review, 45 (15 December 1962), 30.
   Review of The Dumb Waiter and The Collection, New York production.

1009 H. G. M. "The Caretaker." Theatre World, 56, No. 425 (June 1960), 8-9.
   Review.

1010 _____. "The Collection and Playing With Fire." Theatre World, 58, No. 45 (August 1962), 6.
   Review.

1011 HIBBIN, NINA. "A Man's Film: But It Got Me in the End." London Morning Star, 11 February 1967, p. 3.
   Film review of Accident.

1012 _____. "Pulling in Different Directions." London Daily Worker, 18 July 1964, p. 3.
   Film review of The Pumpkin Eater.

1013 _____. "Wistful, Engaging--But in the End, a Bore." London
        Daily Worker, 14 March 1964, p. 3.
            Review of the film version of The Caretaker.

1014 HIGGINS, DAVID M. "Existential Valuation in Five Contemporary
        Plays." Dissertation Abstracts International, 32:
        4612A. Ph.D. dissertation, Bowling Green University, 1971.
            Genet's The Balcony, Beckett's Waiting for Godot, Pin-
        ter's The Homecoming, Albee's Box-Mao-Box, and Miller's
        The Price are examined from an existential point of view.
        The Homecoming centers on "mind-body dissociation," and
        the unity of life, etc., in Pinter is only illusory.

1015 HIGGINS, JOHN. "The Collection and Playing with Fire."
        London Financial Times, 20 June 1962, p. 20.
            Review of original stage production of The Collection.

*1016 HILSKY, MARTIN. "The Two Worlds of Harold Pinter's Plays."
        In Bohumil Trunka and Adenek Stribrny, Acta Universitatis
        Carolinae. Philologica 3 (1969). Prague Studies in
        English, 13. Prague: Universitis Karlova, 1969, pp.
        109-15.

1017 HINCHCLIFFE, ARNOLD P. The Absurd. The Critical Idiom
        Series, 5. London: Methuen, 1969. Reprinted: New York:
        Barnes and Noble, 1969.

1018 _____. "Book Review." Modern Drama, 13, No. 4 (February
        1971), 449-50.
            Book review of Gordon's Stratagems to Uncover Nakedness
        (See no 911).

1019 _____. British Theatre: 1950-1970. Totowa, New Jersey:
        Rowman and Littlefield, 1974.
            Includes an examination of Pinter's works.

*1020 _____. "Drama." The Twentieth Century Mind, Vol. 3 (1945-
        65). Edited by C. B. Cox and A. E. Dyson. London:
        Oxford University Press, 1972, pp. 414-39.

1021 _____. Harold Pinter. New York: Twayne, 1967. Twayne's
        English Authors Series. Reprinted London: Macmillan,
        1976.
            Traces Pinter's development, concentrating on the
        meaning of individual plays and the use of language.
        Although there are some holes, it is the most complete
        study prior to Esslin's. Includes first printing of the
        revue sketch, "Special Offer." Reviewed: See no. 1486.

Hinchcliffe

1021a   ____. Modern Verse Drama. New York: Barnes and Noble, 1977.
           Vol. 32 in the Critical Idiom Series.
               Through a discussion of the modern verse drama genre,
           with specific attention to the work of Eliot and Fry,
           Hinchcliffe shows how Pinter's poetic theatre is an
           evolutionary outgrowth of the general trends in the form.

1022   ____. "Mr. Pinter's Belinda." Modern Drama, 11, No. 3
           (September 1968), 173-79.
               Sexual matters form the core of many of Pinter's plays,
           with women filling the roles of wife, mother, mistress,
           and whore.

1023   HIPP, EDWARD SOTHERN. "'Caretaker' Excels." Newark Evening
           News, 5 October 1961, p. 54.
               Review of New York production of The Caretaker.

1024   ____. "'Homecoming.'" Newark Evening News, 6 January 1967,
           p. 54.
               Review of The Homecoming (New York).

1025   ____. "'The Birthday Party.'" Newark Evening News, 4 Octo-
           ber 1967, p. 66.
               Laudatory review of The Birthday Party (New York) as
           a "tantalizingly implicit" black comedy.

1026   ____. "Two Pinter Playlets." Newark Evening News, 3 April
           1970, p. 16.
               Review of Landscape and Silence (New York).

1027   HINXMAN, MARGARET. "Films." Queen, 15 February 1967, pp.
           20-21.
               Film review of Accident.

1028   HIRSCHBERG, STUART. "Pinter's Caricature of Howard's End
           in The Homecoming." Notes on Contemporary Literature,
           4, No. 4 (1974), 14-15.

1029   HOBE. "The Birthday Party." Variety, 248 (11 October 1967),
           104.
               Review of New York production of The Birthday Party
           which states that the play will appeal to afficionados,
           but bore others.

1030   ____. "The Homecoming." Variety, 245 (11 January 1967),
           72, 76.
               Review of The Homecoming (New York).

1031   _____. "Landscape and Silence." Variety, 258 (8 April 1970),
        122.
            Review of Landscape and Silence (New York).

1032   HOBSON, HAROLD. "Accidental Achievement." Drama, 117
        (Winter 1975), 20-21.
            In a review of Terry Browne's Playwrights' Theatre
        (See no. 508), Hobson faults the Royal Court Theatre for
        not producing The Birthday Party.

1033   _____. "The Arts in Form Again." The Sunday Times (London),
        22 January 1961, p. 33.
            Review of original stage production of A Slight Ache,
        extremely lavish in praise.

1034   _____. "A Change of Taste." The Sunday Times, 24 July
        1960, p. 31.
            Review of The Birthday Party.

1035   _____. "The Dumb Waiter. The Room." The Sunday Times
        (London), 13 March 1960, p. 25.
            Review of The Dumb Waiter and The Room.

1036   _____. "The Importance of Fantasy." The Sunday Times (Lon-
        don), 22 September 1963, p. 33.
            Review of The Dwarfs and The Lover.

1037   _____. "Life Outside London." The Sunday Times (London),
        15 June 1958, p. 11.
            Review of the first run of The Birthday Party.

1038   _____. "Living Together." The Sunday Times (London), 27
        April 1975, p. 37.
            Very short review of No Man's Land.

1039   _____. "Old Times." The Sunday Times (London), 6 June
        1971, p. 29.
            Review of the play.

1040   _____. "Paradise Lost." The Sunday Times (London), 6 July
        1969, p. 52.
            A laudatory review dealing with the theme of memory in
        Landscape and Silence and the continuing influence the
        past exercises on the present.

1041   _____. "Pinter Minus the Moral." The Sunday Times (London),
        6 June 1965, p. 39.
            Review of the original production of The Homecoming

Hobson

which praises the aesthetic of the play, but faults it for its "moral vacuum."

1042 _____. "Pinter's No-Contest 'Old Times.'" Christian Science Monitor, 14 June 1971, p. 4.
Review.

1043 _____. "Real and Romantic Agony." The Sunday Times (London), 5 March 1972, p. 34.
Review of The Caretaker.

1044 _____. "Remembrance of Things Past." The Sunday Times (London), 6 June 1971, p. 29.
Review of Old Times.

1045 _____. "The Screw Turns Again." The Sunday Times (London), 25 May 1958, p. 11.
Review of the first run of The Birthday Party. Calling Pinter "the most original, disturbing, and arresting talent in theatrical London," Hobson comments on the theme of omnipresent terror.

*1046 _____. "Theatre." The Sunday Times (London), 31 December 1957.
Admiring review of the first performance of The Room. Reference in Hinchcliffe (See no 1021), p. 41.

1047 _____. "Theatre." The Sunday Times (London), 24 January 1960, p. 23.
Review of New York production of The Dumb Waiter and The Room.

1048 _____. "Things Are Looking Up." The Sunday Times (London), 5 June 1960, p. 25.
Review of original production of The Caretaker.

1049 _____. "Vagaries of the West End." The Sunday Times (London), 31 January 1960, p. 23.
Review of New York production of The Dumb Waiter and The Room unreservedly approving of Pinter's ability to captivate audiences.

1050 HODGENS, R. M. "The Guest." Film Quarterly, 18, No. 1 (Fall, 1964), 61.
Review of the film version of The Caretaker.

1051 HOEFER, JACQUELINE. "Pinter and Whiting: Two Attitudes Towards the Alienated Artist." Modern Drama, 4, No. 4. (February 1962), 402-08.

A comparison of The Birthday Party and Whiting's Saint's Day which examines the artist-vs.-society theme, concluding that where society is the victim in Whiting's drama, it becomes the villain in Pinter's. Hoeffer also mentions the influences of Kafka and Beckett.

1052   HOLDEN, DAVID. "Books in Brief." Modern Drama, 14, No. 1 (May 1971), 125-26.
Includes brief review of Hollis's Harold Pinter: The Poetics of Silence (See no. 1055).

*1053   HOLLAND, JULIAN. "The No. 296 All-Night Bus to Success." London Evening News, 14 May 1960.
Cited in Imhof (See no. 1098), p. 13.

1054   HOLLAND, MARY. "Theatre." Queen, 16 June 1965, p. 15.
Review of the original production of The Homecoming.

1055   HOLLIS, JAMES R. Harold Pinter: The Poetics of Silence. Crosscurrents/Modern Critiques Series. Carbondale: Southern Illinois University Press, 1970.
Another "introduction" volume mostly devoted to summaries of plot and interpretations dealing with the "linguistic and metaphoric patterns of the major plays," as well as a study of alienation and a need for but denial of transcendental experience. Purports to focus on Pinter's "relationship to and utilization of language." Reviewed: See nos. 684 and 1052.

1056   HOLMSTROM, JOHN. "Rambler." New Statesman, 2 April 1965, p. 547.
Review of television production of Tea Party.

1057   HOMAN, R. L. "T. S. Eliot's The Confidential Clerk: Prelude to Pinter?" Educational Theatre Journal, 28 (October 1976), 398-404.

1058   HOPE-WALLACE, PHILIP. "The Birthday Party." Manchester Guardian, 19 June 1964, p. 11.
Review of The Birthday Party revival, now considered a "modern classic."

1059   _____. "The Dumb Waiter. The Room." Manchester Guardian, 9 March 1960, p. 7.
Review of New York production of The Dumb Waiter and The Room.

Hope-Wallace

1060   ____. "Harold Pinter Double Bill." Manchester <u>Guardian</u>, 18 September 1970, p. 8.
      Review of <u>Tea Party</u> and <u>The Basement</u> (London).

1061   ____. "Mixed Doubles." Manchester <u>Guardian</u>, 10 April 1969, p. 9.
      Review of <u>Night</u>.

1062   ____. "New Pinter Play." Manchester <u>Guardian</u>, 19 June 1962, p. 7.
      Review of original stage production of <u>The Collection</u>.

1063   ____. "New Pinter Play at the Aldwych." Manchester <u>Guardian</u>, 2 June 1971, p. 8.
      Review of <u>Old Times</u>.

1064   ____. "Pinter's 'The Homecoming.'" Manchester <u>Guardian</u>, 4 June 1965, p. 11.
      Review.

1065   ____. "Pinter Plays." Manchester <u>Guardian</u>, 3 July 1969, p. 10.
      Review of <u>Landscape</u> and <u>Silence</u>.

1066   ____. "Three from Dublin." Manchester <u>Guardian</u>, 3 October 1961, p. 7.
      Review of <u>A Night Out</u>.

1067   ____. "Treble Chance." Manchester <u>Guardian</u>, 19 January 1961, p. 9.
      Review of original stage production of <u>A Slight Ache</u>.

1068   ____. "Two Pinter Plays." Manchester <u>Guardian</u>, 19 September 1963, p. 9.
      Review of <u>The Dwarfs</u> and <u>The Lover</u>. Both are concerned with ontology and are "pure Pinterism."

*1069   HOPPER, STANLEY ROMAINE. "Irony--The Paths of the Middle." <u>Crosscurrents</u>, Winter 1962, pp. 31-40.

1069a   HORNBY, RICHARD. <u>Script into Performance: A Structuralist View of Play Production</u>. Austin, Texas: University of Texas Press, 1977.
      <u>The Homecoming</u> is used as an example to show how performance is viewed as a function of the script.

*1070   HORTMANN, WILHELM. Englische Literatur im 20. Jahrhundert
         (Bern, 1965), pp. 177-78.
              Cited in Imhof (See no. 1098), p. 13.

*1071   HOUGHTON, NORRIS. Drama and Theatre of the Twentieth Century.
         New York: 1971.
              Cited in Imhof (See no. 1098), p. 13. This may be a
         reference to The Exploding Stage (See no. 1072).

1072   _____. The Exploding Stage: An Introduction to Twentieth-
         Century Drama. New York: Weybright and Talley, 1971;
         New York: Delta, 1971.
              A two-page summary of critical opinions regarding
         Pinter's work is included. Houghton thinks that The
         Birthday Party is Pinter's best play and that Pinter's
         dramas are fairly meaningless, though interesting in terms
         of technique. The brief section on Pinter concentrates
         on how he is different from Beckett (the former is con-
         cerned with anxiety, the latter with "emptiness" and
         "meaninglessness"). Although Pinter's verbal skill is
         praised, Houghton questions whether there is any substance
         to the plays.

1073   HOUSTON, PENELOPE. "Losey's Hand in Pinter's Glove." The
         Spectator, 17 February 1967, p. 195.
              Film review of Accident.

1074   _____. "The Quiller Memorandum." Sight and Sound, 36, No.
         1 (Winter 1966-67), 48.
              Film review of The Quiller Memorandum.

1075   HUDGINS, CHRISTOPHER CHAPMAN. "Dance to a Cut-Throat Temper:
         Audience Response, Identity, and the Mass-Media Influences
         in the Absurdist Work of Harold Pinter." Dissertation
         Abstracts International, 37: 4367-68A. Ph.D. dissertation,
         Emory University, 1976.
              An examination of Pinter's works, including his early
         poems and the unfinished novel, The Dwarfs, which demon-
         strates that dominance/subservience is a main theme. A
         psychologically based argument featuring Hans Robert
         Jauss's theories of audience response is used to show how
         Pinter represents his concepts of the relationship between
         reality and identity, especially in his utilization of
         techniques from radio, etc.

1076   HUDSON, ROGER. "Three Designers." Sight and Sound, 34, No.
         1 (Winter 1964-65), 26-31.
              Includes an interview with Richard MacDonald, Losey's
         set designer.

1077   HUGHES, ALAN. "'They Can't Take That Away from Me'; Myth and
        Memory in Pinter's <u>Old Times</u>." <u>Modern Drama</u>, 17, No. 4.
        (December 1974), 467-76.
            A brief examination of <u>Old Times</u> in which the past is
        seen as a cause and the present as its effect.

1078   HUGHES, CATHERINE. "'The Birthday Party.' how can I be
        certain of what I see?" <u>America</u>, 118 (6 January 1968),
        10-12.
            Review of <u>The Birthday Party</u> (New York).

1079   _____. Book review of Esslin's <u>The Peopled Wound</u>. <u>Catholic</u>
        <u>World</u>, 213 (April 1971), 48-49. (<u>See</u> no. 755).

1080   _____. "New York." <u>Plays and Players</u>, 17 (June 1970),
        16-17, 33.
            Includes review of <u>Landscape</u> and <u>Silence</u> (New York).

1081   _____. "Pinter and 'Pinteresque.'" <u>America</u>, 135 (11 Decem-
        ber 1976), 424.
            A production review of <u>No Man's Land</u> which is called
        "archetypal Pinter."

1082   _____. "Pinter is as Pinter Does." <u>Catholic World</u>, 210
        (December 1969), 124-26.
            Review of <u>Landscape</u> and <u>Silence</u>: Pinter's "refusal to
        make contact has been carried to its farthest extreme
        so far."

1083   _____. "Pinter Revisited." <u>America</u>, 125 (7 August 1971),
        70-71.
            Pinter's characters and techniques in <u>The Homecoming</u>
        are discussed briefly and highly approvingly.

1084   _____. "Pinter's 'Old Times.'" <u>America</u>, 125 (4 December
        1971), 485.
            Pinter is becoming Pinteresque (style seems more
        important than substance).

1085   HUMM. "Tea Party and The Basement." <u>Variety</u>, 252 (30 Octo-
        ber 1968), 75.
            Review of <u>Tea Party</u> and <u>The Basement</u> (New York). These
        plays are "clearly open to the charge of being 'Pinterish.'"

*1086   HUNT, ALBERT. "Around Us...Things Are There." <u>Encore</u>, 8,
        No. 6 (1961), 24-32.
            Cited in Imhof (<u>See</u> no. 1098), p. 13.

*1087   ____. "Pinter and Coward." New Society, 24 June 1976,
        pp. 696-97.
            Cited in British Humanities Index, 2 (April-June 1976),
        114.

1088   HUNT, JOSEPH A. "Interaction Process Analysis of Harold
        Pinter's The Homecoming: Toward a Phenomenological
        Criticism of Drama." Dissertation Abstracts International,
        32: 4159A. Ph.D. dissertation, University of New Mexico,
        1972.
            Robert F. Bale's system for determining Interaction
        Process Analysis is applied to The Homecoming, including
        computer tabulations and schematic drawings, to reveal the
        leader in the struggle for dominance.

1089   HUNTER, C. K. "English Drama, 1900-1960." In The Twentieth
        Century, Sphere History of Literature in the English
        Language Series, Vol. 7, edited by B. Bergonzi (See no.
        431), pp. 310-33.

1090   HURREN, KENNETH. "Familiar Ground." Spectator, 225 (26
        September 1970), 341-42.
            Review of Tea Party and The Basement (London).

1091   ____. "These Foolish Things." Spectator, 12 June 1971, p.
        821.
            Review of Old Times.

1092   HURT, JAMES, ed. Focus on Film and Theatre, Englewood
        Cliffs, N.J.: Prentice-Hall, 1974.
            Includes reprint of Downer and Pinter's "Filming 'The
        Caretaker'" (See no. 82) and Lindsay's "Thirty Differences
        Between the Photoplays and the Stage" (See no. 1343).

1093   HUTCHINGS, PATRICK. "The Humanism of a Dumb Waiter."
        Westerly, No. 1 (1963), pp. 56-63.
            A study of The Dumb Waiter as a play concerning
        alienation which is expressed in terms of a "farcical
        inconsequential, nightmarish" plot and dramatic enigmas.

1094   IBSEN, ELIZABETH. "Blind Man's Buff." Dissertation
        Universitetsbiblioteket, Bergen, 1969.
            A study of the theme of isolation in The Room, The
        Birthday Party, The Dumb Waiter, and The Caretaker.

*1095   IMHOF, RUDIGER. "Forschungsberichte und Bibliographien zu
        Harold Pinter." Anglia, 93, Nos. 3-4 (1975), 413-23.
            Cited in 1975 MLA International Bibliography, 1, p. 126.

Imhof

*1096 _____. "Harold Pinters gestalterische Mittel im Zusammenhang
seines dramatischen Gesamtwerkes (1957-73)." Dissertation,
Marburg, 1974.
In German. Cited in Imhof (See no 1098), p. 13.

*1097 _____. "Harold Pinters revue sketches als Schullektüre der
gymnasialen Oberstufe (Sekundarstufe II)." Die Neueren
Sprachen, 5 (October 1975), 390-401.

1098 _____. Pinter: A Bibliography. London: T Q Publications,
1975.
Checklist with an emphasis on London productions and
German studies. Perpetuates a few errors.

1099 _____. "The Pinter Problem." Modern Drama, 9, No. 4
(December 1976), 426-30.
Book review of Austin Quigley's linguistic study of
Pinter's work (See no. 1595).

1100 _____. "Pinter's Silence: The Impossibility of Communication." Modern Drama, 17, No. 4 (December 1974), 449-60.
Silence deals with the impossibility of communication
between the characters.

1101 ITZIN, CATHERINE. "Birthday Party." Plays and Players, 22
(March 1975), 26-27.
Review.

1102 _____. "Lookin Back on the Absurd." Theatre Quarterly,
Vol. 14, No. 16 (November 1974-January 1975), 91.
A retrospective book review of Esslin's Theatre of the
Absurd (See no. 761).

1103 _____. "The Pinter Enigma." Theatre Quarterly, 14, No. 13
(February-April 1974), 95.
Book reviews of Esslin (See no. 755), Trussler (See no.
1877) and Baker and Tabachnick (See no. 386).

1104 IVASK, IVOR and GERO VON WILPERT, eds. World Literature
Since 1945. New York: Ungar, 1973, pp. 95, 98-101,
484.
Briefly touches on Pinter.

1105 JACKSON, FRANK. "The New Shows." London Sunday Citizen, 25
May 1958, p. 7.
Review of original production of The Birthday Party.

1106   JACKSON, PETER. "The Birthday Party." Plays and Players, 5,
        No. 10 (July 1958), 16.
            Review of the original production of The Birthday Party
        which "could not be more logical" and which would receive
        the acclaim it deserves if Pinter were a foreigner.

1107   JACOB, GILES. "Joseph Losey, or the Camera Calls." Sight
        and Sound, 35, No. 2 (Spring 1966), 62-67.
            Discussion of Losey's style and the question of whether
        he should be considered an auteur. Praiseful recognition
        that Pinter's writing changes. Landscape and Silence
        are "evocations from certain lives that have been lived
        in certain juxtapositions."

1108   JAPA. "The Birthday Party." Variety, 253 (18 December 1968),
        26.
            Review of film version of The Birthday Party. Objects
        to close-ups as distracting from dialogue.

1109   JEFFREYS, ALLAN. "'Tea Party' and 'The Basement.'" For WABC-
        7 television, 15 October 1968; in New York Theatre Critic's
        Reviews, 30 December 1968, p. 142.
            Review.

1110   JENNINGS, ANN S. "The Reactions of London's Drama Critics to
        Certain Plays by Henrik Ibsen, Harold Pinter, and Edward
        Bond." Dissertation Abstracts International, 34: 2067A.
        Ph.D. dissertation, Florida State University, 1973.
            An interesting study in which The Birthday Party, The
        Caretaker, and The Homecoming are used in tracing the
        process by which plays originally rejected by drama
        critics become accepted and assimilated into the general
        cultural consciousness.

1111   JENSEN, TH. BORUP. Udgivet au Dansklaererforeninged.
        Copenhagen: Gyldendal, 1972.
            Includes "Dramaturgisk analyse," pp. 89-123, and
        "Arbejdssp∅rgsmål," pp. 125-34, and reprints The Care-
        taker (See no. 96).

1112   J. F. "Pinter Masterpiece." Jewish Chronicle, 13 March
        1964, p. 48.
            Review of the film version of The Caretaker.

1113   _____. "Unforgettable Stage Experience." Jewish Chronicle,
        27 September 1963, p. 42.
            Review of The Lover and The Dwarfs.

Jha

1114 JHA, A. "Christopher Fry and the Theatre of the Absurd."
      Indian Journal of English Studies, 8 (March 1967), 106-23.
      Fry is a precursor of Pinter in suspecting that the
      universe is meaningless.

1115 JIGI, VERA M. "Pinter's Four Dimensional House: The Home-
      coming." Modern Drama, 17, No. 4 (December 1974), 433.
      Audiences find The Homecoming powerful and satisfying
      because of three related factors: "our collective
      inheritance, our infantile fantasies and memories, and
      our subconscious present-day responses."

1116 JOHANSON, ELAINE. "Bravo, Mr. Pinter!" Letter to the Editor.
      New York Times, 9 January 1972, Sec. 2, pp. 6, 10.
      Concerned with Old Times.

1117 JONES, D. A. N. "Chic and Cute." Listener, 24 September
      1970, p. 433.
      Review of Tea Party and The Basement (London).

1118 _____. "Corruption." Listener, 82 (10 July 1969), 60-61.
      Review of Landscape and Silence.

1119 _____. "Silent Censorship in Britain." Theatre Quarterly,
      1, No. 1 (January-March 1971), 22-28.

1120 _____. "Yorubaland." New Statesman, 16 December 1966,
      p. 916.
      Review of The Homecoming.

1121 JONES, EDWARD T. "Summer of 1900: A la Recherche of 'The
      Go-Between.'" Literature Film Quarterly, 1, No. 2 (April
      1973), 154-60.
      Discussion of the theme of time in The Go-Between and
      speculation on possible application to Proust's work.

1122 JONES, JOHN BUSH. "Stasis as Structure in Pinter's No Man's
      Land." Modern Drama, 19, No. 3 (September 1976), 291-304.
      The meaning of No Man's Land is in part derived through
      its references to T. S. Eliot's "The Love Song of J.
      Alfred Prufrock" and Beckett's Endgame.

1123 JONES, PAUL D. "The Intruder in the Drama of Harold Pinter:
      A Functional Analysis." Dissertation Abstracts Interna-
      tional, 32: 4758-59A. Syracuse University, 1972.
      A "functional" (theatrical) analysis of Pinter's work
      and the dramatic presentation of intruders.

1124 JORDAN, RENÉ. "The Go-Between." Film Quarterly, 25, No. 3
      (Spring 1972), 37–41.
           Film review: an excellent film, though adaptation is
      called uninteresting.

1125 J. S. "Counter-Point." Daily Worker, 4 October 1961, p. 2.
           Review of A Night Out.

1126 _____. "Pinter and the Malignant Dwarfs." London Daily
      Worker, 20 September 1963, p. 2.
           Review of The Dwarfs and The Lover. The Dwarfs is a
      "dead end of fantasy and despair."

1127 KAEL, PAULINE. "The Comedy of Depravity: Accident." In
      Kiss Kiss Bang Bang (See no. 1132), pp. 129–34.
           An interesting review of the film Accident, which Kael
      likes in spite of its faults, this selection contains an
      accurate discussion of Pinter's failings as a scenarist:
      "In movies Pinter doesn't avoid exposition--he's just no
      good at it."

1128 _____. "The Current Cinema: The Birthday Party." New
      Yorker, 49 (21 December 1973), 90–91.
           Review of The Birthday Party.

1129 _____. "The Current Cinema: Humanoids and Androgynes."
      New Yorker, 49 (26 November 1973), 185–86.
           Film review of the movie version of The Homecoming
      which concludes that the play does not come off well as
      a film. Kael says that the fault lies in the original
      material which is filled with "cheap-theatricals" and is
      "corny."

1130 _____. "The Current Cinema: Stallone and Stahr." New
      Yorker, 52 (29 November 1976), 154, 157–60, 163.
           Includes movie review of The Last Tycoon, which Kael
      finds an almost complete failure. As usual, Kael deems
      Pinter's script the major problem with the film, though
      directing (by Elia Kazan), editing, acting, and even
      make-up and lighting are also "ineffective."

1131 _____. Going Steady. New York: Bantam, 1971.
           Includes another disparaging review, this time of the
      cinematic version of The Birthday Party (pp. 260–61).
      Pinter fails because he is "the actor as dramatist" whose
      writing does not transfer to the screen because the
      magnetism of live acting becomes rigid on film.

Kael

1132   _____. Kiss Kiss Bang Bang. New York: Little, Brown, 1968.
        Reprinted: New York: Bantam, 1969.
             Includes reprints of "The Comedy of Depravity: Accident"
        (See no 1127) and "A Sense of Disproportion" (See no.
        1133).

1133   _____. "Movies: A Sense of Disproportion." New Republic,
        14 January 1967, p. 42. Reprinted in Kiss Kiss Bang Bang
        (See no. 1132), pp. 7-12.
             Film review of The Quiller Memorandum.

1134   KAHANE, ERIC. "Pinter et le réalisme irréel." L'Avant-Scène
        (15 April 1967), p. 9.
             In French. Discusses dialogue and man's isolation.

1135   KAHL, KURT. "Harold Pinter: Der Hausmeister." Theater Heute,
        3, No. 5 (1962), 48.
             Review of The Caretaker (in German).

*1136   KAHLER, KLAUS. "Die Syntax des Dialogs im modernen Englisch
        untersucht an Werken von Harold Pinter und Graham Greene."
        Zeitschrift für Anglistik und Amerikanistik, 23, No. 1
        (1975), 41-63.
             Cited in 1975 MLA International Bibliography, 1, p. 118.

1137   KAISER, JOACHIM. "Der Fall Pinter: die Heimkehr in den
        Munchen Kammerspielen." Theater Heute, 7, No. 4 (1966),
        37-38.
             Review of The Homecoming (in German).

1138   KALEM, T. E. "Is Memory a Cat or a Mouse?" Time, 97 (29
        November 1971), 70-71.
             A disparaging review of the New York production of Old
        Times, a "bit of a bore" that is evidence that in this
        treatment of memory Pinter "has mistaken a dead end for
        a new road."

1139   _____. "Pinter Patter." Time, 107 (12 July 1976), 68.
             Review of David Mamet's Duck Variations and Sexual
        Perversity in Chicago in which characters hide behind
        masks of words a là Pinter.

1140   _____. "Roomer." Time, 96 (12 October 1970), 60-61.
             Essentially a book review of Esslin's The Peopled
        Wound (See no. 755).

1141   _____. "The Theatre: Spirited Skull-Puzzler." Time, 97 (22
        February 1971), 52.
             Review of The Birthday Party, an excellent production.

1142 KANTERS, ROBERT. "De Grands Moments de Theatre." In "La
Critique: Le Retour." L'Avant-Scene, 15 April 1967, p. 29.
Concerns The Homecoming.

1143 KARASEK, H. "Pinter-Einakter bei Leitzau." Die Zeit, 16
January 1970, p. 16.
Discusses the German production of Silence (in German).

*1144 KARRER, WOLFGANG, and EBERHARD KREUTZER. Daten der englischen
und amerikanischen Literatur von 1890 bis zur Gegenwart
(Munich, 1973), pp. 225, 235, 259.
In German. Cited in Imhof (See no. 1098), p. 13.

1145 KASTOR, FRANK S. "Pinter and Modern Tragicomedy." Wichita
State University Bulletin: University Studies, 46, No.
84 (August 1970), 1-13.
In Pinter, realistic settings, characters, and dialogue
operate within an absurd totality.

1146 _____. "The Theatre of Harold Pinter." Speech given at
the University of Southern California, 22 April 1968.
An overview of themes and techniques.

1147 KAUFFMANN, STANLEY. "Bergman and Pinter." New Republic, 3
January 1969, p. 34.
Review of The Birthday Party.

1148 _____. "The Birthday Party." New Republic, 4 January 1969.
Reprinted in his Figures of Light: Film Criticism and
Comment (See no. 1149), pp. 128-29.
A review of The Birthday Party film, which Kauffmann
feels is inferior to both the play and the movie version
of The Caretaker, in part because The Birthday Party is
not as strong a play and in part because director William
Friedkin is distractingly clever.

1149 _____. Figures of Light: Film Criticism and Comment. New
York: Harper and Row/Colophon, 1971, pp. 128-29.
Contains Kauffmann's "The Birthday Party" (See no.
1148).

1150 _____. "Films: Real, Real, Super-Real." New Republic, 150
(25 January 1964), 26ff.
A positive review of the film version of The Caretaker
(The Guest) which states that the film enhances the play--
subtleties and nuances lend greater implications to the
silence.

Kauffmann

1151 _____. "The Guest." New Republic, 25 January 1964. Reprinted in: A World on Film: Criticism and Comment (See
no. 1163), pp. 213-15.
    A review of the film version of The Caretaker, comment-
ing on Pinter's technical artistry and drawing the conclusion that the piece is "fully revealed" as a movie.

1152 _____. "High Life Below Stairs." New Republic, 150 (21
March 1964), 27-28.
    Film review of The Servant which finds that the
characters and plot are well delineated in the first
half of the movie, but everything falls apart in the
second half.

1153 _____. "The Homecoming." New Republic, 8 December 1973,
pp. 22+. See also no. 1620.
    Film review.

1154 _____. "Landscape and Silence." New Republic, 162 (25 April
1970), 20, 31. Reprinted in: Kauffmann, Persons of the
Drama (See no. 1156). See also no. 1620.
    Review.

1155 _____. Living Images: Film Comment and Criticism. New York:
Harper, 1975.
    Contains film reviews of The Go-Between and The Home-
coming (pp. 242-46).

1156 _____. Persons of the Drama: Theatre Criticism and Comment.
New York: Harper, 1976.
    Includes reprints of the production reviews "Landscape/
Silence," pp. 201-04, and "Pinter and Sexuality: Notes
Mostly on Old Times," pp. 335-48. See nos. 1154 and 1157.

1157 _____. "Pinter and Sexuality: Notes, Mostly on Old Times."
American Poetry Review, 3, No. 3 (July-August 1974),
39-41. Reprinted in: Kauffmann, Persons of The Drama.
See also no. 950.
    Review.

1158 _____. "Stanley Kauffmann on Films: The Go-Between." New
Republic, 165 (11 September 1971), 26, 33.
    Pinter's script is called no better or worse than
"several dozen other professionals might have done."
Interestingly, in the note in "Films Worth Seeing"
(New Republic, 18 December 1971, p. 20), Kauffmann
calls the film vacuous, though he recommends it and
praises the good performances and directing.

1159 _____. "Stanley Kauffmann on Films: The Last Tycoon." New
Republic, 175 (4 December 1976), 20-21.
Film review of The Last Tycoon.

1160 _____. "Stanley Kauffmann on Theatre." New Republic, 165
(18 December 1971), 20, 29-30.
Highly approving opinion of Pinter given, though Old
Times is not seen as being as strong as some of the playwright's earlier pieces.

1161 _____. "Stanley Kauffmann on theatre: no man's land." New
Republic, 175 (11 December 1976), 24-25.
An approving review of No Man's Land.

1162 _____. "Stanley Kauffmann on Theatre: Three Cities." New
Republic, 8 December 1973, p. 22.
Film review which praises the movie version of The
Homecoming and gives four responses to the film: 1)
comedy; 2) characters as mediums; 3) language; 4) sequence
in Pinter's work.

1163 _____. A World on Film: Criticism and Comment. New York:
Dell/Delta, 1966.
Includes reprint of "The Guest" pp. 213-15. (See
no. 1151).

1164 KAUFMAN, GERALD. "No Message." The Listener, 9 March 1967,
p. 330.
Film review of Accident.

1165 KAUFMAN, MICHAEL W. "Actions that a Man Might Play: Pinter's
The Birthday Party." Modern Drama, 16 (1973), 167-78.
Uses The Birthday Party to show that Pinter treats
absolute Truth and Reality with a Pirandellan contempt
in trying to show the individual's experience of living.
The game of blind man's buff is an appropriate climax to
the ritual man goes through as his "inner life" threatens
him with chaos until order is imposed from without.

*1166 KAWAGUCHI, KYŌICHI. "Harold Pinter: Society and Literature."
Eigo Kyōiku, May 1973.
In Japanese.

1167 KEE, ROBERT. "The Lover and The Dwarfs." Queen, 9 October
1963, p. 16.
Review.

Kemper

1168   KEMPER, ROBERT. "One Man's Family." Christian Century,
        84 (1 March 1967), 276-77.
                Concerned with The Homecoming as a theological allegory.
        Unconvincing.

1169   KENN. "The Caretakers." Variety, 233 (12 February 1964), 82.
                Review of the film version of The Caretaker (The Guest).

1170   ____. "The Dumb Waiter and The Collection." Variety, 229
        (5 December 1962), 58.
                Review of The Dumb Waiter and The Collection, New York
        production. "Uneven, seemingly lacking in substance,"
        these plays are "not Pinter at his best."

1171   ____. "The New Pinter Plays." Variety, 237 (16 December
        1964), 66.
                Review of New York production of A Slight Ache and The
        Room.

1172   ____. "Play and The Lover." Variety, 233 (22 January 1964),
        92.
                Review of The Lover (New York).

*1173   KENNARD, JEAN E. The Literature of the Absurd. New York:
        Harper.

*1174   KENNEDY, ANDREW E. K. "Language and Modern English Drama."
        Ph.D. dissertation, Bristol University, 1971-1972.
                Cited in Index to Theses (London: Aslib, 1974).

1175   ____. "Old and New in London Now." Modern Drama, 11, No.
        4 (February 1969), 437-46.
                Brief review of the radio version of Landscape included.

1176   ____. Six Dramatists in Search of a Language: Shaw, Eliot,
        Beckett, Pinter, Osborne, Arden. Cambridge: Cambridge
        University Press, 1974.
                Taking into account the texts, performances, and
        author's intents, Kennedy analyzes modern drama through
        theatrical language--"practical criticism" as opposed to
        a narrowly linguistic approach. Includes a chapter on
        Pinter's use of language (pp. 165-91). In contrast to
        Beckett and Ionesco, Pinter "has created his dialogue
        out of the failures of language that might occur as
        English is spoken." An extended examination, drawing on
        other scholars fairly heavily. Reviewed: See nos. 960
        and 1789.

1177   KEOWN, ERIC. "At the Play." Punch, 30 September 1959, pp. 252-53.
         Revue sketches reviewed.

1178   ____. "At the Play." Punch, 16 March 1960, p. 400.
         Review of The Room and The Dumb Waiter.

1179   ____. "At the Play." Punch, 238 (11 May 1960), 665.
         Review of original production of The Caretaker, which depends upon superb acting for its success.

1180   ____. "At the Play." Punch, 240 (25 January 1961), 186.
         Review of original stage production of A Slight Ache.

1181   ____. "At the Play." Punch, 242 (27 June 1962), 987.
         Review of original stage production of The Collection.

1182   KERNAN, MARGOT S. "Accident." Film Quarterly, 20, No. 4 (Summer 1967), 60-63.
         Film review.

1183   KERR, JEAN. "'Waiting for Pinter': A Play." New York Times, 12 December 1971, Sec. 2, pp. 3, 5.
         Review of Old Times.

1184   KERR, WALTER. "A Break with Anything Pinter Has Done Before." New York Times, 12 April 1970, Sec. 2, p. 3.
         Review of Landscape and Silence (New York).

1185   ____. "'The Caretaker.'" New York Herald Tribune, 5 October 1961, p. 16.
         Review of New York production of The Caretaker.

1186   ____. "The Dumbwaiter and The Collection." New York Herald Tribune, 27 November 1962, p. 20.
         Review of The Dumb Waiter and The Collection, New York production. The Collection deals with the "problem of transposed identities."

1187   ____. "First Night Report: 'The Caretaker.'" New York Herald Tribune, 5 October 1961, p. 16. Reprinted in: New York Theatre Critics' Reviews, 9 October 1961, p. 250.
         Review of The Caretaker.

1188   ____. God on the Gymnasium Floor, and Other Theatrical Adventures. New York: Simon and Schuster, 1972.

Kerr

Includes a chapter on Pinter: "The Playwright as
Existentialist," pp. 127-58. Basically a rewrite of
Kerr's Columbia University pamphlet, Harold Pinter (See
no 1189).

1189   ____. Harold Pinter. Columbia Essays on Modern Writers,
No. 27. New York: Columbia University Press, 1967;
London, 1967. See also no. 1620.
Pinter not only states existential themes, his plays
"function according to existential principle," Kerr asserts.

1190   ____. "Is Mr. Pinter Telling Us Less Than He Knows?" New
York Times, 28 November 1971, Sec. 2, pp. 1, 7.
Review of Old Times.

1191   ____. "Kerr Reviews Pinter's 'Room' and 'Slight Ache.'"
New York Herald Tribune, 10 December 1964, p. 16.
Review.

1192   ____. "A Majestic Joke from Harold Pinter." New York Times,
21 November 1976, Sec. 2, pp. 3, 22.
Review of No Man's Land (New York).

*1193   ____. "Making a Cult of Confusion." Horizon, 5 (September
1962), 33-41.

1194   ____. "Pinter's Balance of Terror." New York Herald Tribune,
27 December 1964, p. 17.
Review of The Room and A Slight Ache.

1195   ____. "'Play' and 'The Lover'--Twin Bill at Cherry Lane."
New York Herald Tribune, 6 January 1964, p. 12.
Review of The Lover (New York). The resolution is "not
surprising."

1196   ____. "A Pox on Shocks." New York Times, 15 January 1967,
Sec. 2, p. 11.
A review of Pinter's The Homecoming, which Kerr feels
contradicts our attempts to deal with the world logically
and rationally.

1197   ____. "Put Off--Or Turned On--By Pinter." New York Times,
15 October 1967, Sec. 2, p. 1. Reprinted in Kerr's Thirty
Plays Hath November (See no. 1203).
Offers reasons why most people would not like The Birthday Party. The reasons include length, lack of concrete
action, a feeling that Stanley could escape if he really
wanted to.

1198   ____. "The Something That Pinter Holds Back." <u>New York Times</u>, 3 November 1968, Sec. D, p. 7.
        Review of <u>Tea Party</u> and <u>The Basement</u>.

1199   ____. "The Struggle to See." In Kerr's <u>Thirty Plays Hath November</u> (See no. 1203), pp. 41-49.
        Concerns <u>The Birthday Party</u>.

1200   ____. <u>The Theatre in Spite of Itself</u>. New York: Simon and Schuster, 1963.
        Discusses <u>The Caretaker</u>, pp. 116-19. <u>See also</u> "The Hey, Wait a Minute Theatre," pp. 29-41.

1201   ____. "Theater Is the Victim of a Plot." <u>New York Times</u>, 25 June 1967, Sec. 4, p. 10.
        Kerr speaks of the theatre as mostly unchanging, though Pinter (especially in <u>The Homecoming</u>) is getting away from the conventional.

1202   ____. "The Theater: Pinter's <u>Homecoming</u>." <u>New York Times</u>, 6 January 1967, p. 29.
        An unfavorable report on <u>The Homecoming</u>.

1203   ____. <u>Thirty Plays Hath November</u>. New York: Simon and Schuster, 1969.
        Includes "Put Off-Or Turned On-By Pinter" (See no. 1197) and "The Struggle to See: The Moment of Pinter" (See no. 1199), pp. 41-46.

1204 KERSHAW, JOHN. <u>The Present Stage</u>. London: Collins, 1966.
        Includes "Harold Pinter, Dramatist" (pp. 70-78) and "The Language of Silence" (pp. 79-87). Discusses <u>The Caretaker</u>. Basically a repetition of previous critical concerns and conclusions.

*1205 KESTING, MARIANNE. "Harold Pinter." <u>Panorama des zeitgenos-sischen Theaters</u> (Munich, 1969), pp. 243-48.
        Cited in Imhof (See no 1098), p. 13.

1206 KILLINGER, JOHN. <u>World in Collapse: The Vision of Absurd Drama</u>. New York: Delta, 1971.
        Includes a discussion of Pinter's work.

1207 KILPATRICK, ROSS S. "A Note on <u>The Room</u> by Harold Pinter." <u>Theatre Annual</u>, 31 (1975), 55-56.

1208 KING, FRANCIS. "Television." <u>The Listener</u>, 1978 (23 February 1967), 271.
        Review of television production of <u>A Night Out</u>.

King

1209   KING, KIMBALL. <u>Twenty Modern British Dramatists: A Bibliography, 1956 to 1976</u>. New York: Garland, 1977, pp. 125–92.
      A bibliography, including a section on Pinter. Useful
for cross-references.

1210   KINGSTON, JEREMY. "At the Play." <u>Punch</u>, 246 (24 June 1964),
941.
      Review of <u>The Birthday Party</u> revival: the three acts
represent Stanley's birth, life, and death.

1211   _____. "At the Theatre." <u>Punch</u>, 257 (9 July 1969), 73–74.
      Review of <u>Landscape</u> and <u>Silence</u>.

1212   _____. "Theatre." <u>Punch</u>, 248 (16 June 1965), 901.
      Review of the original production of <u>The Homecoming</u>.
Pinter is approaching self-parody.

1213   _____. "Theatre." <u>Punch</u>, 16 June 1971, pp. 826–27.
      Review of <u>Old Times</u>.

1214   KIRBY, MICHAEL S. <u>The New Theatre</u>. New York: New York
University Press, 1974.
      Performance documentation.

*1215   KISHI, TETSUO. "The Ambiguity of Harold Pinter." <u>Eigo
Bungaku Sekai</u>, June 1966.
      In Japanese. Cited by Kishi in personal correspondence.

*1216   _____, ed. <u>Gendai Engeki</u> (Modern Drama). Tokyo: Gakusei-
sha, 1975.
      A record of a symposium on modern drama, including
Pinter. In Japanese. Cited by Kishi in personal
correspondence.

1217   _____, ed. <u>Pinta Gikyoku Zenshu</u> (Collected Plays of Harold
Pinter). Tokyo: Takeuchi Shotem, 1970.
      <u>See</u> no. 108 for listing of translated plays included.

*1218   _____. "The New Kind of Reality in Pinter's Plays." <u>Gunzo</u>,
January 1969.
      In Japanese. Cited by Kishi in personal correspondence.

*1219   _____. "A Survey of Modern English and American Drama." In <u>A
Survey of Modern World Drama</u>. Tokyo: Hakusuisha, 1972.
      In Japanese. Cited by Kishi in personal correspondence.

*1220 _____. "Theatre of Loquaciousness." Eigo Seinen, May-June
1970.
In Japanese. Cited by Kishi in personal correspondence.

*1221 _____. "Theatre of Silence." Shingeki, September 1970.
In Japanese. Cited by Kishi in personal correspondence.

*1222 KISSELL, HOWARD. Review of The Last Tycoon, Women's Wear
Daily, November 1976.
Film review. Quoted in New York Times advertisement.

*1223 KITCHEN, LAURENCE. "Backwards and Forwards." Twentieth
Century, 169, No. 1008, 168-69.

1224 _____. Drama in the Sixties: Form and Interpretation.
London: Faber, 1966.
See "Compressionism. The Form," pp. 45-53.

1225 _____. Mid-Century Drama. Second edition. London: Faber,
1962.
"Compressionism" is seen as Pinter's main technique in
both language and dramatic situation. Mentions similarity
to Chekhov. See pp. 119-22.

1226 _____. "Realism in the English Mid-Century Drama." World
Theatre, 14, No. 1 (January 1965), 17-26.
A tracing of influences on contemporary English real-
ists, citing a mastery of experimental staging, scenery,
and dialect as praiseworthy and unprecedented graces.

1227 KLINEMAN, NEIL. "Naming of Names." In Pinter's Optics
(See no 311), pp. 4-5.
Edward in A Slight Ache is a "composite of the
Enlightenment Man."

*1228 KLOTZ, FRIEDRICH. "Jean Tardieu: Theatre de Chambre." Der
Fremdsprachliche Unterricht, 4, No. 13 (February 1970),
69-83.
Cited in Imhof (See no. 1098), p. 14.

1229 KLOTZ, GUNTHER. "Individuum und Gesellschaft im Englischen
Drama der Gegenwart: Arnold Wesker und Harold Pinter."
Weimarer Meiträge, 9, No. 10 (1973), 187-91.
Analyzes the relationship between the individual and
society as reflected in the plays of Wesker and Pinter.
Klotz sees Pinter as a "modernist" whose plays are not
socially significant and who denies the social function
of art. In German.

1230   KNIGHT, ARTHUR. "The Birthday Party."
        An interview with director William Friedkin, 18 Decem-
        ber 1968, on tape (T277) and held at the University of
        Southern California Doheny Library.

1231   ____. "SR Goes to the Movies: The Mechanics of Laughter."
        Saturday Review, 47 (15 February 1964), 33.
        Film review of The Caretaker (The Guest).

1232   KNIGHT, G. WILSON. "The Kitchen Sink: On Recent Developments
        in Drama." Encounter, 21, No. 6 (December 1963), 48-54.
        Pinter, as a member of the Kitchen Sink school of
        dramatists, is depicted as trying to reestablish human
        values by balancing "mental discontinuities" with "objec-
        tive absurdities."

1233   KOEGLER, HORST. "Plays and Players Abroad: Dusseldorf."
        Plays and Players, 8, No. 8 (May 1961), 17.
        Review of The Caretaker.

*1234   KOSOK, HEINZ. "Das moderne englische Kurzdrama." Neusprach-
        liche Mitteilungen aus Wissenschaft und Praxis, 3 (1970),
        131-41.
        In German. Cited in 1970 MLA International Bibliography,
        1, p. 82.

*1235   KOSTELANETZ, RICHARD. On Contemporary Literature. New York:
        Avon, 1969.
        Includes John Lahr's "Harold Pinter" (See no. 1263),
        and John Russell Taylor's "British Drama of the 50's"
        (See no. 1813).

1236   KOTLOWITZ, ROBERT. "Performing Arts: Four Films from
        Europe." Harper's, 324 (June 1967), 110-11.
        A film review of Accident in which Pinter's screen-
        play (dialogue, ambiguity) is lambasted.

*1237   KOTT, JAN. "The Icon and the Absurd." The Drama Review, 14
        (Fall 1969), 17-24.

1238   KRAFT, DAPHNE. "Two Pinter Plays." Newark Evening News, 16
        October 1968, p. 56.
        Review of Tea Party and The Basement (New York) which
        sees man's total isolation as the theme of these plays.

1239   KRETZMER, HERBERT. "Fight Against Time by New Caretaker."
        London Daily Express, 3 March 1972, p. 12.
        Review.

1240 ____. "Freaky Night at the Pintermime." London <u>Daily</u>
<u>Express</u>, 19 September 1963, p. 4.
    Review of <u>The Dwarfs</u> and <u>The Lover</u>. <u>The Lover</u> is
repetitive in style.

1241 ____. "The Laughs Grow--But Should Pinter be Happy?"
London <u>Daily Express</u>, 19 June 1964, p. 6.
    People accept the revival of <u>The Birthday Party</u> because
they are familiar with Pinter, not because the play
deserves any acclaim.

1242 ____. "The Magic Touch that Falters." London <u>Daily Express</u>,
19 June 1962, p. 4.
    Review of original stage production of <u>The Collection</u>.
Comments on audience familiarity with Pinter: "Nothing
will destroy Mr. Pinter's effects and influence more
swiftly than [a] kind of public cosiness, since it completely destroys the kind of hallucination that haunted
his earlier plays."

1243 ____. "Pinter Caught Fast in a Rut." London <u>Daily Express</u>,
2 June 1971, p. 14.
    Review of <u>Old Times</u>.

1244 ____. "That Break Through Becomes a Cliche." London <u>Daily</u>
<u>Express</u>, 4 June 1965, p. 4.
    Review of <u>The Homecoming</u>.

1245 ____. "Up to Pinter's Larks--But Arid...." London <u>Daily</u>
<u>Express</u>, 3 July 1969, p. 8.
    Review of <u>Landscape</u> and <u>Silence</u>.

1246 ____. "Where Marriage Is a Prison Sentence." London <u>Daily</u>
<u>Express</u>, 10 April 1969, p. 12.
    Review of <u>Night</u>.

1247 KROLL, JACK. "Blood from Stones." <u>Newsweek</u>, 70 (16 October
1967), 104, 106.
    Review of New York production of <u>The Birthday Party</u>.

1248 ____. "Britain Onstage." <u>Newsweek</u>, 22 March 1976, pp.
74-78.
    Discussion of the New National Theatre, mentioning
Pinter and productions of his works.

1249 ____. "Camera Obscura." <u>Newsweek</u>, 78 (29 November 1971),
110-11.
    Review of <u>Old Times</u> which sees Pinter as being repetitive.

Kroll

1250   _____. "Dark Secrets." Newsweek, 72 (28 October 1968), 135.
      Review of Tea Party and The Basement (New York).

1251   _____. "Falling Stahr." Newsweek, 88, No. 21 (22 November
      1976), 107-08, 110.
      Film review of The Last Tycoon which finds the movie
      "by far the best" translation of F. Scott Fitzgerald to
      the screen to date, but still a disappointment.

1252   _____. "Harold and Sam." Newsweek, 75 (13 April 1970), 83.
      Review of Landscape and Silence.

1253   _____. "Malice Domestic." Newsweek, 64 (21 December 1964),
      75-76.
      Review of A Slight Ache and The Room, neither of which
      yet fulfill Pinter's promise.

1254   _____. "One Man's Family." Newsweek, 77 (31 May 1971), 42.
      Reprinted in: New York Theatre Critics' Reviews, 14 June
      1971, p. 262.
      The Homecoming is a "beautifully ambiguous" play, in
      Kroll's opinion.

1255   _____. "The Puzzle of Pinter." Newsweek, 88 (29 November
      1976), 74-78, 81.
      A review of No Man's Land which is also part overview
      and part biography. Language, T. S. Eliot, symbolism,
      the nature of art, and the theme of identity-seeking are
      discussed.

*1256 KUNKEL, FRANCIS L. "Dystopia of Harold Pinter." Renascence,
      21 (Autumn 1968), 17-20.
      Cited in Herman Schroll (See no. 1700), p. 104.

1257 LAHR, JOHN. "An Actor's Approach." In Lahr, A Casebook on
      Harold Pinter's The Homecoming (See no. 1260), pp. 137-50.
      An interview with John Normington, Sam in The Homecoming.

1258   _____. "An Actor's Approach." In Lahr, A Casebook on Harold
      Pinter's The Homecoming (See no. 1260), pp. 151-74.
      An interview with Paul Rogers, Max in The Homecoming.

1259   _____. Astonish Me: Adventures in Contemporary Theatre.
      New York: Viking, 1973.
      Includes reprint of "Pinter and Chekhov: The Bond of
      Naturalism" (See no. 1265).

1260   _____, ed. A Casebook on Harold Pinter's The Homecoming.
        New York: Grove Press, 1971.
            An interesting collection of essays on meaning, language,
        characterization, etc.: by Martin Esslin, "The Homecoming:
        An Interpretation" (See no. 752); Irving Wardle, "The
        Territorial Struggle" (See no. 1939) and "A Director's
        Approach" (See no. 1925); Margaret Croyden, "Pinter's
        Hideous Comedy" (See no. 647); John Russell Taylor,
        "Pinter's Game of Happy Families" (See no. 1823); Steven
        M. L. Aronson, "Pinter's Family and Blood Knowledge" (See
        no. 376); Rolf Fjelde, "Plotting Pinter's Progress" (See
        no. 787); Bernard Dukore, "A Woman's Place" (See no. 720);
        Augusta Walker, "Why the Lady Does It" (See no 1914); and
        pieces by Lahr (See nos. 1257, 1258, 1262, 1266, and
        1268). Interviews with the director, set designer, and
        two actors prove surprisingly useful--insights and infor-
        mation. Reviewed: See no. 818.

1261   _____. "Cracking the Pinter Puzzle." Evergreen Review, 15,
        No. 86 (January 1971), 74-76.
            Book review of Esslin's The Peopled Wound (See no. 755).

1262   _____. "A Designer's Approach." In Lahr, A Casebook on
        Harold Pinter's The Homecoming (See no. 1260), pp. 9-26.
            An interview with John Bury about staging The Homecoming.

1263   _____. "Harold Pinter." In Richard Kostelanetz, On Contem-
        porary Literature (See no. 1235), pp. 682-89.

1264   _____. "The Language of Silence." Evergreen Review, 13,
        No. 64 (March 1969), 53-55, 82-90.
            The idea of the moment is studied as Lahr notes that
        Pinter uses silence as an "articulate energy which gives
        resonance to the spoken word." Pinter, Beckett, Joyce,
        and Kafka use silence as communication.

1265   _____. "Pinter and Chekhov: The Bond of Naturalism." Drama
        Review, 13, No. 2 (1968), 137-45. Reprinted in: Lahr,
        Astonish Me: Adventures in Contemporary Theatre (See no.
        1259). Reprinted in: Ganz, Pinter: A Collection of
        Critical Essays (See no. 843), pp. 60-71.

1266   _____. "Pinter's Language." In Lahr, A Casebook on Harold
        Pinter's The Homecoming (See no. 1260), pp. 123-36.
            Emphasis is on silence.

*1267   _____. "Pinter's Room: Who's There." Arts Magazine, March
        1967, pp. 21-23.

Lahr

1268   _____. "Pinter the Spaceman." Evergreen Review, 12, No. 55
        (June 1968), 49-52, 87-90. Reprinted in: Lahr, Up Against
        the Fourth Wall (See no. 1269), pp. 175-94; reprinted in:
        Lahr, A Casebook on Harold Pinter's The Homecoming (See
        no. 1260), pp. 175-93.
        Pinter's naturalism is discussed.

1269   _____. Up Against the Fourth Wall. New York: Grove Press,
        1969.
        Includes "Pinter the Spaceman" (See no. 1268).

1270   LAMBERT, J. W. "The Caretaker." The Sunday Times (London),
        1 May 1960, p. 25.
        Review of original production of The Caretaker, which
        deals with human relationships.

1271   _____. "Dogs Beneath the Skin." The Sunday Times (London),
        20 September 1970, p. 29.
        Review of Tea Party and The Basement.

1272   _____. "Introduction." New English Dramatists 3, edited by
        Tom Maschler. Harmondsworth: Penguin, 1961, pp. 7-10.

1273   _____. "Plays in Performance." Drama, 56 (Spring 1960),
        20-27.
        Review of The Room and The Dumb Waiter.

1274   _____. "Plays in Performance." Drama, 57 (Summer 1960),
        18-25.
        Review of The Caretaker.

1275   _____. "Plays in Performance." Drama, 60 (Spring 1961),
        20-26.
        Includes a review of A Slight Ache.

1276   _____. "Plays in Performance." Drama, 66 (Autumn 1962),
        18-25.
        Review of The Collection.

1277   _____. "Plays in Performance." Drama, 71 (Winter 1963),
        18-26.
        Review of The Lover and The Dwarfs.

1278   _____. "Plays in Performance. London." Drama, 94 (Autumn
        1969), 14.
        Review of Landscape and Silence: "a marked shrinkage."

1279   ____. "Plays in Performance." <u>Drama</u>, 99 (Winter 1970), 22-23.
      Review of <u>Tea Party</u> and <u>The Basement</u> (London).

1280   ____. "Plays in Performance." <u>Drama</u>, 102 (Autumn 1971), 12-30.
      Review of <u>Old Times</u>.

1281   ____. "Plays in Performance." <u>Drama</u>, 116 (Spring 1975), 47-49.
      Production review of <u>The Birthday Party</u>.

1282   ____. "Plays in Performance." <u>Drama</u>, 117 (Summer 1975), 37-55.
      Praiseful review of <u>No Man's Land</u>: exposes "the desperate shifts that human nature is sometimes put to at the behest of the will to live."

1283   ____. "Plays in Performance." <u>Drama</u>, 118 (Autumn 1975), 42-59.
      Review of <u>Otherwise Engaged</u>. Pinter's directing "has often been ponderous," but this is an exception.

1284   ____. "A Stitch in Time." <u>The Sunday Times</u> (London), 24 June 1962, p. 35.
      Review of original stage production of <u>The Collection</u>.

1285   ____. "Trial by Laughter." <u>The Sunday Times</u> (London), 21 June 1964, p. 33.
      Review of <u>The Birthday Party</u> revival.

1286 LAMONT, ROSETTE C. "Pinter's <u>The Homecoming</u>: The Contest of the Gods." <u>Far-Western Forum</u>, 1 (1974), 47-73.

1287 LANDSTONE, CHARLES. "From John Osborne to Shelagh Delaney." <u>World Theatre</u>, 8 (1959), 203-16.

1288   ____. "Revolts and Fascinates." <u>Jewish Chronicle</u>, 11 June 1965, p. 38.
      Review of <u>The Homecoming</u>.

1289 LANE, JOHN FRANCIS. "No Sex Please, I'm English: John Francis Lane on the Pinter-Visconti Case." <u>Plays and Players</u>, 20, No. 10 (July 1973), 19-21.

1290 LANE, STEWART. "An Eerie Affair." London <u>Daily Worker</u>, 24 March 1960, p. 2.
      Review of British television production of <u>The Birthday Party</u>, in which nothing is said.

Lane

1291   _____. "New Director? Let's Call in the Head Shrinker."
London <u>Daily Worker</u>, 30 March 1963, p. 2.
    Review of television production of <u>The Lover</u> which,
although "laden with sexual symbolism," is "little more
than a Pinterish exercise."

1292   _____. "Pinter's Hero Loses Control of his Destiny." London
<u>Daily Worker</u>, 27 March 1965, p. 2.
    Review of television production of <u>Tea Party</u>.

1293   _____. "Talented Harold Pinter." London <u>Daily Worker</u>, 26
April 1960, p. 3.
    Review of television version of <u>A Night Out</u>.

1294   _____. "Televiews." London <u>Daily Worker</u>, 12 August 1961,
p. 2.
    Review of British television production of <u>The Dumb
Waiter</u>.

1295   _____. "Those Swinging, Way-Out Trendsetters Were a Drag."
London <u>Morning Star</u>, 29 October 1966, p. 2.
    Negative review of the film version of <u>The Caretaker</u>:
"My own search for anything more than technical signifi-
cance was unavailing."

1296 LANGLEY, LEE. "From 'Caretaker' to 'Servant.'" New York
<u>Herald Tribune</u>, 1 March 1964, <u>Magazine</u> section, p. 24.
    Pinter discusses his screenwriting and the nature of
film from the writer's point of view. <u>The Caretaker</u>, <u>The
Pumpkin Eater</u>, <u>The Compartment</u> (from "Project One"), and
<u>The Servant</u> are mentioned.

1297   _____. "Genius--A Change in Direction." London <u>Daily Telegraph Magazine</u>, 23 November 1973, pp. 30-36.
    Combination reminiscence, article, and interview, with
focus on Pinter's direction of the film version of <u>Butley</u>.

1298 LAWS, FREDERICK. "Drama and Light Entertainment." <u>The
Listener</u>, 15 April 1965, p. 575.
    Review of television production of <u>Tea Party</u>.

1299   _____. "Man of Blood." <u>The Listener</u>, 8 December 1960, p.
1078.
    Review of radio version of <u>The Dwarfs</u>.

1300 LEAHY, JAMES. <u>The Cinema of Joseph Losey</u>. London: Zwemmer,
1967; Cranbury, New Jersey: A. S. Barnes, 1967.

1301　LECHLER, HANS-JOACHIM. "Harold Pinters Sketch Last to Go." Der fremdsprachliche Unterricht, 4, No. 13 (February 1970), 29-37.

*1302　LECLERC, GUY. Review of Le Gardien. L'Humanitè, 28 January 1961, p. 2.
　　　　Review of The Caretaker. Cited in Elliott (See no. 733), p. 558.

*1303　LEE, N. F. A. H. "The Deliberate Use of Shock Techniques in the Post-War Theatre in England and France." M. A. thesis, Manchester, 1967-68.
　　　　Cited in Index to Theses (London: Aslib).

1304　LEECH, CLIFFORD. The Dramatist's Experience: with other Essays in Literary Theory. New York and London: Chatto and Windus, 1970.

1305　_____. "Two Romantics: Arnold Wesker and Harold Pinter." The Contemporary Theatre, 20 (1962), 11-31.
　　　　Leech feels that Pinter and Wesker share with Wordsworth and Coleridge and each other a similar view and approach to the inner and outer life of man.

1306　LE MARCHAND, JACQUES. "Caliban nu." In "La Critique: Le Retour." L'Avant-Scène, 15 April 1967, p. 29.
　　　　Concerns The Homecoming.

1307　LEON, GEORGES. "Des Artistes admirables." In "La Critique: Le Retour." L'Avant-Scène, 15 April 1967, p. 29.
　　　　Concerns The Homecoming.

1308　LEONARD, HUGH. "Television Plays." Plays and Players, 10, No. 9 (June 1963), 41.
　　　　Review of The Lover.

1309　LESSER, S[IMON] O. "Reflections on Pinter's The Birthday Party." Contemporary Literature, 13 (Winter 1972), 34-43.
　　　　Examines affinities between The Birthday Party and Kafka's The Trial.

1310　_____. Tragedy. The Critical Idiom Series, Vol. 1. New York: Harper and Row, 1969. Reprinted: London: Methuen.
　　　　A study of tragedy which includes Pinter's work as a notable example of contemporary tragedy.

Levedova

1311   LEVEDOVA, I. "A New Hero Appears in the Theatre." Inostrannaya
        Literatura, No. 1 (January 1962), pp. 201-08.
              Pinter (and Osborne, Wesker, Behan, Delaney) has
        created a protesting plebeian hero.

1312   LEVIN, BERNARD. "The Last Laugh for Mr. Pinter?" London
        Daily Mail, 19 June 1964, p. 14.
              Review of The Birthday Party.

*1313 LEVITAN, SYLVIA. "Chance to Think." Letter to the Editor.
        New York Times, 17 December 1967, Sec. 2, p. 14.
              Cited in Elliott (See no. 733).

1314   ____. "My Index Finger Itches." London Daily Mail, 20
        September 1963, p. 3.
              Review of The Dwarfs and The Lover.

1315   ____. "Nowhither and Doing Nowhat." London Daily Express,
        22 January 1960, p. 4.
              Review of The Room and The Dumb Waiter.

1316   ____. "One Times Three is a Sum that Pleases Me!" London
        Daily Express, 19 January 1961, p. 8.
              Review of original stage production of A Slight Ache
        highly appreciative of the play's emotional effects and
        the economy of style.

1317   ____. "There's Truth in This Man's Every Twitch." London
        Daily Express, 2 May 1960, p. 4.
              Highly approving review of original production of The
        Caretaker.

1318   ____. "Three-Line Cut Lets Everyone See This Play." London
        Daily Express, 31 May 1960, p. 16.
              Highly approving review of original production of The
        Caretaker.

1319   LEWIS, ALLAN. The Contemporary Theatre. New York: Crown,
        1971.
              Includes A. Lewis's "The English Theatre-Osborne, Pinter,
        Shaffer" (See no. 1320).

1320   ____. "The English Theatre--Osborne, Pinter, Shaffer." In
        Oscar Lewis, Anthropological Essays (See no. 1329), pp.
        315-35. Reprinted In: A. Lewis, The Contemporary Theatre
        (See no. 1319).

1321   LEWIS, JACK. "Accident." London <u>Sunday Citizen</u>, 12 February 1967, p. 16.
     Film review.

1322   _____. "The Little Man's Secret Urge to Kill." London <u>Sunday Citizen</u>, 22 September 1963, p. 22.
     Review of <u>The Dwarfs</u> and <u>The Lover</u>. <u>The Dwarfs</u> is "formless rubbish" which "appears to have nothing to do with anything at all."

1323   _____. "Macabre." London <u>Sunday Citizen</u>, 6 June 1965, p. 25.
     Review of the original production of <u>The Homecoming</u>.

1324   _____. "Occult." London <u>Sunday Citizen</u>, 21 June 1964, p. 20.
     Review of <u>The Birthday Party</u>.

1325   _____. "Shaw Has Plenty of Ideas for 1961." London <u>Reynolds News</u>, 8 October 1961, p. 11.
     Review of <u>A Night Out</u>.

1326   _____. "Theatre and Cinema." London <u>Sunday Citizen</u>, 15 March 1964, p. 24.
     Review of film version of <u>The Caretaker</u>.

1327   _____. "The Value of Virtue." London <u>Sunday Citizen</u>, 24 June 1962, p. 8.
     Review of original stage production of <u>The Collection</u>.

1328   _____. "When Love's Labour's Lost." London <u>Sunday Citizen</u>, 19 July 1964, p. 20.
     Review of <u>The Pumpkin Eater</u>.

1329   LEWIS, OSCAR, editor. <u>Anthropological Essays</u>. New York: Random House, 1970.
     Includes Allan Lewis's "The English Theatre--Osborne, Pinter, Shaffer" (<u>See</u> no. 1320), pp. 315-35.

1330   LEWIS, PETER. "The Caretaker." London <u>Daily Mail</u>, 3 March 1972, p. 19.
     Review.

1331   _____. "An Exciting Menu of Brevity." London <u>Daily Mail</u>, 10 April 1969, p. 12.
     Review of <u>Night</u>.

1332   _____. "Fascinated by Unsatisfactory People." <u>Time and Tide</u>, 21 June 1962, pp. 16-17.
     <u>The Collection</u> is regarded as a typical Pinter play.

Lewis

1333   ____. "A Small Pinter But Deftly Done." London <u>Daily Mail</u>,
       3 October 1961, p. 3.
          Review of <u>A Night Out</u>.

1334   ____. "Straightforward? Well, No, But Highly Entertaining."
       London <u>Daily Mail</u>, 22 July 1960, p. 14.
         Review of British television production of <u>Night School</u>.

1335   ____. "Turn On, Tune In to Pinter's Magic." London <u>Daily
       Mail</u>, 26 April 1968, p. 16.
         Review of radio version of <u>Landscape</u>; praises Pinter's
       "delicate" writing.

1336   LEWIS, ROBERT. "The Quality of Imports." <u>New Leader</u>, 11
       December 1961, p. 31.
         Review of New York production of <u>The Caretaker</u>.

1337   LEWIS, THEOPHILUS. "The Birthday Party." <u>America</u>, 117 (28
       October 1967), 487.
         Review of <u>The Birthday Party</u> (New York).

1338   ____. "The Homecoming." <u>America</u>, 116 (11 March 1967), 353.
         Review of <u>The Homecoming</u> (New York).

1339   ____. "The Teaparty. The Basement." <u>America</u>, 119 (9
       November 1968), 447.
         Review of <u>Tea Party</u> and <u>The Basement</u> (New York).

1340   ____. "Theatre." <u>America</u>, 106 (9 December 1961), 376.
         Plot summary style review of the New York production
       of <u>The Caretaker</u>.

1341   LEYBURN, ELLEN D. "Comedy and Tragedy Transposed." <u>Yale
       Review</u>, 53, No. 4 (Summer 1964), pp. 553-62.
         The traditional distinction between comedy and tragedy
       has broken down with Pinter's plays asking the "ultimate
       questions" of tragedy and using the comedy to arouse a
       "tragic involvement" in the audience (also true of Miller,
       Williams, Osborne, Beckett, Ionesco, and Durrenmatt).

1342   L. G. S. "Comic Horror of <u>The Birthday Party</u>." <u>The Stage</u>,
       22 May 1958, p. 12.
         Review.

1343   LINDSAY, VACHEL. "Thirty Differences Between the Photoplays
       and the Stage." In James Hurt, ed., <u>Focus on Film and
       Theatre</u> (<u>See</u> no. 1092), pp. 18-28.

1344   LIPSETT, RICHARD. Book review of The Caretaker. The Theatre,
       April 1961, p. 49.

1345   LOCKHARDT, FREDA BRUCE. "Television." Time and Tide, 30
       April 1960, p. 483.
           Review of television version of A Night Out.

1346   LOCKWOOD, LYN. "Pinter at his Puzzles Again." London Daily
       Telegraph, 11 August 1961, p. 12.
           Review of British television production of The Dumb
       Waiter.

1347   _____. "Pinter Play's Message is Received." London Daily
       Telegraph, 29 March 1963, p. 16.
           Review of television production of The Lover.

1348   LONEY, GLENN. "Broadway and Off-Broadway Supplement."
       Educational Theatre Journal, 19 (May 1967), 198-204.
           Includes a review of The Homecoming (New York), which
       Loney thinks is seen by critics in their own terms rather
       than its own.

1349   _____. "Broadway in Review." Educational Theatre Journal,
       19 (December 1967), 511-17.
           Review of New York production of The Birthday Party.

1350   _____. "Theatre of the Absurd: Is It Only a Fad?" Theatre
       Arts, 46, No. 11 (November 1962), 20, 22, 24, 66-68.

1351   LOSEY, JOSEPH. Losey on Losey, edited by Tom Milne. Garden
       City, N. Y.: Doubleday, 1968.

1352   _____. "The Monkey on My Back." Films and Filming, 19, No.
       1 (October 1963), 11, 54.
           Discussion of interference by producers, especially in
       regards to The Servant.

1353   _____. "The Servant." Sight and Sound, 33, No. 2 (Spring
       1964), 66-67.
           Discusses The Servant.

1354   LUBBREN, RAINER. "Das ABC des Hausmeisters." Theater und
       Zeit, 9 (1961-62), 245-51.
           Discussion of The Caretaker   In German.

*1355 _____. "Robbe-Grillet, Pinter, und 'Die blaue Villa in Hong-
       kong.'" Die Neue Rundschau, 78, No. 1 (1967), 119-26.
       In German.

Lumley

1356   LUMLEY, FREDERICK. New Trends in Twentieth Century Drama:
        A Survey Since Ibsen and Shaw. New York: Oxford Universi-
        ty Press; and London: Barrie and Rockliff, 1967. Fourth
        edition, 1972.
            Includes "Harold Pinter" (pp. 269-76), a very super-
        ficial discussion of The Birthday Party and The Caretaker
        criticizing Pinter for not creating memorable characters or
        stimulating ideas, though Lumley likes the short plays.
        He finds the characters in Pinter's plays typically British
        and states that The Birthday Party is representative, since
        the dramatist "cannot be said to have advanced since then."

*1357   LÜTHE, RUDOLF. "Umkehrung der drammatischen Ironie: Über-
        legungen zu H. Pinters frühen Dramen." Germanisch-Roman-
        ische Monatsschrift, 24 (December 1974), 472-80.

1358   LYONS, JEFFREY. Review of The Last Tycoon. WCBS Radio.
        November 1976.
            Film review. Quoted in New York Times advertisement.

1359   MC AULEY, GAY. "The Problem of Identity: Theme, Form, and
        Theatrical Method in Les Nègres, Kaspar and Old Times."
        Southern Review, 8, No. 1 (March 1975), 51-65.
            Discusses the differences and similarities between the
        three plays, themes and techniques.

1360   MC CARTEN, JOHN. "Amorphous Doings." New Yorker, 42 (14
        January 1967), 48.
            Review of The Homecoming (New York).

1361   _____. "Down, way down by the Seaside." New Yorker, 43
        (14 October 1967), 151.
            Review of New York production of The Birthday Party.

1362   MC CLAIN, JOHN. "Entrancing, Unusual Drama." New York
        Journal American, 5 October 1961, p. 19.
            Review of New York production of The Caretaker.
        Especially praises the cast.

1363   _____. "Pinter Fuzzy in Dual Bill." New York Journal
        American, 10 December 1964, p. 19.
            Review of New York production of A Slight Ache and
        The Room.

1364   _____. "Two New Plays by Pinter Prove Only Irritating." New
        York Journal American, 27 November 1962, p. 17.
            Review of The Dumb Waiter and The Collection, New York
        production.

1365 _____. "Two Plays: Abstract But Clear." New York Journal
        American, 6 January 1964, p. 13.
                Review of The Lover (New York).

1366 MC CRINDLE, JOSEPH F., ed. Behind the Scenes: Theatre and
        Film Interviews from the Transatlantic Review. New York:
        Holt, Rinehart and Winston, 1971.
                Includes reprint of Pinter and Donner's "Filming 'The
        Caretaker'" (See no. 82).

1367 MAC DONALD, DWIGHT. "Films." Esquire, October 1964, pp.
        62-65ff.
                Film review: Pinter's script of The Servant inter-
        mittently comes to life.

1368 _____. "Films." Esquire, January 1965, p. 116.
                Film review of The Pumpkin Eater which is largely a
        plot synopsis, though Macdonald expresses dislike for
        Pinter's screenplay, finding fault with the repetitious
        and realistic (boring) dialogue.

1369 MC GARRY, MARY ANNE. "The Adaptation Process as Seen through
        Selected Plays and Screenplays by Harold Pinter." Ph.D.
        dissertation, Northwestern University, 1976.
                The first dissertation to deal entirely with Pinter's
        films, this study examines the use of off-stage space on
        the screen, cinematic transitional devices, dialogue
        additions and omissions, and the different circumstances
        under which the plays and the films were produced. Chap-
        ters are devoted to The Birthday Party, The Caretaker, and
        The Homecoming.

1370 McLAUGHLIN, JOHN. "Harold Pinter and PBL." America, 10 Feb-
        ruary 1968, p. 193.
                Discussion of American television presentation of The
        Dwarfs.

1371 MacNEICE, LOUIS. Varieties of Parable. Cambridge, England:
        Cambridge University Press, 1965, pp. 121-23.
                A "whole sheaf of meanings" develops through the
        technique of "apparent straightforwardness" in Pinter.

1372 McVAY, DOUGLAS. "The Pumpkin Eater." Film, No. 41 (1964),
        12-13.
                Film review.

McWhinnie

1373   McWHINNIE, DONALD. "Donald McWhinnie, Interviewed by Robert
Rubens." <u>Transatlantic Review</u>, No. 12 (Spring 1963),
34-38.
      The director stresses the importance of words, using
<u>The Caretaker</u> as an example.

*1374   MAIN, WILLIAM W. "The Meaning of Meaninglessness: A Clue
to Contemporary Art and Literature." <u>Western Humanities
Review</u>, 12 (1958), 241-49.

1375   MAJSTRAK, MANFRED, and HANS ROSSMAN. "Harold Pinter."
<u>Bibliographie der Interpretationen: Englisch</u> (Dortmund,
1972), pp. 117-20.
      Check list. In German.

1376   MALKIN, LAWRENCE. "Pinter's New World." <u>Time</u>, 19 May 1975,
p. 80.
      Review of <u>No Man's Land</u> which sees the "dark inevita-
bility of the future...of death in life" as the drama's
concern. The play becomes "exhilerating theatre" because
it is "very funny."

1377   MALLET, RICHARD. "At the Cinema." <u>Punch</u>, 18 February 1970,
p. 276.
      Film review of <u>The Birthday Party</u>.

1378   _____. "At the Pictures." <u>Punch</u>, 25 March 1964, p. 468.
      Review of the film version of <u>The Caretaker</u>.

1379   _____. "Cinema." <u>Punch</u>, 29 July 1964, p. 169.
      Film review of <u>The Pumpkin Eater</u>.

1380   _____. "Cinema." <u>Punch</u>, 16 November 1966, p. 748.
      Film review of <u>The Quiller Memorandum</u>.

1381   _____. "Cinema." <u>Punch</u>, 16 February 1967, p. 241.
      Film review of <u>Accident</u>.

1382   MALPAS, EDWARD R. H. "A Critical Analysis of the Stage
Plays of Harold Pinter." <u>Dissertation Abstracts Inter-
national</u>, 27: 1955A. Ph.D. dissertation, University of
Wisconsin, 1965.
      Pinter is seen as being unable to evaluate his own
work because he is not aware of his own power of poetry
and his instinct for the theatre.

*1383   MANDER, GERTRUD. "Die jungen englischen Dramatiker." Neue
          deutsche Hefte, 83 (1961), 104-30.
          In German. Cited in Imhof (See no 1098), p. 15.

*1384   _____. "Wie langweilig is das Ordinare?" Theater Heute,
          February 1966, pp. 4-5.
          In German. Cited in Imhof (See no. 1098), p. 15.

1385   MANNES, MARYA. "Just Looking, Thanks." Reporter, 13 Octo-
          ber 1960, pp. 48-51.
          Review of The Caretaker: "Pinter's talent lies as much
          in his silences as in his talk: his timing is masterly,
          his dialogue hypnotic in its repetition either of absurd
          clichés or plain human confusion."

1386   _____. "Movies: Some to see and some to flee." McCalls,
          96 (February 1969), 48, 131.
          A film review of The Birthday Party--which should
          have remained a one-act play, according to Mannes.

1387   _____. "What's Pinter Up To?" New York Times, 5 February
          1967, Sec. 2, p. 1.
          Review of The Homecoming.

1388   MANVELL, ROGER. "The Decade of Harold Pinter." Humanist,
          132 (April 1967), 112-15.

1389   _____. "Pinter Through French Eyes." Humanist, 134 (May
          1969), 142-44.
          An interview with Daniel Salem.

1390   MARCEL, GABRIEL. "Une Odeur de Putréfaction." In "La
          Critique: Le Retour." L'Avant-Scène, 15 April 1967, p. 29.
          Discusses The Homecoming.

1391   MARCUS, FRANK. "A Couple of Half-Pinters." London Sunday
          Telegraph, 6 July 1969, p. 14.
          Review of Landscape and Silence: "Studies in loneli-
          ness: memory plays illustrating man's isolation."

1392   _____. "End of the Beginning." London Sunday Telegraph, 20
          September 1970, p. 14.
          Review of Tea Party and The Basement (London).

1393   _____. "Pinter: The Pause That Refreshes." New York Times,
          12 July 1969, Sec. D, p. 8.

Marker

> The use of language and non-language (especially pauses and silences) to convey meaning in Landscape and Silence is discussed in a review of the two plays.

1394 MARKER, FREDERICK J. "Pinteresque." Modern Drama, 17, No. 4 (December 1974), 361-62.
> Introduction to special all-Pinter issue.

1395 MAROWITZ, CHARLES. "Biography." New York Times, 1 October 1967, Sec. 6, p. 36.

1396 ____. "Butley." New York Times, 8 August 1971, Sec. 2, p. 3.
> Simon Gray's play directed by Pinter.

1397 ____. "Can Pinter Be Beckett?" New York Times, 13 June 1971, Sec. 2, pp. 1, 3.
> Review of Old Times.

1398 ____. Confessions of a Counterfeit Critic: London Theatre Notebook. London: Eyre Methuen, 1973.
> Includes discussion of The Caretaker, pp. 47-49; Landscape and Silence, pp. 163-65; and Old Times, pp. 184-88.

1399 ____. "Heroes and Un-Heroes." Drama, 60 (Spring 1961), 39-43.

1400 ____. "New Wave in a Dead Sea." Quarterly Review, 1 (October 1960), 270-77.
> Comments on Pinter, the most important of the "New Wave" dramatists, to the effect that his poetic drama depends on symbols and "mood concept" to "bypass the cerebrum and plunge directly into the [non-Freudian] psyche." Pinter, Wesker, Osborne, Behan, and Simpson are compared. Pinter emulates contemporary French playwrights (Joan Littlewood's Theatre Workshop has supplied the impetus for such emulation).

1401 ____. "Notes on the Theater of Cruelty." Tulane Drama Review, 11 (Winter 1966), 152-56.
> Artaud's "Theatre of Cruelty" and its effect on young playwrights.

1402 ____. "'Pinterism' Is Maximum Tension Through Minimum Information." New York Times, 1 October 1967, pp. 36-37.
> Generally a character sketch of Pinter, with some relating of facts to plays, especially the early ones.

1403 _____. "Theatre Abroad." Village Voice, 1 September 1960.
       Pinter is questioned about the meaning of The Caretaker.
       He claims it is about "love"--which Marowitz equates with
       "need."

1404 _____, TOM MILNE, and OWEN HALE, eds. The Encore Reader: A
       Chronicle of the New Drama. London: Methuen, 1965.
       Includes Wardle's "Comedy of Menace" (See no. 1924),
       pp. 86-91.

1405 _____ and SIMON TRUSSLER. Theatre at Work: Playwrights in
       the Modern British Theatre. Introduction by Irving Wardle.
       London: Methuen, 1967. Reprinted: New York: Hill and
       Wang, 1968.
       Includes Bensky's "Harold Pinter: An Interview" (See
       no. 427).

1406 MARRIOTT, R. B. "Harold Pinter's First Play is Revived."
       The Stage, 25 June 1964, p. 13.
       Review of The Birthday Party.

1407 _____. "Mortimer, Simpson, and Pinter, All in One Evening."
       The Stage, 26 January 1961, p. 13.
       Includes a review of A Slight Ache.

1408 _____. "No Caretaker Needed in Harold Pinter's Sinister
       House." The Stage, 10 June 1965, p. 13.
       Review of The Homecoming.

1409 _____. "Pinter Double Bill: The Lover and The Dwarfs."
       The Stage, 26 September 1963, p. 22.
       Review.

1410 _____. "Strindberg's Couples, Pinter's Too." The Stage, 21
       June 1962, p. 13.
       Review of The Collection.

1411 MARSHALL, NORMAN. "The Plays of Rodney Ackland." London
       Magazine, April 1965, pp. 62-67.
       Ackland's plays are forerunners of Pinter.

1412 MARTIN, BRUCE. "Accident." Take One, 1, No. 5 (June 1967),
       28.
       Film review.

1413 MARTINEAU, STEPHEN. "Pinter's Old Times: The Memory Game."
       Modern Drama, 16, No. 4 (December 1973), 287-97.
       The contest in the play is not for the wife, but for her
       past.

Maschler

1414　MASCHLER, TOM, ed. New English Dramatists, No. 3. London:
　　　　Penguin, 1961.
　　　　　　Includes a reprint of The Dumb Waiter.

*1415　MAST, GERALD. "Harold Pinter and the Modern Premise." Ph.D.
　　　　dissertation, University of Chicago, 1968.

1416　_____. "Pinter's Homecoming." Drama Survey, 6, No. 3
　　　　(Spring 1968), 266-77.
　　　　　　Consistent personalities of the characters "absolutely
　　　　determine" the action in the play. Pinter transforms the
　　　　natural into the strangely unfamiliar.

1417　MATLAW, MYRON. Modern World Drama. New York: Dutton, 1972,
　　　　pp. 606-07.
　　　　　　Very brief biography.

*1418　MATSUBARA, TADASHI. "A Question about Pinter's Plays."
　　　　Phoenix, No. 29, December 1968.
　　　　　　In Japanese.

1419　MATTHEWS, HONOR. The Primal Curse: The Myth of Cain and
　　　　Abel in the Theatre. London: Chatto and Windus, 1967.
　　　　Reprinted: New York: Schocken Books, 1967.
　　　　　　See pp. 22-23, 198-201, (481-90 in the Schocken
　　　　edition) for a discussion of The Collection and The Dumb
　　　　Waiter.

1420　MAYERSBERG, PAUL. "Harold Pinter's 'The Collection.'"
　　　　Listener, 5 July 1962, p. 26.
　　　　　　Review of original stage production of The Collection,
　　　　comparing Pinter with Ionesco to show that he is "not a
　　　　dramatist of the Absurd."

1421　MELCHINGER, SIEGFRIED. The Concise Encyclopedia of Modern
　　　　Drama. Translated by George Wellwarth. Edited by Henry
　　　　Popkin. New York: Horizon, 1964.
　　　　　　Contains a short biography.

1422　MELLOAN, GEORGE. "Pinter's Abstract Dramatic Art." Wall
　　　　Street Journal, 18 November 1971, p. 22.
　　　　　　A review of Old Times which sees the play as a poetic
　　　　abstract, meaning that the drama appeals to our emotions,
　　　　and has no message!

1423　MENNEMEIER, FRANZ M. Das moderne Drama des Auslandes.
　　　　Dusseldorf: Franz Norbert Bagel, 1961.

1424   MESSENGER, ANN P. "Blindness and the Problem of Identity in
        Pinter's Plays." <u>Die Neueren Sprachen</u>, 8 (August 1972),
        481-90.
            Blindness is equated with spiritual death in Pinter's
        plays.

1425   MIKHAIL, E. H. <u>Contemporary British Drama: 1950-1976</u>.
        Totowa, New Jersey: Rowman and Littlefield, 1976.
            An annotated bibliography of British drama (160 pages).
        Forward by William A. Armstrong.

1426   MILBERG, RUTH. "1 + 1 = 1: Dialogue and Character Splitting
        in Harold Pinter." <u>Die Neueren Sprachen</u>, 73 (NS 23),
        No. 3 (June 1974), 225-33.

1427   MILLER, MARY JANE. "Pinter as a Radio Dramatist." <u>Modern
        Drama</u>, 17, No. 4 (December 1974), 403-12.
            Discusses <u>A Slight Ache</u>, <u>A Night Out</u>, and <u>The Dwarfs</u>.
        Alterations of the radio versions for the stage are seen
        mainly as an attempt to simplify the intellectual content.

1428   MILNE, TOM. "Accident." <u>Sight and Sound</u>, 36, No. 2 (Spring
        1967), 56-59. Reprinted in: Boyum and Scott, <u>Film as
        Film: Critical Responses to Film Art</u> (<u>See</u> no. 473), pp.
        38-44.
            A review and explication of the film <u>Accident</u>.

1429   _____. "Double Pinter." <u>Encore</u>, 7, No. 2 (1960), 38-40.
            Review of <u>The Room</u> and <u>The Dumb Waiter</u>.

1430   _____. "The Hidden Face of Violence." <u>Encore</u>, 7, No. 1
        (1960), 14-20. Reprinted in: J. R. Brown, <u>Modern British
        Dramatists</u> (<u>See</u> no. 501), pp. 38-46.
            <u>The Birthday Party</u> is discussed, along with Whiting's
        <u>Saint's Day</u> and Arden's <u>Serjeant Musgrave's Dance</u> in an
        effort to explain their commercial failure.

*1431   MINETA, E[ISAKU]. "On H. Pinter." <u>Waseda Review</u>, No. 4,
        May 1966.
            In Japanese. Cited by Tetsuo Kishi in correspondence.

*1432   _____. "On H. Pinter." <u>Jissen Eibungaku</u>, No. 5, December
        1973.
            In Japanese. Cited by Tetsuo Kishi in correspondence.

*1433   _____. "An Introduction to Pinter." <u>Bulletin of Jissen
        Women's College</u>, No. 5.
            In Japanese. Cited by Tetsuo Kishi in correspondence.

1434 MINOGUE, VALERIE. "Taking Care of The Caretaker." Twentieth
Century, No. 168 (September 1960), 243-48. Reprinted
in: Ganz, Pinter: A Collection of Critical Essays (See
no. 843), pp. 72-77.
The Caretaker is a dramatic expression of Pinter's
concepts about the evasion of communication. It concerns
the fight of three men against nonentity.

1435 MISHKIN, LEO. "Birthday Party." New York Morning Telegraph,
10 December 1968, p. 3.
Review of the film version of The Birthday Party which
is called "just as cryptic [and] puzzling" as the stage
play, and close-ups create "more terror."

1436 _____. "'The Guest' Weird, Fascinating Film." New York
Morning Telegraph, 21 January 1964, p. 2.
Review of the film version of The Caretaker.

1437 _____. "One-Act Pinter Plays Purely 'Experimental.'" New
York Telegraph, 4 April 1970, p. 3.
Review of Landscape and Silence (New York).

1438 MITCHELL, ADRIAN. "Pinter's Quiet Scream." London Sun, 26
March 1965, p. 16.
Review of television production of Tea Party.

1439 M. M. "A Collection of Characters." London Daily Worker, 29
April 1960, p. 2.
Review of original production of The Caretaker which
depends upon superb acting for its success.

1440 _____. "Theatre Three." London Daily Worker, 20 January
1961, p. 3.
Review of original stage production of A Slight Ache.

1441 MÖLLER, JOACHIM. "Vergangenheit und Gegenwart im dramatischen
Werk Harold Pinters" (Past and Present in the Dramatic
Works of Harold Pinter). Masters thesis, Justus Liebig-
Universität, Giessen (West Germany), 1972.

*1442 MOORE, MAVOR. "The Decline of Words in Drama." Canadian
Literature, No. 46 (1970), 11-18.

1443 MORGAN, DEREK. "These Our Actors...." Reporter, 23 February
1967, pp. 46-48.
Review of The Homecoming (New York) which is seen
abstractly as a bad dream Teddy is having "back there 'on
the old campus.'"

1444   MORGAN, RICKI. "What Max and Teddy Come Home to in The Homecoming." Educational Theatre Journal, 25 (1973), 490-99.
In a savage world the characters' protective illusions
are stripped from them.

1445   MORGENSTERN, JOSEPH. "Breaking the Bond." Time, 88 (23
December 1966), 75-76.
Film review of The Quiller Memorandum which praises
Pinter's script.

1446   _____. "Stalking Stanley." Newsweek, 23 December 1968, pp.
89-90.
Review of the film version of The Birthday Party.

1447   MORLEY, SHERIDAN. Theatre 71. London: Hutchinson, 1971, pp.
208-33.
Includes Billington's "Our Theatre in the Sixties"
(See no. 444).

1448   MORRIS, IVAN. "The Room and A Slight Ache, 'bitter, offbeat
humour.'" Vogue, 145 (1 February 1965), 98.
Review of New York production of A Slight Ache and The
Room.

1449   MORRIS, KELLY. "The Homecoming." Tulane Drama Review, 11,
No. 2 (Winter 1966), 185-91.
The Homecoming is seen as a sort of comedy of manners
in the tradition of Ibsen and Strindberg combined with
the aggressive nature of the family and a confusion of
sexual roles.

1450   MORRISON, KRISTIN. "Pinter and the New Irony." Quarterly
Journal of Speech, 55, No. 55 (December 1969), 388-93.
The Birthday Party, The Room, A Slight Ache, The Caretaker, and The Dumb Waiter all contain characters who become aware of death before the audience does, a reversal
of traditional dramatic irony.

1451   MORTIMER, JOHN. "Now This is What I call Great Acting."
London Evening Standard, 31 May 1960, p. 12.
Review of The Caretaker.

1452   MORTLOCK, C. B. "The Homecoming." London City Press, 25
June 1965, p. 11.
Disapproving review of the original production of The
Homecoming: "I hope I may never see a nastier play."

Mortlock

1453 _____. "She's a Poppet." London City Press, 18 March 1960,
    p. 8.
    Review of New York production of The Dumb Waiter and
    The Room.

1454 _____. "Sir Laurence With No Heroics." London City Press,
    6 May 1960, p. 13.
    Review of original production of The Caretaker, compared
    to Waiting for Godot.

1455 _____. "Two Casualties." London City Press, 3 June 1960,
    p. 10.
    Review of original production of The Caretaker.

1456 MOSLEY, LEONARD. "Three So Splendid." London Daily Express,
    12 March 1964, p. 4.
    Review of film version of The Caretaker.

1457 MUIR, KENNETH. "Verse and Prose." In Contemporary Theatre,
    edited by John Russell Brown and Bernard Harris (See no.
    503), pp. 97-115.
    Pinter creates "unrealistic drama" out of a prose
    poetry producing a Kafkaesque effect.

1458 MULLER, ROBERT. "An Evening like this Revives One's Faith."
    London Daily Mail, 19 June 1962, p. 3.
    Review of original stage production of The Collection
    in which he claims that Pinter creates a compelling world,
    though Pinter must be allowed to grow.

1459 _____. "Hate Yourself Though You May, You'll Enjoy These
    Plays." London Daily Mail, 19 January 1961, p. 3.
    Review of original stage production of A Slight Ache:
    a "brilliantly sinister tour de force" (reason for con-
    clusion not explained).

1460 _____. "The Small World of Harold Pinter." London Daily
    Mail, 30 April 1960, p. 3.
    Review of The Caretaker.

*1461 MÜNDER, PETER. Harold Pinter und die Problematik des Absurden
    Theaters. Bern: Lang, 1976.
    Cited in Modern Drama, 20, No. 2 (June 1977), 182.

1462 MURPHY, MARESE. "Pinter and Visconti." Drama, No. 109
    (Summer 1973), p. 45.

1463   MURPHY, ROBERT P. "Non-Verbal Communication and the Over-
        looked Action in Pinter's The Caretaker." Quarterly Jour-
        nal of Speech, No. 58 (February 1972), 41-47.
            The actions of the characters in The Caretaker are as
        important as the dialogue in determining the meaning of
        the play: attention to non-verbal communication shows
        that Mick and Aston consciously set out to destroy Davies'
        psyche.

1464   _____. "Sean O'Casey and The Bald Primaqueera." James Joyce
        Quarterly, 8, No. 1 (Fall 1970), 96-110.
            An answer to O'Casey's article, "The Bald Primaqueera,"
        which states that O'Casey does not understand Pinter (See
        no. 1499).

1465   M. W. W. "The Birthday Party." Manchester Guardian, 21 May
        1958, p. 5.
            Review.

1466   MYSON, MIKE. "Horror 'comic.'" London Daily Worker, 26 May
        1958, p. 2.
            The Birthday Party is a power struggle between the weak
        and the strong, but is still "symbolism in the lunatic
        horror style."

1467   NADEL, NORMAN. "'The Caretaker' at Lyceum." New York World
        Telegram and Sun, 5 October 1961, p. 16. Reprinted in:
        New York Theatre Critics' Reviews, 9 October 1961, p. 250.
            Review of New York production of The Caretaker.

1468   _____. "'Homecoming' Unfathomable." New York World Journal
        Tribune, 6 January 1967, p. 14.
            Review of The Homecoming (New York).

1469   _____. "Pinter is Peerless as Ruler of Enigma." New York
        World Telegram and Sun, 10 December 1964, p. 13.
            Review of New York production of A Slight Ache and The
        Room.

1470   _____. "Playgoing is an Adventure with Barr, Wilder and Albee."
        New York World Telegram and Sun, 6 January 1964, p. 14.
            Review of The Lover included.

1471   _____. "Two Pinter Plays at Cherry Lane." New York World
        Telegram and Sun, 27 November 1962, p. 20.
            Review of The Dumb Waiter and The Collection, New York
        production.

Naismith

*1472   NAISMITH, W. "Dramatic Structure in the Plays of Harold
        Pinter." Masters thesis, Cardiff: University of Wales,
        1967-68.
            Cited in Index to Theses (London: Aslib).

1473   NATHAN, DAVID. "Oh, Mr. Pinter, What a Way to Write a Play."
        London Daily Herald, 9 March 1960, p. 3.
            Review of New York production of The Dumb Waiter and
        The Room, both of which confuse the critic completely.

1474   _____. "Pinter Looks at Loving." London Daily Herald, 19
        June 1962, p. 7.
            A review of original stage production of The Collection.

1475   _____. "Pinter on the Road to Nowhere." London Sun, 3 July
        1969, p. 7.
            Review of Landscape and Silence.

1476   _____. "Pinter's Poetic but Puzzling Private World." London
        Daily Herald, 19 September 1963, p. 3.
            Review of The Dwarfs and The Lover.

1477   _____. "Same Again from Puzzling Mr. Pinter." London Sun,
        4 June 1965, p. 10.
            Negative review of the original production of The
        Homecoming: "To what Pinteresque purpose?"

1478   _____. "This is Life Over the Hill." London Daily Herald,
        19 January 1961, p. 3.
            Review of A Slight Ache.

*1479   NELSON, BENJAMIN. "Avant-Garde Dramatists from Ibsen to
        Ionesco." Psychoanalytic Review, 55 (1968), 505-12.
            Cited in Elliott (See no. 733), p. 551.

1480   NELSON, GERALD. "Harold Pinter Goes to the Movies." Chicago
        Review, 19, No. 1 (Summer 1966), 33-43.
            Pinter's work in film (e.g., The Caretaker/The Guest)
        shows both great freedom and control of movement in
        creating "real human personalities," moving away from
        Beckett and Ionesco.

1481   NELSON, HUGH. "The Homecoming: Kith and Kin." In Modern
        British Dramatists, edited by J. R. Brown (See no. 501),
        pp. 145-63.
            Biblical and Shakespearean references are explored to
        back Nelson's contention that The Homecoming is basically
        a traditional play which demonstrates that function is more
        important than blood ties in family relationships.

1482 NELSON, R. J. Book review of <u>Old Times</u>. <u>Prairie Schooner</u>, Spring 1972, p. 81. (<u>See</u> no. 22).

1483 NICOLL, ALLARDYCE. <u>English Drama: A Modern Viewpoint</u>. London: Harrap, 1968. Reprinted: New York: Barnes and Noble, 1968, pp. 140-44.
      Mentions Pinter.

1484 NIGHTINGALE, BENEDICT. "Even Pinter Is Being Pinteresque." <u>New York Times</u>, 11 May 1975, Sec. D, p. 5.
      Review of <u>No Man's Land</u>, seen as being repetitious.

1485 _____. "<u>The Homecoming</u>." Manchester <u>Guardian</u>, 27 March 1965, p. 6.
      Review of <u>The Homecoming</u>.

1486 _____. "Human Zoo." <u>Encounter</u>, 48 (February 1977), 71-74.
      Discussing the simplicity and conflict in Pinter's dramas, Nightingale examines <u>The Homecoming</u> briefly. Included are Pinter's comment on Peter Terson, and Nightingale's opinion of the criticism of Quigley (<u>See</u> no. 1595), Hinchcliffe (<u>See</u> no. 1021), and Bryden (<u>See</u> no. 527).

1487 _____. "Inaction Replay." <u>New Statesman</u>, 2 May 1975, p. 601.
      Review of <u>No Man's Land</u> as unsuccessful because Pinter's preoccupations have led him to repetition and "resurrecting mannerisms." The part of Spooner is more memorable than the play itself, according to Nightingale.

1488 _____. "Love Plays." <u>New Statesman</u>, 18 April 1969, pp. 561-62.
      Review of <u>Night</u>.

1489 _____. "Outboxed." <u>New Statesman</u>, 80 (25 September 1970), 394-95.
      Review of <u>Tea Party</u> and <u>The Basement</u> (London).

*1490 _____. "Taking Bloody Liberty." <u>New Statesman</u>, 78 (18 July 1969), 83.

1491 _____. "Three's a Crowd." <u>New Statesman</u>, 11 June 1971, p. 817.
      Review of <u>Old Times</u>.

Nightingale

1492   _____. "To the Mouth of the Cave." New Statesman, 78 (11
        July 1969), 57.
            Review of Landscape and Silence. Plays lack depth
        and have nothing new to say.

1493   NOLLAU, MICHAEL. "Texterfahrung als Selbsterfahrung: die
        Lektüre von Harold Pinters Fernsehspiel The Basement and
        seines Vortrages 'Writing for the Theatre' in Klasse 12,"
        Die Neueren Sprachen, 73, (NS 23), No. 6 (December 1974),
        495-511.
            In German.

1494   NORMAN, BARRY. "Getting Nowhere in Great Style." London
        Daily Mail, 4 July 1969, p. 14.
            Review of Landscape and Silence. Not recognizing that
        Pinter's style has changed, the critic claims that he is
        running in place.

*1495   NÜNNING, JOSEFA, ed. Das englische Drama. Darmstadt:
        Wissenschaftliche Buchgesellschaft, 1973.
            Includes Paul Goetsch's "Das englishe Drama seit Shaw"
        (See no 899). Cited in Imhof (See no. 1098).

1496   NYSZKIEWICZ, HEINZ. "The Dumb Waiter/The Caretaker."
        Zeitgenossische englische Dichtung, Bd. 3 (Frankfurt,
        1968), 210-33.
            In German.

1497   OAKES, PHILIP. "Masterly Who's Whose." London Sunday Tele-
        graph, 17 November 1963.
            Film review of The Servant.

1498   _____. "Pinter's Worthy Pioneer." London Sunday Telegraph,
        15 March 1964, p. 14.
            Review of the film version of The Caretaker.

1499   O'CASEY, SEAN. "The Bald Primaqueera." In Ayling, Blasts
        and Benedictions (See no. 380), pp. 71-72.
            Discusses The Birthday Party (See also Robert P. Murphy,
        "Sean O'Casey and 'The Bald Primaqueera,'" no. 1464).

1500   O'CONNOR, JOHN J. "The Theater. Songs and Sciences." Wall
        Street Journal, 4 April 1970, p. 18. Reprinted in: New
        York Theatre Critics' Reviews, 1 June 1970, p. 246.
            Review of Landscape and Silence (New York).

1501   O'CONNOR, PATRICK. "Theatre." Furrow, 16 (August 1965),
        495-97.
            Review of the original production of The Homecoming.

*1502   ODASHIMA, YŪSHI. "Contemporary English Theatre." Studies
        in English Literature, 42, No. 1 (September 1965).
            In Japanese. Cited by Tetsuo Kishi in personal
        correspondence.

*1503   _____. "Pinter Notes." Eigo Seinen, 115 (July 1969), 416-96.
            In Japanese. Cited by Tetsuo Kishi in personal
        correspondence.

1504   O'GORMAN, NED. "Entertainment." Jubilee, 40 (December 1963),
        p. 40.
            Misguided review of The Dumb Waiter and The Collection,
        New York production: "the dry rot of a stricken language,
        banal violence and existential prattle."

*1505   OKOCHI, YASUYUKI. "Dramatic Style of Harold Pinter."
        Humanities Bulletin of Nūgata University, No. 45 (n. d.).
            In Japanese. Cited by Tetsuo Kishi in personal
        correspondence.

*1506   _____. "Listen and Arrange: Double Structure of
        Pinter's Plays." Eigo Seinen, November 1971.
            In Japanese. Cited by Tetsuo Kishi in personal
        correspondence.

1507   OLIVER, EDITH. "The Bum in the Attic." New Yorker, 14
        October 1961, p. 162.
            Discusses The Caretaker as a non-allegorical play.

1508   _____. "Comedies of Terror." New Yorker, 38 (8 December
        1962), 148-50.
            Review of The Dumb Waiter and The Collection, New York
        production.

1509   _____. "Doing Pinter Proud." New Yorker, 39 (11 January
        1963), 69-70.
            Review of The Lover (New York).

1510   _____. "Good Shepard." New Yorker, 46 (11 April 1970),
        82-84.
            Review of Landscape and Silence (New York).

Oliver

1511 _____. "Hooray!" New Yorker, 40 (19 December 1964), 66-71.
Review of New York production of A Slight Ache and The
Room.

1512 _____. "The Theatre: Off Broadway." New Yorker, 46 (13
February 1971), 78.
A review of the revival of The Birthday Party which is
highly approving.

1513 _____. "The Theatre: Off Broadway." New Yorker, 47 (29
May 1971), 55.
Review of The Homecoming. A strong script survives a
weak production at New York's Bijou Theatre.

1514 _____. "Threats and Games." New Yorker, 44 (26 October
1968), 140-41.
Review of Tea Party and The Basement (New York). Not
Pinter's best, but still better than most other contemporary plays.

1515 OLIVER, WILLIAM I. "Between Absurdity and the Playwright."
In Modern Drama: Essays in Criticism, edited by T. M.
Bogart and W. I. Oliver (See no. 456), pp. 3-19.

1516 OPENHEIMER, GEORGE. "A Most Arcane Work." Newsday, 17
November 1971.
Review of Old Times.

1517 _____. "Pinter's 'Homecoming' Continues Its Magic."
Standard Star (New Rochelle, N. Y.), 19 May 1971, p. 23.
Review.

1518 ORLEY, RAY. "Pinter and the Menace." Drama Critique, 2
(1968), 124-48.
"Dramatically, as well as politically, terror and
menace are most essential elements of Harold Pinter's
vision of life: the horror of existence presented in
truly threatening and frightening terms."

1519 OSHEROW, ANITA R. "Mother and Whore: The Role of Woman in
The Homecoming." Modern Drama, 17, No. 4 (December 1974),
423-32.
Ruth's role as victim and victimizer (and ultimately
the triumpher) and allusions to Jessie are used to examine
the ambiguous view of women given in The Homecoming.

1520   OULAHAN, RICHARD. "Happiness Is Another Baby." Life, 57 (13
             November 1964), 15.
                 Film review of The Pumpkin Eater which focuses on Anne
             Bancroft's acting.

1521   PACEY, ANN. "Marriage--Stripped to its Tortured Heart."
             London Daily Herald, 15 July 1964, p. 169.
                 Film review of The Pumpkin Eater.

1522   _____. "Pinter's Party Piece." London Daily Herald, 19 June
             1964, p. 5.
                 Review of The Birthday Party.

1523   _____. "Three Men in a House of Dreams." London Daily Herald,
             13 March 1964, p. 6.
                 Review of the film version of The Caretaker saying that
             it fails to create the claustrophobic effect of the stage
             play.

1524   PACKARD, WILLIAM. "An Interview with Harold Pinter." First
             Stage, 6, No. 2 (Summer 1967), 82.
                 Pinter says that he has not read Freud and that the
             plays are "about what the titles say."

1525   PAGET, JEAN. "Une Sorte de Tendresse Étrange." In "La
             Critique: Le Retour." L'Avant-Scène, 15 April 1967, p. 29.
                 Concerns The Homecoming.

1526   PALATSKY, GENE. "Cherry Lane Pair Incisive." Newark Evening
             News, 6 January 1964, p. 16.
                 Review of The Lover (New York).

1527   _____. "Dramatic Revival." Newark Evening News, 31 January
             1964, p. 14.
                 Review of the film version of The Caretaker (The Guest).

1528   PÁLFY, ISTVÁN. "Modern English Drama Through Hungarian Eyes."
             Hungarian Studies in English, 5 (1971), 137-49.

1529   PALLAVINCINI, ROBERTO. "Aspetti della drammaturgia contempo-
             ranea." Aut, Aut, No. 81 (May 1964), pp. 68-73.
                 Failure to fulfill the social function of drama in
             terms of audience involvement. In Italian.

1530   PALMER, DAVID S. "A Harold Pinter Checklist." Twentieth
             Century Literature, 16, No. 4 (October 1970), 287-96.
                 Some errors in citations.

1531 PANTER-DOWNES, MOLLIE. "Letter from London." New Yorker, 36 (9 July 1960), 57-61.
 Review of original production of The Caretaker.

1532 _____. "Letter from London." New Yorker, 39 (30 November 1963), 202-09.
 Includes a review of The Servant, a "brilliantly original and haunting film."

1533 _____. "Letter from London." New Yorker, 41 (31 July 1965), 59-66.
 Review of original production of The Homecoming.

1534 _____. "Letter from London." New Yorker, 47 (3 July 1971), 64-65.
 Review of Old Times included.

1535 _____. "Letter from London." New Yorker, 12 May 1975, pp. 115-18.
 Brief review of No Man's Land included--"a pastiche of Pinter...a great London theatre occasion."

1536 PARKER, R. B. "Force and Society: the Range of Kingsley Amis." Wisconsin Studies in Contemporary Literature, 11, No. 3 (Fall 1961), 27-38.
 Amis is similar to Pinter in his combining of reality and fantasy.

1537 _____. "The Theory and Theatre of the Absurd." Queens Quarterly, 73 (Autumn 1966), 421-41.
 Pinter (Beckett, Ionesco, and Genet) never "negates negation" to conform to the theory of the Absurd advanced by Camus in The Myth of Sisyphus.

1538 PARR, RONALD. "Nottingham." Plays and Players, 9, No. 9 (June 1962), 43 f.
 Review of The Birthday Party.

*1539 PEACOCK, D. K. "The Examination of the Nature of Violence in the Plays of Four Modern Dramatists: John Whiting, Harold Pinter, John Arden, David Rudkin." Ph.D. dissertation, Exeter, 1971-72.
 Cited in Index to Theses (London: Aslib).

1540 PEASE, NICHOLAS B. "Role, Ritual and Game in the Plays of Harold Pinter." Dissertation Abstracts International, 32: 3324A. Ph.D. dissertation, Buffalo: State University of New York, 1971.

162

A critical interpretation based on "modern psychological and sociological theory," the primary sources for which are Ewing Goffman (Interaction Ritual) and Eric Berne (Games People Play). The final chapter compares Pinter to Pirandello, Strindberg, Genet, and Beckett.

1541   PEEL, MARIE. "Violence in Literature." Books and Bookmen, 17, No. 5 (February 1972), 20–24.
In a discussion of "serious" writers' approaches to violence (people are seen more as victims than as agents of violence), Pinter, Hemingway, James Baldwin, Norman Mailer, Edward Bond, David Storey, and John Osborne are mentioned.

1542   PELSWICK, ROSE. "British Entry Has Vague Story Line." New York Journal American, 21 January 1964, p. 11.
Review of the film version of The Caretaker.

*1543   PERKYNS, R. J. H. "The Impact of the Expressionist Movement on British and American Drama and Theatre Practices." Ph.D. dissertation, London: Kings College, 1967–1968. Cited in Index to Theses (London: Aslib).

1543a   PERRY, GEORGE. The Great British Picture Show: From the 90's to the 70's. New York: Hill and Wang, 1974.
Mentions Pinter's screenwriting in passing.

1544   PESTA, JOHN. "Pinter's Usurpers." Drama Survey, 6, No. 1 (Spring 1967), 54–65. Reprinted in: Ganz, Pinter: A Collection of Critical Essays (See no. 843), pp. 123–35.
In Pinter's dramas, from The Room through The Homecoming, man's existential security is threatened by a "usurper."

1545   PETRULIAN, CATRINEL. "Între realism și absurd—Harold Pinter." Revista de Istorie si Theorie Literara, 21 (1972), pp. 533–39.
Cited in 1972 MLA International Bibliography, p. 122.

*1546   PHILLIPS, GENE. "The Critical Camera of Joseph Losey." Cinema, 4, No. 1 (Spring 1968), 23.

1547   PHILLIPS, PEARSON. "Another Look at Classic Pinter." London Daily Mail, 18 September 1970, p. 10.
Review of Tea Party and The Basement.

Phillips

1548　PHILLIPS, PHILIP. "It's a Pity I Couldn't Laugh Last Night."
　　　London Daily Herald, 22 July 1960, p. 3.
　　　　　Review of television version of Night School.

1549　P. H. S. "Americans Film Pinter." The Times (London), 9
　　　January 1968, p. 6.
　　　　　Review of The Birthday Party film.

1550　_____. "Evacuees Look Back." The Times (London), 4 November
　　　1967, p. 8.

1551　_____. "Losey-Pinter's The Go-Between." The Times (London),
　　　2 December 1968, p. 10.
　　　　　Discusses the filming of The Go-Between.

1552　_____. "The Making of a Book." The Times (London), 22 July
　　　1968, p. 6.
　　　　　Concerned with The Homecoming.

1553　_____. "Pinter--a New Play." The Times (London), 10 January
　　　1968, p. 8.
　　　　　Review of radio production of Landscape.

1554　_____. "Pinter Axed." The Times (London), 9 October 1968,
　　　p. 10.
　　　　　Concerned with The Homecoming.

1555　_____. "Shorter Pinter." The Times (London), 11 April 1970,
　　　p. 10.
　　　　　Review of Landscape and Silence.

1556　_____. "Thames Scrap Play on Legal Advice." The Times
　　　(London), 16 July 1971, p. 12.
　　　　　Concerned with The Homecoming.

1557　_____. "The Times Diary." The Times (London), 7 October
　　　1969, p. 8.

1558　PIERCE, ROGER N. "Three Plays Analyses." Dissertations
　　　Abstracts International, 30: 2660A. Ph.D. dissertation,
　　　University of Iowa, 1969.
　　　　　Includes a hierarchical analysis of The Homecoming.

1559　PILER, JACK. "Pinter's Play Makes a Real 'Night Out.'"
　　　London Daily Herald, 3 October 1961, p. 9.
　　　　　Review of A Night Out.

1560   POPKIN, HENRY. "The Lover and Play, 'Curiosities.'" Vogue,
         143 (15 February 1964), 22.
            Review of The Lover (New York).

1561   _____, ed. Modern British Drama (originally The New British
         Drama). New York: Grove, 1964.
            Includes a reprint of Pinter's "Writing for the Theatre"
         (See no 54).

1562   PORTER, PETER. "Foreplay." New Statesman, 7 August 1970,
         pp. 159-60.
            Review of Landscape and Silence.

1563   PORTERFIELD, CHRISTOPHER. "Memories as Weapons." Time, 97
         (14 June 1971), 49.
            Review of Old Times.

1564   POSTLEWAIT, THOMAS ELWOOD. "The Design of the Past: Uses of
         Memory in the Drama of Henrik Ibsen, Samuel Beckett and
         Harold Pinter." Dissertation Abstracts International, 37:
         3605A, Ph.D. dissertation, University of Minnesota, 1976.
            In their battles for dominance, Pinter's characters
         control or remake the past.

1565   POTTER, DENNIS. "Pinter Play a Sizzling Triumph." London
         Daily Herald, 29 March 1963, p. 7.
            Review of television production of The Lover.

1566   POWELL, DILYS. "Solitaries in an Attic." The Sunday Times
         (London), 15 March 1964, p. 21.
            Review of the film version of The Caretaker.

1567   _____. "View from a Death." The Sunday Times (London), 12
         February 1967, p. 49.
            Film review of Accident.

1568   POWLICK, LEONARD. "A Phenomenological Approach to Harold
         Pinter's A Slight Ache." Quarterly Journal of Speech, 60
         (1974), 25-32.

1569   _____. "The Terror of Temporality: The Phenomenology of
         Change in Six Early Plays of Harold Pinter." Dissertation
         Abstracts International, 35: 1668A. Ph.D. dissertation,
         University of Pittsburgh, 1974.
            Powlick examines time in Pinter's plays, especially in
         relation to characters undergoing changes in their identi-
         ties.

Prentice

1570   PRENTICE, PENELOPE A. "An Analysis of Dominance and Sub-
          servience as Technique and Theme in the Plays of Harold
          Pinter." Dissertation Abstracts International, 32:
          7000A. Ph.D. dissertation, Loyola University (Chicago),
          1972.
              Pinter poses questions about the nature of dominance and
          subservience in modern life, but no easy affirmative
          answers are given in his works.

1571   _____, ed. Pinter on Pinter. An edition of Pinter's essays,
          interviews, and profiles in preparation for Seabury Books
          (Viking Press), New York.

1572   PRICE, JAMES. "Words and Pictures." London Magazine, Octo-
          ber 1964, pp. 66-70.
              Film review of The Pumpkin Eater.

1573   PRICKETT, STEPHEN. "Three Modern English Plays." Philo-
          logica Pragensia, 10 (1967), 12-21.
              Discusses major influences on the British theatre from
          abroad (Brecht and Beckett), with The Caretaker used as
          an example of those plays moving away from naturalistic
          speech and action patterns.

1574   PRIDEAUX, TOM. "The Adventurous Play--Stranger to Broadway."
          Life, 3 March 1967, p. 6. Reprinted in: The Discovery
          of Drama, edited by Thomas E. Sanders (See no. 1673), pp.
          624-27.
              Review of The Homecoming (New York).

1575   PRITCHETT, OLIVER. "'Definitive Pinter' is Film's Aim."
          Washington Post, 2 June 1968, Sec. F, p. 1.
              Pre-release comments on the film version of The Birth-
          day Party.

1576   _____. "Fried-Up Pinter." Manchester Guardian, 27 April
          1968, p. 7.
              Review of film version of The Birthday Party.

1577   PROBST, LEONARD. "The Homecoming." For NBC-4 television,
          18 May 1971. In New York Theatre Critics' Reviews, 14
          June 1971, p. 263.
              Review.

1578   _____. "Landscape and Silence." For NBC-4 television, 2
          April 1970. In New York Theatre Critics' Reviews, 1 June
          1970, p. 248.
              Review.

1579 _____. "'Tea Party' and 'The Basement.'" For NBC-4 television, 15 October 1968. In New York Theatre Critics' Reviews, 30 December 1968, p. 141.
Review.

1580 PRYCE-JONES, ALAN. "At the Theatre. O'Neill's Last Phase."
London Observer, 24 January 1960, p. 21.
Review of The Dumb Waiter and The Room: "studies in
treachery...almost too conveniently polished off with a
sudden act of violence." Also praises emotional effects.

1581 _____. "Is a National Theatre Necessary." London Magazine,
7, No. 7 (July 1960), 25-30.
Discusses the difficulty of understanding the new wave
of playwrights in the English theatre, including Pinter
(The Birthday Party).

1582 _____. "Mathematics of the Heart." London Observer, 13
March 1960, p. 23.
Review of The Room and The Dumb Waiter.

1583 _____. "Openings/New York." Theatre Arts, 47 (January
1963), 10-11.
Review of The Dumb Waiter and The Collection, New York
production.

1584 _____. "The Party's Over." Spectator, 26 June 1964, p. 854.
Review of The Birthday Party.

1585 _____. "Through the Looking-Glass." London Observer, 1 May
1960, p. 23.
Review of The Caretaker which sees "individuality" as
the play's theme.

1586 PUGH, MARSHALL. "Trying to Pin Down Pinter." London Daily
Mail, 7 March 1964.
An interview with Pinter.

1587 PURSER, PHILIP. "How to Take Part." London Sunday Telegraph,
26 February 1967, p. 11.
Review of the television version of The Basement which
praises Pinter's skill in the medium of television, but
feels that there is nothing in the play "to occupy the
mind."

1588 _____. "Mr. Bell's Fare Sums up a Revolution." London News
Chronicle, 25 April 1960, p. 3.

Purser

        Review of British television production of <u>The Birthday Party</u> which sees the play as a failure because of the audience's lack of empathy for Stanley.

1589   ____. "Pinter's Boxes." London <u>Sunday Telegraph</u>, 14 May 1961, p. 10.
        Review of television production of <u>The Collection</u>.

1590   ____. "Sense of Occasion." London <u>Sunday Telegraph</u>, 28 March 1965, p. 15.
        Review of television production of <u>Tea Party</u>.

1591   ____. "Winning a Fixed Race." London <u>Sunday Telegraph</u>, 31 March 1963, p. 13.
        Review of television production of <u>The Lover</u> which is by Pinter's standards "an easy, even lightweight [and "predictable"] piece."

1592   P. W. B. "Disappointing Pinter." <u>The Stage</u>, 10 July 1969, p. 13.
        Review of <u>Landscape</u> and <u>Silence</u>.

1593   QUIGLEY, AUSTIN E[dmund]. "<u>The Dwarfs</u>: A Study in Linguistic Dwarfism." <u>Modern Drama</u>, 17, No. 4 (December 1974), 413–22.
        Sees <u>The Dwarfs</u> as an important step in Pinter's development in terms of relating linguistic patterns to social relationships.

1594   ____. "The Dynamics of Dialogue: The Plays of Harold Pinter." <u>Dissertation Abstracts International</u>, 33: 6928A. Ph.D. dissertation, University of California, Santa Cruz, 1973.
        A linguistic analysis of Pinter's work which concentrates on <u>The Room</u>, <u>The Caretaker</u>, and <u>Landscape</u>.

1595   ____. <u>The Pinter Problem</u>. Princeton, N. J.: Princeton University Press, 1975.
        Attempts to examine Pinter's plays from a linguistic perspective to show the diversity of ways in which languages can transmit information. An expansion of "The Dynamics of Dialogue: The Plays of Harold Pinter" (<u>See</u> no. 1594). Reviewed: <u>See</u> nos. 735, 817, 960, 1099, 1486, 1638, and 1746.

1596   ____. "A Stylistic Analysis of Harold Pinter's <u>The Dwarfs</u>." Masters thesis, University of Birmingham, 1969.
        "The thesis examines the usefulness of an experimental stylistic approach to a prose text."

1597   QUIGLY, ISABEL. "Home Fires." The Spectator, 17 July 1964, p. 84.
         Film review of The Pumpkin Eater.

1598   ____. "Pinter's Marks." The Spectator, 20 March 1964, pp. 380-81.
         Review of the film version of The Caretaker stressing the language.

1599   R. B. M. "Mr. Pinter Has Written a Fine Play in The Caretaker." The Stage, 5 May 1960, p. 21.
         Review.

1600   REED, REX. Conversations in the Raw. New York: Signet, 1970, pp. 116-20.
         Interview with director Joseph Losey praising the terseness of Pinter's scripts.

1601   ____. "A New Puzzle from Pinter." New York Sunday News, 1 August 1971, Sec. S, p. 9.
         Concerned with Old Times.

1602   ____. "Rex Reed at the Movies: The Birthday Party." Holiday, 45 (March 1969), 26-31.
         Includes a review of the film version of The Birthday Party, a "good stage-to-screen transition."

1603   RICH, FRANK. Review of The Last Tycoon. New York Post, November 1976.
         Film review. Quoted in New York Times advertisement.

1604   RICHARDS, DICK. The Curtain Rises. London: Trewin, 1966.
         Includes Evan's "Pinter's Black Magic" (See no. 764).

1605   ____. "Subtle Goonery." London Daily Mirror, 31 May 1960, p. 18.
         Review of original production of The Caretaker.

1606   ____. "Talent in the Attic." London Daily Mirror, 13 March 1964, p. 21.
         Review of the film version of The Caretaker.

*1607 RICHARDS, MICHAEL. "Harold Pinter." In Englische Dichter der Modern, edited by R. Suhnel and D. Riesner (See no. 1791), pp. 578-87.
         Cited in 1975 MLA International Bibliography, 1, p. 126.

Richardson

1608   RICHARDSON, GINA. "Alarms and Diversions." Time and Tide,
          23-29 July 1964, p. 84.
             Film review of The Pumpkin Eater.

1609   _____. "Taking Care." Time and Tide, 19-25 March 1964, p. 26.
             Review of film version of The Caretaker.

1610   RICHARDSON, JACK. "English Imports on Broadway." Commentary,
          43 (January 1967), 73-75.
             Review of The Homecoming (New York) which is concerned
          with whether or not the characters' motives are convincing-
          ly presented.

1611   RICHARDSON, MAURICE. "Eyes behind the Iron Curtain." London
          Observer, 14 May 1961, p. 27.
             Review of British television production of The Collec-
          tion.

1612   _____. "Life with the Dolphins." London Observer, 26 Febru-
          ary 1967, p. 25.
             Review of television version of The Basement.

1613   _____. "Mr. Pinter's Night Thoughts." London Observer, 24
          July 1960, p. 24.
             Review of television version of Night School.

1614   _____. "Oedipus of the Sixth Form." London Observer, 27
          March 1960, p. 25.
             Review of British television production of The Birthday
          Party.

1615   _____. "Paranoid's Progress." London Observer, 28 March
          1965, p. 25.
             Review of television production of Tea Party.

1616   _____. "The Pilkington Network." London Observer, 8 October
          1961, p. 27.
             Review of The Room and The Dumb Waiter.

1617   _____. "Pinter Among the Pigeons." London Observer, 31
          March 1963, p. 39.
             Review of television production of The Lover.

1618   _____. "Rope's End and Stop Watch." London Observer, 4 May
          1960, p. 19.
             Review of television version of A Night Out.

1619   RICKERT, ALFRED E. "Perceiving Pinter." English Record, 22,
        No. 2 (1971), 30-35.
            Pinter concentrates on the individual, rather than on
        social problems.

1620   RILEY, CAROLYN, ed. Contemporary Literary Criticism.
        Detroit: Gale, 1973, Vols. 1 and 5.
            Vol. 1 includes extracts from Walter Kerr's Harold
        Pinter (See no. 1189), Martin Esslin's Theatre of the
        Absurd (See no. 761), and Robert Brustein's "A Naturalism
        of the Grotesque" (See no. 514); pp. 266-69. Vol. 5 in-
        cludes extracts from George Wellwarth's The Theatre of
        Protest and Paradox (See no. 1967), Robert Brustein's
        The Third Theatre (See no. 518), John Simon on The Home-
        coming (See no. 1745), John Gassner's Dramatic Soundings
        (See no. 852), Stanley Kauffmann on The Homecoming, Land-
        scape and Silence (See nos. 1153 and 1154), Jay Cock's
        "Fire and Ice" (See no. 593), Robert Heilman's "Demonic
        Strategies: The Birthday Party and The Firebugs" (See
        no. 987), and "Theatre Without Adventure" (See no. 354).

1621   RIVERS, LARRY. "'Begin Anywhere.'" New York Times, 5 Febru-
        ary 1967, Sec. 2, p. 3.
            Review of The Homecoming.

1622   ROBERTS, EDWIN A., Jr. "A Very Cluttered Room." Wall Street
        Journal, 6 October 1961, p. 10.
            Review of New York production of The Caretaker.

1623   ROBERTS, P. Book review of Five Screenplays. Stand, 12,
        No. 4, 60 (See no 33).

1624   _____. Book review of Tea Party and Other Plays, Stand, 12,
        No. 1, 64 (See no. 17).

*1624a _____. Review of Mixed Doubles. Stand, 12, No. 1, p. 64.
            Concerns Night. Cited in An Index to Book Reviews in
        the Humanities (1973).

1625   ROBERTS, PATRICK. The Psychology of Tragic Drama. Boston:
        Routledge and Kegan Paul, 1975.
            Includes a Freudian analysis of the "tragic consequences
        of childhood responses to child-parent relationships" in
        Pinter's work.

1626   ROBERTS, PETER. "The Caretaker." Plays and Players, 7
        (July 1960), 15.
            Review of original production.

Roberts

1627 _____. "The Dumb Waiter. The Room." Plays and Players, 7
      (April 1960), 16.
        Review of New York production of The Dumb Waiter.

*1628 ROBERTSON, RODERICK. "A Theatre of the Absurd: The Passion-
      ate Equation." Drama Survey, 2, No. 1 (June 1962), 24-43.
        Cited in Schroll (See no. 1700), p. 105.

1629 ROBINSON, DAVID. "The Improved Pumpkin Eater." London
      Financial Times, 17 July 1964, p. 24.
        Film review of The Pumpkin Eater.

1630 _____. "Tensions Below." London Financial Times, 10 Febru-
      ary 1967, p. 27.
        Film review of Accident.

1631 _____. "Trios." London Financial Times, 13 March 1964, p.
      26.
        Review of the film version of The Caretaker.

1632 ROBINSON, ROBERT. "Meeting of the Twain." London Sunday
      Telegraph, 12 February 1967, p. 12.
        Film review of Accident.

1633 _____. "Radio." London Sunday Times, 25 December 1960, p.
      32.
        Review of radio version of The Dwarfs which Robinson
      finds "boring" because it lacks form.

1634 _____. "With Proper Humility." The Sunday Times (London),
      2 August 1959, p. 14.
        Review of the radio version of A Slight Ache.

*1635 RODGER, IAN. "The Moron as Hero." Drama, 59 (Winter 1960),
      36-39.
        Cited in Imhof (See no. 1098).

1636 _____. "The Wrong Audience." The Listener, 29 March 1962,
      p. 573.
        Review of radio production of The Caretaker.

1637 ROGERS, RODNEY O[UTHWAITE]. "Harold Pinter: Essays on the
      Metaphysics of His Theatre." Dissertation Abstracts
      International, 35: 2295A. Ph.D. dissertation, University
      of Virginia, 1974.
        In Pinter's dramas man is isolated from the world he
      inhabits.

1638 _____. South Carolina Quarterly [1977].
Review of The Pinter Problem by Austin Quigley (See no. 1595).

1639 ROGOFF, GORDON. "Following Beckett." New Leader, 20 January 1964, pp. 29-30.
Review of The Lover (New York).

1640 _____. "Richard's Himself Again." Tulane Drama Review, 11, No. 2 (Winter 1966), 29-40.

1641 ROLAND, ALAN. "Pinter's Homecoming: Imagoes in Dramatic Action." Psychoanalytic Review, 61 (1974), 415-28.

1642 ROLL-HANSEN, DIDERIK. "Harold Pinter og det absurde drama." Samtiden, 74 (September 1965), 435-40.
Influences on Pinter of European dramatic traditions. In Norwegian.

1643 RONAN, MARGARET. "Films: Faces of War, Faces of the Past." Senior Scholastic, 99 (18 October 1971), 20.
Film review of The Go-Between.

1644 _____. "Following the Films." Senior Scholastic, 94 (7 March 1969), 26.
Review of The Birthday Party film, which is seen as enigmatic.

1645 ROSELLI, JOHN. "Between Farce and Madness." Manchester Guardian, 29 April 1960, p. 13.
Review of original production of The Caretaker.

*1646 ROSENBERG, JAMES. European Influences on the American Theatre, 1959-60.
Discusses The Caretaker.

1647 ROTHSCHILD, ELAINE. "The Pumpkin Eater." Films in Review, 15, No. 10 (December 1964), 633.
Film review; essentially a synopsis.

1648 ROUD, RICHARD. "All Done Without Mirrors." Manchester Guardian, 9 February 1967, p. 5.
Review of Accident film.

1649 _____. "Going Between." Sight and Sound, 40, No. 3 (Summer 1971), 158-59.
Discussion of the transformation of The Go-Between from novel to film.

1650 ROY, EMIL. British Drama Since Shaw. Crosscurrents/Modern
Critiques Series. Carbondale: Southern Illinois Universi-
ty Press, 1972.
Includes discussion of Pinter, pp. 115-23.

1651 RUBENS, ROBERT. "Donald McWhinnie." Transatlantic Review,
No. 12 (Spring 1963), pp. 34-38. See no. 1373.

1652 RUNDALL, JEREMY. "On the Beach." The Sunday Times (London),
28 April 1968, p. 53.
Review of the radio version of Landscape.

1653 RUSINKO, SUSAN. Book review of Esslin's The Peopled Wound.
Modern Drama, 14, No. 1 (May 1971), 114-15 (See no. 755).

1654 _____. "Stratagems of language in the Poems and Plays of
Harold Pinter: A Study of Text, Sub-Text and Conscious
Sub-Text." Dissertation Abstracts International, 32:
6451A. Ph.D. dissertation, Pennsylvania State Univer-
sity, 1972.
Language, especially in relation to silence, is examined.

1655 RUSSELL, FRANCIS. "A Pinter Pickled Peppers." National
Review, 21 March 1967, pp. 316-17.
Review of The Homecoming (New York).

*1656 RUSSELL, LEONARD. Correspondence in The Times (London), 14
August 1960, p. 21.
An open letter to Pinter regarding audience laughter
at the London production of The Caretaker--answered by
the playwright (See no. 68). Cited in Elliott (See no.
733); also cited in Esslin (See no. 755), p. 45, no date
or pagination given.

1657 RYAN, STEPHEN P. "The London Stage." America, 106, No. 12
(23-30 December 1961), 756-58.
Review of The Collection.

1658 _____. "The London Stage." America, 107 (27 October 1962),
956-58.
Review of original stage production of The Collection
placing Pinter in the "Theatre of the Absurd."

1659 SAINER, ARTHUR. The Sleepwalker and the Assassin. New York:
Bridgehead Books, 1964, pp. 99-102.
Includes the section "A Slight Ache."

1660 SAHAI, SURENDRA. "Harold Pinter: Room Without View." Ph.D.
dissertation, London University, 1976.

*1661   SAKAMOTO, FUMIKO. "An Essay on Harold Pinter--The Role of an
         Intruder in the Theatre of the Absurd." Metropolitan, 14.
             In Japanese. Cited by Tetsuo Kishi in personal
         correspondence.

1662   SALE, JAMES. "The Film of the Play." Queen, 11 March 1964,
         p. 17.
             Review of the film version of The Caretaker.

1663   _____. "Savage Success." Queen, 11 March 1964, p. 17.
             Film review of The Pumpkin Eater.

1664   SALEM, DANIEL. Book review of Landscape, Silence, Night, and
         Old Times. Etudes Anglaises, October-December 1972, p.
         578 (See nos. 21 and 22).

1665   _____. Harold Pinter, dramaturge de l'ambiguité. Paris:
         Denoël, 1968.
             Considered the only important book-length study of
         Pinter in French.

1666   _____. "Les adaptations cinematographiques de Pinter."
         Etudes Anglaises, 25, No. 4 (1972), 493-505.
             Discusses Pinter's cinematic adaptions.

1667   _____. "La blessure peuplee de Pinter." Les Langues Modernes,
         67 (1973), 84-85.

1668   _____. "Le Gardien: Analyse d'un personnage de Pinter."
         Les Langues Modernes, 67 (1973), 67-71.
             Discussion of Davies in The Caretaker.

1669   SALEM, JAMES M. A Guide to Critical Reviews: Part III:
         British and Continental Drama from Ibsen to Pinter. Metu-
         chen, New Jersey: Scarecrow Press, 1968.

1670   SALMON, ERIC. "Harold Pinter's Ear." Modern Drama, 17, No.
         4 (December 1974), 363-75.
             Unconvincingly discusses Pinter's use of language,
         claiming that critics have been unprepared to study the
         imagistic and ritualistic language Pinter uses to "es-
         tablish the right relationship between the surface-
         portraiture of naturalistic versimilitude...and the inner
         sense of life." Using Synge's language in comparison,
         Salmon concludes that "Synge is by far the greater artist."

Samuel

1671   SAMUEL, F. H. "Clayton's Masterpiece." Jewish Chronicle, 17
       July 1964, p. 32.
          Film review of The Pumpkin Eater.

1672   _____. "Student Affairs." Jewish Chronicle, 10 February
       1967, p. 26.
          Film review of Accident.

1673   SANDERS, THOMAS E., ed. The Discovery of Drama. Glenville,
       Illinois: Scott, Foresman, 1968.
          Includes reprint of Prideaux's "The Adventurous Play--
       Stranger to Broadway" (See no. 1574), pp. 624-27.

1674   SANDERS, WALTER E. "The English-Speaking Game Drama."
       Dissertation Abstracts International, 30: 5001A-02A.
       Ph.D. dissertation, Northwestern University, 1969.
          In Beckett, Pinter, and Albee the game is central in
       both structure and theme.

1675   SANDIER, GILLES. "Comme dans la Vie...." In "La Critique:
       Le Retour." L'Avant-Scène, 15 April 1967, p. 29.
          Concerns The Homecoming.

1676   SARNE, MIKE. "Accident." Films and Filming, 13, No. 7
       (April 1967), 4-5.
          Film review.

1677   SARRIS, ANDREW. "Accident." Village Voice, 18 May 1967.
       Reprinted in: Boyum and Scott, Film as Film (See no. 473),
       pp. 31-34.
          A review of the film Accident. The movie is too
       static to be successful.

1678   _____. The American Cinema: Directors and Directions, 1929-
       1968. New York: Dutton, 1968.
          In dealing with various directors (Anderson, Losey),
       Sarris comments that Pinter's scripts are responsible
       for their successes.

1679   _____. Confessions of a Cultist: On the Cinema, 1955-1969.
       New York: Simon and Schuster, 1970.
          Includes "The Birthday Party," pp. 409-14, a film
       review.

1680   _____. "Films in Focus." The Village Voice, 12 August 1971,
       p. 43.
          Film review of The Go-Between.

1681 _____. "The Guest." The Village Voice, 30 January 1964, p. 16.
     Review of the film version of The Caretaker.

1682 _____. "The Homecoming." The Village Voice, 29 December 1973.
     Review of the film version of The Homecoming.

1683 _____. "The Pumpkin Eater." The Village Voice, 19 November 1964, p. 16.
     Review of the film.

1684 _____. "The Quiller Memorandum. The Village Voice, 19 January 1967, p. 27.
     A review of the film.

1685 _____. Review of The Last Tycoon. Village Voice, November 1976.
     Film review. Quoted in New York Times advertisement.

1686 _____. "Second Thoughts About Accident." The Village Voice, 8 June 1967. Reprinted in: Boyum and Scott, Film as Film (See no. 473), pp. 34-35.
     Decides that there is more to the movie than he first thought, though he still feels the film fails.

1687 _____. "The Servant." The Village Voice, 26 March 1964, p. 17.
     A film review.

1688 _____. "What Does 'Mean' Mean." The Village Voice, 19 December 1968, p. 51.
     Review of the film version of The Birthday Party.

1689 SAY, ROSEMARY. "Pinter Looks Back." London Sunday Telegraph, 6 June 1971, p. 14.
     Review of Old Times.

1690 SCHECHNER, RICHARD. "Puzzling Pinter." Tulane Drama Review, 11, No. 2 (Winter 1966), 176-84.
     Pinter's plays rely on the audience to supply the outside-world framework necessary to elicit the subtextual meanings which are conveyed through implication. See also Anthony Callen's response (See no. 541).

*1691 SCHEEHAN, PETER J. "Theatre of the Absurd: a Child Studies Himself." English Journal, 58, No. 4 (April 1969), 561-65.

177

Schenker

*1692   SCHENKER, UELI. "Versuche zur Ordnung: Harold Pinter und
        sein Caretaker." Neue Zürcher Zeitung, 13 April 1969.
        In German.

1693   SCHICKEL, RICHARD. "The Most Dour Spy of Them All." Life,
        27 January 1967, p. 15.
            Movie review of The Quiller Memorandum.

1694   _____. "When Croquet Was in Flower." Life, 71 (1 October
        1971), 10.
            Film review of The Go-Between. Pinter fails to make
        anything of the book, which Schickel finds "no master-
        piece."

1695   SCHIFF, ELLEN F. "Pancakes and Soapsuds: A Study of
        Childishness in Pinter's Plays." Modern Drama, 16 (June
        1973), 91-101.

1696   SCHLEGELMILCH, WOLFGANG. "Der Raum des Humanen: Zu Harold
        Pinters The Caretaker." Die Neueren Sprachen, 13 (1964),
        328-33.
            The disorderly room in The Caretaker functions
        symbolically. In German.

1697   SCHLESINGER, ARTHUR, Jr. "The Go-Between." Vogue, 158
        (15 September 1971), 88-89.
            A review which states that Pinter's "capacity to evoke
        genuine mystery by words" is the reason this film is so
        outstanding, a "gem."

1698   _____. "Movies." Vogue, 153 (1 January 1969), 66.
            Film review in which approval of the film version of
        The Birthday Party is expressed.

*1699   SCHREY, HELMUT. "Das zeitgenossische englische Drama in
        Schule und Fernsehen." Der fremdsprachliche Unterricht,
        Jg. 4, 13 (February 1970), 2-14.
            Cited in 1970 MLA International Bibliography.

1700   SCHROLL, HERMAN T. Harold Pinter: A Study of His Reputation,
        1958-1969. Metuchen, N. J.: Scarecrow Press, 1971.
            Includes a checklist notable primarily for listing of
        reviews; some errors.

1701   SCHUMACHER, ERNST. "In Munchen Der Hausmeister von Harold
        Pinter." Theater der Zeit, 16, No. 4 (1961), 70-71.
            Review of The Caretaker   In German.

*1702   SCHWARZE, HANS-WILHELM. "Orientierungslosigkeit und
         Betroffensein: Spielelemente in Harold Pinters The
         Birthday Party." Literatur in Wissenschaft und Unter-
         richt, 7, No. 2 (August 1974), 98-114.
             Cited in 1974 MLA International Bibliography.

1703   SCOTT, JAMES F. Film: The Medium and the Maker. New York:
         Holt, Rinehart, 1975.
             Pinter's reputation for adaptation and scenarios,
         psychological complexity, and dialogue have been responsi-
         ble for critical acclaim of Losey.

1704   SEAR, RICHARD. "Diamond Bright Comedy." London Daily Mirror,
         22 July 1960, p. 16.
             Review of television version of Night School.

1705   _____. "A Glittering Haze." London Daily Mirror, 12 May
         1961, p. 20.
             Review of British television production of The Collection.

1706   _____. "A Night Out." London Daily Mirror, 25 April 1960,
         p. 26.
             Review of television version of A Night Out.

1707   _____. "A Play to Scorch Nerve Ends." London Daily Mirror,
         23 March 1960, p. 18.
             Review of British television production of The Birthday
         Party which Sear in part disliked, though he found it
         "astonishingly effective."

1708   _____. "The Quiller Memorandum." Esquire, 67 (April 1967),
         47-49.
             Film review which calls the movie a dud, largely due
         to the poor acting.

1709   _____. "Such an Elegant Love Play." London Daily Mirror,
         29 March 1963, p. 18.
             Review of British television production of The Lover,
         which he says has "no message."

1710   SEYMOUR-SMITH, MARTIN. Book review of Poems. The Times
         Literary Supplement (London), 31 October 1968, p. 1220
         (See no. 65).

1711   _____. Who's Who in Twentieth-Century Literature. New York:
         McGraw-Hill, 1977.
             Includes a short section on Pinter.

Sharp

1712   SHARP, WILLIAM L. <u>Language in Drama: Meanings for the</u>
<u>Director and the Actor</u>. Scranton, Pa.: Chandler Pub-
lishing Company, 1970.
    Includes a separate chapter on Pinter.

1713   SHEED, WILFRID. "Absurdity Revisited." <u>Commonweal</u>, 30 April
1965, pp. 193-94.
    Review of New York production of <u>A Slight Ache</u> and <u>The</u>
<u>Room</u>, finding both pieces devoid of meaning.

1714   _____. "Films." <u>Esquire</u>, 71 (February 1969), 32, 34.
    Review of film version of <u>The Birthday Party</u> which
calls both <u>The Birthday Party</u> and <u>The Caretaker</u> a "dismal
waste."

1715   _____. <u>The Morning After</u>. London and New York: Farrar,
Straus, 1971.
    Discusses <u>The Birthday Party</u>, pp. 227-29.

1716   _____. "The Stage." <u>Commonweal</u>, 27 January 1967, pp. 459-60.
    Review of <u>The Homecoming</u> (New York).

1717   SHERRILL, R. E. "Religious Imagery in the Plays of Harold
Pinter." <u>Religion in Life</u>, 46 (Spring 1977), 32-43.

*1718   SHIGIHARA, SHINICHI. "Pinter's Sense of Form." <u>Review of</u>
<u>English Literature</u> (Kyoto University), 27, March 1971.
    In Japanese. Cited by Tetsuo Kishi in personal
correspondence.

1719   SHIMANE, KIMIE. "Whose Birthday Party?--The Question Posed
by Harold Pinter's <u>The Birthday Party</u>." <u>Bulletin of</u>
<u>English Literature</u> (Notre Dame Seishin Women's College),
No. 8.

1720   SHORTER, ERIC. "Outrageous and Gruesomely Funny Play."
London <u>Daily Telegraph</u>, 4 June 1965, p. 18.
    Review of the original production of <u>The Homecoming</u>, a
play which has an "unedifying conclusion."

1721   _____. "Pinter Hero Who Loses Confidence." London <u>Daily</u>
<u>Telegraph</u>, 26 March 1965, p. 19.
    Review of television production of <u>Tea Party</u>.

1722   _____. "Pinter Up in the World. Horrors Round the Corner."
London <u>Daily Telegraph</u>, 12 May 1961, p. 17.

Review of the television production of <u>The Collection</u>
which, in spite of a shift to a middle class milieu, is
still "the Pinter world of horrors."

*1723   SHROYER, FREDERICK B. and LOUIS G. GARDEMAL. <u>Types of Drama</u>:
        <u>A Critical and Historical Introduction.</u> Glenview,
        Illinois: Scott, Foresman, 1970.
            Includes a section on "The Development of Drama in the
        Western World," with a subdivision on "Trends in the
        Twentieth Century."

 1724   SHULMAN, MILTON. "Drama--or Confidence Trick?" London
        <u>Evening Standard</u>, 4 June 1965, p. 5.
            Review of <u>The Homecoming</u>.

 1725   _____. "Eight Sharp, Cynical Looks at the Unholiness of
        Marriage." London <u>Evening Standard</u>, 10 April 1969, p. 6.
            Review of <u>Night</u>.

 1726   _____. "Mini-Pinter." London <u>Evening Standard</u>, 3 July 1969,
        p. 17.
            Review of <u>Landscape</u> and <u>Silence</u>. Sees the style as
        disappointing, "minimal drama."

 1727   _____. "Now You See It, Now You Don't...." London <u>Evening
        Standard</u>, 18 September 1970, p. 25.
            Review of <u>Tea Party</u> and <u>The Basement</u> (London).

 1728   _____. "The Party, Mr. Pinter, Is Beginning to Bore...."
        London <u>Evening Standard</u>, 19 June 1964, p. 4.
            Review of <u>The Birthday Party</u>.

 1729   _____. "Pinter in His Best Hypnotic Mood." London <u>Evening
        Standard</u>, 19 June 1962, p. 10.
            Enthusiastic review of original stage production of
        <u>The Collection</u>: "a commentary on the inability of any of
        us to recognize the truth."

 1730   _____. "The Private, Padded World of Mr. Pinter." London
        <u>Evening Standard</u>, 19 September 1963, p. 4.
            Review of <u>The Dwarfs</u> and <u>The Lover</u> which calls these
        plays "far inferior" to his earlier ones.

Shulman

1731   _____. "Sorry, Mr. Pinter, You're Just Not Funny Enough."
        London Evening Standard, 20 May 1958, p. 6.
            Review of the first run of The Birthday Party: a
        naive allegory about messengers of death and "man's
        inability to stand up to the powers of verbal suggestion."

1732   _____. "Terrifying--This Hymn of Hate Against Women." London
        Evening Standard, 3 October 1961, p. 18.
            Review of A Night Out.

1733   _____. "Three for One Give Mr. Williams an Actor's Field
        Day." London Evening Standard, 19 January 1961, p. 14.
            Review of original production of A Slight Ache, which is
        "smaller and less satisfying" than Pinter's other plays
        because it is "uncommitted to any political or social
        solution" and only attempts to create an atmosphere.

1734   SHUTTLEWORTH, MARTIN. "Ambiguities." Listener, 21 June
        1962, pp. 1089-90.
            Review of radio version of The Collection.

1735   SIGAL, CLANCY. "The Collection." Queen, 3 July 1962, p. 17.
            Review.

1736   SILLITOE, ALAN. "Novel or Play?" Twentieth Century, 169
        (February 1961), 206-11.

1737   SILVER, LEE. "Pinter's 'Homecoming' Revived at the Bijou."
        New York Daily News, 19 May 1971. Reprinted in: New
        York Theatre Critics' Reviews, 14 June 1971, p. 261.
            Review of The Homecoming.

1738   SIMON, JOHN. "The Best of Behan." New York, 20 April 1970,
        p. 62.
            Review of Landscape and Silence (New York).

1739   _____. Movies Into Film: Film Criticism, 1967-1970. New
        York: Delta Books, 1971.
            Includes a review of Accident (pp. 337-42) in a chapter
        on "Pseudo-Art" which says some very unflattering things
        about Pinter's technique.

1740   _____. "The Pause That Regresses." New York, 7 June 1971,
        p. 62.
            Review of The Homecoming.

1741   _____. "Pinter, Boy Soprano." <u>Commonweal</u>, 87 (27 October 1967), 122-23.
        Review of New York production of <u>The Birthday Party</u>.

1742   _____. "Pinter Is At It Again." <u>New York</u>, 18 November 1968, p. 44.
        Review of <u>Tea Party</u> and <u>The Basement</u> (New York).

1743   _____. "The Sorcerer and His Apprentices." <u>New York</u>, 13 February 1971, p. 24.
        Review of <u>The Birthday Party</u>.

1744   _____. "Theatre Chronicle." <u>Hudson Review</u>, 14 (1961), 586-92.
        <u>The Caretaker</u> is seen as an almost complete failure in this review.

1745   _____. "Theatre Chronicle." <u>Hudson Review</u>, 20 (Spring 1967), 105-14. <u>See also</u> no. 1620.
        Review of <u>The Homecoming</u> (New York) which claims that Pinter cannot write full-length dramas.

1746   _____. "Theatre Chronicle." <u>Hudson Review</u>, 30, No. 1 (Spring 1977), 100-03.
        Includes a production review of <u>No Man's Land</u>, which Simon feels is a weak play by a playwright whom he does not like or appreciate. Simon also criticises Quigley's <u>The Pinter Problem</u> (See no. 1595).

1747   _____. "Theatre Chronicle." <u>Hudson Review</u>, 30, No. 2 (Summer 1977), 259-69.
        Includes a production review of Simon Gray's <u>Otherwise Engaged</u> with a mention of Pinter's direction, which Simon approves of and calls a "latent talent."

1748 SINGH, MOHINDAR. "Harold Pinter: a Reappraisal." <u>Indian Journal of English Studies</u>, 10 (1969), 81-95.
        Pinter searches for a higher degree of realism than that allowed in the well-made play.

1749 SINGER, ISAAC BASHEVIS. "'Only One Kafka.'" <u>New York Times</u>, 5 February 1967, Sec. 2, p. 3.
        Review of <u>The Homecoming</u>.

1750 SINKO, GREGORZ. "Atara i Mloda Anglia." <u>Dialogue</u>, 60, No. 4 (April 1961), 97-99.
        Claims that the early plays are in the tradition of Kafka. In Polish.

Skloot

1751 SKLOOT, ROBERT. "Putting out the Light: Staging the Theme of Pinter's Old Times." Quarterly Journal of Speech, 61 (October 1975), 265-70.
Concerned with lighting (and shadow) in the staging of Old Times.

1752 SMALLWOOD, CLYDE G. Elements of the Existentialist Philosophy in the Theatre of the Absurd. Dubuque, Iowa: Wm. C. Brown, 1966.
Includes "Harold Pinter," which examines The Room and The Birthday Party for traces of existentialism (pp. 140-45).

1753 SMITH, CECIL. "Pinter: The Compulsion of Playwriting." Los Angeles Times, 3 December 1967, Calendar section, pp. 1, 19.
Pinter discusses his playwriting.

1754 _____. "Pinter's The Homecoming Opens." Los Angeles Times, 7 December 1967, Sec. 4, pp. 1, 9.
A review of The Homecoming, including an interpretation of the characters.

1755 SMITH, FREDERICK N. "Uncertainty in Pinter: The Dwarfs." Theatre Annual, 26 (1970), 81-96.
Traces the influence of Sartre's philosophy on Pinter.

1756 SMITH, LISA GORDON. "The Caretaker." Plays and Players, 7, No. 9 (June 1960), 17.
Review of original production of The Caretaker.

1757 SMITH, R. D. "Back to the Text." In Contemporary Theatre, edited by John Russell Brown and Bernard Harris (See no. 503), pp. 117-37.
Smith feels that too often writers like Pinter are lumped in schools to avoid a need for close examination of their work.

1758 SMITH, WARREN S. "The New Plays in London, II." Christian Century, 8 September 1965, pp. 1096-97.
Review of the original production of The Homecoming.

1759 SORRELL, WALTER. Facets of Comedy. New York: Grosset, 1972.
Deals with Pinter in passing.

1760 SOULE, GEORGE. The Theatre of the Mind. Englewood Cliffs: Prentice-Hall, 1974.

Includes The Dumb Waiter in an anthology emphasizing
the visual, theatrical aspects of drama.

*1761 SPANOS, WILLIAM V. "The Detective and the Boundary: Some
Notes on the Postmodern Literary Imagination." Boundary
2, (Fall 1972), 147-68.
Cited in 1973 MLA International Bibliography, 1, p. 10.

1762 _____. Existentialism 2. New York: Thomas Y. Crowell, 1976.
Includes a reprint of A Slight Ache, pp. 120-41.

1763 _____. "Modern Drama and the Aristotelian Tradition: The
Formal Imperatives of Absurd Time." Contemporary Literature, 12 (1971), 345-72.

1764 SPARK, MURIEL. "An Experiment in Gluttony." London Observer,
13 August 1961, p. 19.
Review of British television production of The Dumb
Waiter.

1765 SPENCER, CHARLES. "Pinter in Print." Jewish Quarterly, 16,
Nos. 2-3 (Autumn 1968), 43.
A review of the limited edition of The Homecoming (See
no. 13).

1766 SPENCER, WALTER. Review of The Last Tycoon. WOR Radio,
November 1976.
Film review. Quoted in New York Times advertisement.

1767 SPIVEY, VIRGIL R. "Psychological Realism and the Absurd: A
Study of Ontological Insecurity in the Plays of Harold
Pinter." Masters thesis, Virginia Polytechnic Institute,
Blacksburg, 1969.
Pinter's progress towards psychological realism is
traced as it is revealed through his use of menace and
insecurity in The Room, The Birthday Party, The Dumb
Waiter, and The Caretaker.

1768 SPRAGUE, CLAIRE. "Possible or Necessary?" New Theatre
Magazine, 8, No. 1 (Autumn 1967), 36-37.
Concerned with The Birthday Party.

1769 SPURLING, HILARY. "In His Own Write." The Spectator, 7
February 1969, p. 183.
Review of The Homecoming.

1770 _____. "Lust and Forgetfulness." The Spectator, 12 July
1969, pp. 49-50.
Review of Landscape and Silence.

185

Starkman

*1771 STARKMAN, ALFRED. "Schweigen--wörtlich genommen." Die Welt,
16 July 1969, p. 7.
In German.

1772 STATES, BERT O. "The Case for Plot in Modern Drama." Hudson
Review, 20 (Spring 1967), 49-61.
Attacks Pinter's formlessness and lack of linear plot
(in answer to John Russell Brown's "Mr. Pinter's Shakespeare"; See no. 500).

1773 ____. Irony and Drama: A Poetics. Ithaca, N. Y.:
Cornell University Press, 1971.

1774 ____. "Pinter's Homecoming: The Shock of Nonrecognition."
Hudson Review, 21 (August 1968), 474-86. Reprinted in:
Ganz, Pinter: A Collection of Critical Essays (See no.
843), pp. 147-60.

1775 STEELE, RICHARD, and JOHN BARNES. "Britain: Hell Hath No
Fury." Newsweek, 85 (11 August 1975), 39-40.
Report of Pinter's affair with Lady Antonia Fraser.

1776 STEIN, KAREN F. "Metaphysical Silence in Absurd Drama."
Modern Drama, 13, No. 4 (February 1971), 423-31.
"Silent characters [in A Slight Ache and The Birthday
Party] are passive vehicles for the talking ones."
Pinter's characters are driven to talking by a fear of
silence.

1777 STEINER, GEORGE. After Babel: Aspects of Language and
Translation. London: Oxford University Press, 1975.
Reprinted: New York, 1976.
Passing comments on Pinter's use of silence and
clichés. Also mentions the interrelationships between
King Lear and The Homecoming, and places Pinter in the
category of those whose techniques "enact a hoarding of
old treasures by means of incisive austerity."

1778 STEPHENS, SUZANNE S. "The Dual Influence: A Dramaturgical
Study of the Plays of Edward Albee and the Specific
Dramatic Forms and Themes which Influence Them." Dis-
sertation Abstracts International, 34: 342A. Ph.D.
dissertation, Miami University, 1973.
The influence of Pinter's technique is studied in
Chapter Three.

1779   STOLL, KARL-HEINZ. The New British Drama: A Bibliography
        with Particular Reference to Arden, Bond, Osborne, Pinter,
        Wesker. Bern: Lang, 1975.
            Very limited (entire volume is only 94 pages).

1780   STORCH, R. F. "Harold Pinter's Happy Families." Massachu-
        setts Review, 8 (August 1967), 703-12. Reprinted in:
        Ganz, Pinter: A Collection of Critical Essays (See no.
        843), pp. 136-46.
            An overview of family relationships in Pinter's plays
        through The Homecoming.

1781   STRAUS, BARRIE RUTH. "Homo Ludens in the Morality Play,
        Medieval and Modern: Everyman and Harold Pinter's The
        Birthday Party." Paper read at the Modern Language
        Association meeting seminar: Homo Ludens at work in
        Medieval Drama and the Theatre of the Absurd; San Fran-
        cisco, 28 December, 1975.
            The affinities between medieval drama and absurdist
        drama are explored, concluding that Everyman and The Birth-
        day Party are both concerned with pointing out "ultimate
        realities" and that attention to play and game demon-
        strates the didactic intent of The Birthday Party in what
        "has become of the medieval morality play."

1782   STREIKER, LOWELL E. D. "Pinter: Artificer of Menacing
        Meaninglessness." Christian Century, 74 (13 December
        1967), 1604.
            Review of New York production of The Birthday Party,
        which is self-defeating because it is "pure Pinterism."

1783   STRICK, PHILIP. "Mice in the Milk." Sight and Sound, 38,
        No. 2 (Spring 1969), 77-79.
            Discussion of Joseph Losey, including material on
        Accident.

1784   STYAN, J. L. The Dark Comedy: The Development of Modern
        Comic Tragedy, Second Edition. Cambridge: Cambridge
        University Press, 1962. Revised 1968.
            Includes "After 'Godot': Ionesco, Genet, and Pinter,"
        pp. 234-50. Discusses The Caretaker, The Collection, and
        The Homecoming. With Beckett and Ionesco, Pinter has
        created a "comic danse macabre."

*1785   _____. "Drama as Ritual." Modern Language Quarterly, 27
        (1966), 323-31.
            Cited in Elliott (See no. 733), p. 552.

Styan

*1786   ____. Drama, Stage and Audience. Cambridge: Cambridge
          University Press, 1975.
                Cited in 1975 MLA International Bibliography, 1, p. 24.

*1787   ____. The Dramatic Experience. Cambridge: Cambridge
          University Press, 1975.
                Possibly a reference to no. 1786.

1788   ____. "The Published Play After 1956: II." British Book
          News, No. 301 (September 1965), pp. 601-05.
                Pinter (drama of the Absurd) and Arden (New Realism)
          are the most exciting of the new British dramatists.

1789   ____. "Six Dramatists in Search of a Language by Andrew
          Kennedy." Modern Drama, 18 (December 1975), 394-95.
                Book review (See no. 1176).

1790   ____. "Television Drama." In Contemporary Theatre, edited
          by Brown and Harris (See no. 503), pp. 185-204.

1791   SUHNEL, R., and D. RIESNER, eds. Englische Dichter der
          Moderne. Berlin: Schmidt, 1971.
                Includes Michael Richards's "Harold Pinter" (See no.
          1607), pp. 578-87.

1792   SUPPLE, BARRY. "Pinter's The Homecoming." Jewish Chronicle,
          25 June 1965, pp. 7, 31.
                Review.

1793   SUSINI, C. "Le lieu et la parole dans le théâtre de Harold
          Pinter." Anglaises et Americaines, 5 (1972), 3-34.

1794   SUTHERLAND, JACK. "Brilliant, Despairing Pinter." London
          Daily Worker, 20 June 1964, p. 3.
                Review of The Birthday Party revival.

1795   ____. "Familiar Themes in Pinter Double Bill." Morning
          Star, 19 September 1970, p. 2.
                Review of Tea Party and The Basement.

1796   ____. "Repellent Play from Pinter." London Daily Worker,
          5 June 1965, p. 2.
                Review of the original production of The Homecoming:
          "entirely worthless and phoney."

1797   ____. "Two New Plays by Pinter." London Morning Star, 4
          July 1969, p. 2.
                Review of Landscape and Silence.

1798   SYKES, ARLENE. <u>Harold Pinter</u>. St. Lucia: University of
        Queensland Press; New York: Humanities Press, 1970.
        A good examination of theatrical techniques, but
        limited in interpretations. Reviewed: <u>See</u> no. 825.

1799   _____. "Harold Pinter's Dwarfs." <u>Komos</u>, 1 (June 1967),
        70-75.
        Attempts to decipher the identity of the title figures.
        Similarities with Beckett's <u>Watt</u> are examined.

1800   _____. "Introduction" to <u>The Caretaker</u>. Sydney: Hicks
        Smith, 1965.

1800a   SYPHER, F. J., ed. <u>The Reader's Adviser: Volume Two: The
        Best in American and British Drama and World Literature
        in English Translation</u>. Ann Arbor, Michigan: R. R.
        Bowker, 1977.
        "Biocritical" sketch with short biography.

1801   TABBERT, REINBERT. "Harold Pinters Dramen der verlorenen
        Identitat." Ph.D. dissertation, University of Tubingen,
        1969.
        In German.

1801a   TABORSKI, B., translator. <u>Dawne Czasy</u> [Old Times]. Dialog,
        No. 122, 1972.
        In Polish.

1802   TALLEY, MARY E. "The Relationship of Theme and Technique in
        Plays of Harold Pinter." <u>Dissertation Abstracts Inter-
        national</u>, 33: 1744-45A. Ph.D. dissertation, Vanderbilt
        University, 1972.
        Pinter's work shows a dramatic integrity in the
        correspondence between his thematic emphasis and his
        dramatic technique.

1803   TALMEY, ALLENE. "People Are Talking About...." <u>Vogue</u>, 15
        January 1971, pp. 52-53.
        Brief pre-release comments about <u>The Go-Between</u>.

*1804   TARN, ADAM. "Die Magie des Absurden." <u>Theatre Heute</u>, 10
        (1965), p. 3.
        In German.

1805   TAUBMAN, HOWARD. "Harold Pinter: His 'Dumbwaiter' and
        'Collection' Arrive." <u>New York Times</u>, 27 November 1962,
        p. 44.
        Review.

Taubman

1806 _____. "A Leap Forward: Pinter Makes Progress in 'The Caretaker.'" New York Times, 15 October 1961, Sec. 2, p. 1.
Comment on Pinter's rapid progression in ability from The Birthday Party to The Caretaker. The characters are not symbols in The Caretaker, but interpretation is still valid. Praises Pinter's work--well written.

1807 _____. "Shared Quicksand: Our Reality Is Infirm, Says Pinter, as His Plays Probe Silence." New York Times, 9 December 1962, Sec. 2, p. 5.
Comment on Pinter's style, especially in The Caretaker and The Dumb Waiter; The Collection is mentioned. There is a passage contrasting Pinter and Robert Bolt.

1808 _____. "Theater: Dual Offering." New York Times, 6 January 1964, p. 35.
Review of The Lover (New York): "not a remarkably fresh idea."

1809 _____. "Theater: Modern Parable of Scorn and Sorrow." New York Times, 5 October 1961, p. 42.
Review of New York production of The Caretaker.

1810 _____. "Theater: Two Early Pinter Dramas." New York Times, 10 December 1964, p. 62.
Review of A Slight Ache and The Room.

1811 TAYLOR, JOHN RUSSELL. "Accident." Sight and Sound, 103 (Autumn 1966), 179-84.
A review of the film Accident. Interviews members of the film company, including Pinter.

1812 _____. Anger and After: A Guide to New British Drama. London: Methuen, 1962. Revised 1969. Published under the title The Angry Theatre in America; New York: Hill and Wang, 1963. Revised 1969. Translated by Tetsuo Kishi, Koshi Nakanori, and Toshehiko Shibata, Tokyo: Kenkyusho [1977].
Includes an important chapter on Pinter as a writer whose "unique eminence" entitles him to be studied by himself. A study of each play through Landscape which includes a rational discussion of Pinter's techniques (especially in relation to "casting doubt upon everything by matching each apparently clear and unequivocal statement with an equally clear and unequivocal statement of

its contrary"), and concludes that Pinter's work is the "most 'musical'" [i.e., poetic], "of the new British drama." See also nos. 843, 1823, 1826.

1813 _____. "British Drama of the 50's." World Theatre, Vol 11 (Autumn 1962), 241-54. Reprinted in Kostelanetz, On Contemporary Literature (See no. 1235), pp. 90-96.
Pinter is studied among the "non-realists" as one of the most interesting writers (along with Arden) in English --part of "an explosion" of activity in the English theatre.

1814 _____. "Cuckoo in the Nest." Plays and Players, 9, No. 11 (August 1962), 20 f.
Review of The Collection.

1815 _____. "The Go-Between." Sight and Sound, 39, No. 4 (Autumn 1970), 202-03.
Film review.

1816 _____. "The Guest." Sight and Sound, 33, No. 1 (Winter 1963-64), 38-39.
Review of the film versions of The Caretaker and The Servant.

1817 _____. "Half Pints of Pinter." Plays and Players, 11 (November 1963), 38-39.
Review of The Dwarfs and The Lover.

1818 _____. Harold Pinter. Longmans' Writers and Their Work Series, No. 212. London: Longmans Green, 1969.
This short study traces Pinter's development (up to and including Landscape, Silence, and Night) from the comedies of menace to the questions of identity and verification explored in the later plays. Reviewed: See no. 818.

1819 _____. "The Losey Film Everyone Has Been Waiting For." The Times (London), 9 February 1967, p. 4.
Film review of Accident.

1820 _____. "Old Times." Plays and Players, 18, No. 10 (July 1971), 28-29.
Review.

1821 _____. "Pinter Pointers." The Times Literary Supplement (London), 1 July 1965, p. 552.
Book review of The Homecoming (See no. 13).

Taylor

1822 _____. "A Pinter Power Struggle." Plays and Players, 12
      (August 1965), 34-35.
      Review of The Homecoming.

1823 _____. "Pinter's Game of Happy Families." In Lahr, A Casebook
      on Harold Pinter's The Homecoming (See no. 1260), pp. 57-66.
      Essentially The Homecoming section from Anger and After
      (See no. 1812).

1824 _____. "Rags to Riches." Plays and Players, 11 (August 1964),
      28-29.
      Review of The Birthday Party revival.

1825 _____. The Rise and Fall of the Well-Made Play. New York:
      Hill and Wang, 1967.
      Mentions Pinter in passing (pp. 142, 162, 163).

1826 _____. "A Room and Some Views: Harold Pinter." In Ganz,
      Pinter: A Collection of Critical Essays (See no. 843),
      pp. 105-22.
      An excerpt from Anger and After (See no. 1812).

1827 _____. "Tea Party and The Basement." Plays and Players, 18
      (November 1970), 36-39.
      Review of the London production.

1828 _____. "What's Happened to the New Dramatists?" Plays and
      Players, 11, No. 11 (August 1964), 8-9.

1829 TAYLOR, STEPHEN. "The Pumpkin Eater." Film Quarterly, 18
      No. 3 (Spring 1965), 45-48.
      Film review.

1830 TENER, ROBERT L. "Uncertainty as a Dramatic Formula."
      Humanities Association Bulletin, 24, No. 3 (1973), 175-82.
      Pinter develops the inconsistency between human behav-
      ior (impulsive) and linguistic labels applied to reality.
      The search for identity and myths of humanity in The Lover,
      The Homecoming, and The Caretaker are explored through
      language and movement in the three plays.

1831 THIRKELL, ARTHUR. "The Abnormal from Pinter." London Daily
      Mirror, 19 September 1963, p. 18.
      Review of The Dwarfs and The Lover.

1832 _____. "Empty." London Daily Mirror, 19 June 1962, p. 24.
      Review of original stage production of The Collection.

1833 _____. "Fine Focus on Marriage." London <u>Daily Mirror</u>, 10
April 1969, p. 13.
Review of <u>Night</u>.

1834 _____. "First Night." London <u>Daily Mirror</u>, 19 June 1964,
p. 18.
Review of <u>The Birthday Party</u> revival: "a piece of
artsy-crafty nonsense."

1835 _____. "First Night." London <u>Daily Mirror</u>, 4 June 1965,
p. 18.
Review of the original production of <u>The Homecoming</u>.

1836 _____. "Gales of Mirth." London <u>Daily Mirror</u>, 3 March 1972,
p. 16.
Review of <u>The Caretaker</u>.

1837 _____. "Theatre." London <u>Daily Mirror</u>, 18 September 1970,
p. 16.
Review of <u>Tea Party</u> and <u>The Basement</u>.

1838 _____. "Theatre." London <u>Daily Mirror</u>, 2 June 1971, p. 18.
Review of <u>Old Times</u>.

1839 _____. "Why Silence Was Best...." London <u>Daily Mail</u>, 3 July
1969, p. 14.
Review of <u>Landscape</u> and <u>Silence</u>.

1840 THOMAS, JOHN. "The Servant." <u>Film Society Review</u>, May 1967,
pp. 20-22.
Film review.

1841 THOMPSON, HARRY. "Harold Pinter Replies." <u>New Theatre
Magazine</u>, 31, No. 2 (January 1961), 8-10.
Interview in which Pinter discusses his choice of
subject matter and approach to writing.

1842 _____. "Mr. Pinter Pursues an Elusive Reality." <u>The Times</u>
(London), 19 September 1963, p. 16.
Review of <u>The Dwarfs</u> and <u>The Lover</u> which sees the plays
as showing an "incurable obsession with the elusiveness
of reality."

1843 _____. "A Slight Case of Conversation." <u>The Times</u> (London),
23 June 1962, p. 4.
Review of the original stage production of <u>The Collec-
tion</u> in which the presentation of the play in three different media (radio, television, stage) is discussed.

Thompson

1844   THOMPSON, JACK. "Perfect Work in 'Caretaker.'" New York
       Journal American, 31 January 1964, p. 19.
         Review of the film version of The Caretaker (The Guest).

1845   THOMPSON, J. W. M. "High Voltage Shocks." London Evening
       Standard, 28 April 1960, p. 19.
         Review of original production of The Caretaker.

1846   THOMPSON, MARJORIE. "The Image of Youth in the Contemporary
       Theater." Modern Drama, 7 (February 1965), 443-45.
         Discusses Pinter in terms of new young heroes who are
       reacting against materialism, etc.

1847   THOMPSON, THOMAS. "A New Twist on the Decadence Bit." Life,
       56 (10 April 1964), 12.
         Movie review of The Servant. The film, which is more
       Losey's than Pinter's, does not add much to an old theme,
       Thompson feels.

1848   THOMSON, PHILIP. The Grotesque. London: Methuen, 1972.
         Includes discussion of Pinter, pp. 29-32.

1849   THORNTON, PETER C. "Blindness and the Confrontation with
       Death: Three Plays by Harold Pinter." Die Neueren
       Sprachen, 17 (5 May 1968), 213-23.
         Blindness is seen as symbolic of a confrontation with
       death in The Room, The Birthday Party, and A Slight Ache.

1850   THORPE, M. Book review of Tea Party and Other Plays.
       English Studies, June 1968, p. 274 (See no. 17).

1851   TOWEY, DENIS J. "Form and Content in Selected Plays of
       Harold Pinter." Dissertation Abstracts International, 34:
       3609A. Ph.D. dissertation, New York University, 1973.
         The relationship between form and content in The Dumb
       Waiter, The Homecoming, Silence, and Old Times is discussed.

1852   TREWIN, J[OHN] C[OURTENAY]. "All Change." Illustrated
       London News, August 1971, p. 45.
         Review of Old Times.

1853   _____. "Battle Area." Illustrated London News, 11 June
       1960, p. 1036.
         Review of The Caretaker.

1854   _____. "Cutting it Short." Illustrated London News, 238
        (4 February 1961), 192.
            Highly disapproving review of original stage production
        of A Slight Ache as being "just silly" and weary, saying
        nothing.

*1855   _____. Drama in Britain: 1951–1964. London, 1965.
            Cited in Palmer (See no. 1530), p. 292.

1856   _____. "Fantastic Exploit." Illustrated London News, 19
        April 1969, p. 33.
            Review of Night.

1857   _____. "Mixed Drinks." Illustrated London News, 5 October
        1963, p. 526.
            Review of The Lover and The Dwarfs.

1858   _____. "The New Plays." Lady, 4 February 1960, pp. 150 f.
            Review of The Room and The Dumb Waiter.

1859   _____. "The New Plays." Lady, 12 May 1960, pp. 715–16.
            Review of The Caretaker.

1860   _____. "The New Plays." Lady, 5 July 1962, pp. 2–3.
            Review of The Collection.

1861   _____. "The New Plays." Lady, 3 October 1963, p. 441.
            Review of The Lover and The Dwarfs.

1862   _____. "Mr. Pinter Says That There's No Place Like Home."
        Illustrated London News, 246 (19 June 1965), 30.
            Review of the original production of The Homecoming.

1863   _____. "Pinter's Parodies." Illustrated London News, 250
        (12 July 1969), 29.
            Review of Landscape and Silence. As usual, Trewin
        finds Pinter and his work minor.

1864   _____. "Plays in Performance." Drama, 78 (Autumn 1965),
        16–23.
            Includes review of The Homecoming.

1865   _____. "The Right Approach." Illustrated London News, 19
        March 1960, p. 486.
            Review of The Room and The Dumb Waiter.

Trewin

1866 ____. "The World of the Theatre. After the Party."
Illustrated London News, 232 (31 May 1958), 932.
Review of the first run of The Birthday Party.

1867 ____. "The World of the Theatre. Between the Lines."
Illustrated London News, 240 (30 June 1962), 1058.
Review of original stage production of The Collection,
a "full-hearted bore" and another instance of Pinter's
persistence in failure.

1868 ____. "The World of the Theatre. Four in Hand." Illustrated London News, 236 (14 May 1960), 850.
Review of The Caretaker. Characterization is cited as
a major reason for Pinter's success.

1869 ____. "The World of the Theatre: Guessing Game."
Illustrated London News, 245 (4 July 1964), 28.
Review of The Birthday Party revival: a minor play
by a minor dramatist.

1870 ____. "The World of the Theatre. Thick and Clear."
Illustrated London News, 236 (6 February 1960), 226.
Review of New York production of The Dumb Waiter and
The Room.

1871 TRILLING, OSSIA. "The New English Realism." Tulane Drama
Review, 7, No. 2 (Winter 1962), 184-93.
Pinter follows the tradition begun with Osborne's
Look Back in Anger in hostility toward the English
institution of class structure and living under the
modern world's threat of nuclear annihilation.

*1872 ____. "Standort ungewiss. Uberblick der neuren englischen
Dramatiker." Theater der Zeit, 15, No. 9 (1960), 23-28.
In German. Cited in Imhof (See no. 1098), p. 18.

1873 ____. "The Young British Drama." Modern Drama, 3 (May
1960), 168.
Theatres and their productions in England are examined,
especially the Lyric Opera House in Hammersmith where The
Birthday Party and The Caretaker have been staged. Trilling lauds Pinter's "insight into the psychological com-
plexity of the broken-down members of human society."

1874 TRUE, WARREN ROBERTS. "Chekhovian Dramaturgy in the Plays of
Tennessee Williams, Harold Pinter, and Ed Bullins." Dissertation Abstracts International, 37: 5131A, Ph.D.
dissertation, University of Tennessee, 1976.

True finds a relationship between Pinter's "rambling, apparently pointless dialogue" and Chekhov's techniques.

1875　TRUSSLER, SIMON. "Farcical Tragedy." Tribune, 18 July 1969, p. 11.
　　　Review of Landscape and Silence.

1876　_____. "Lots of Sound and Fury." Tribune, 16 December 1966, p. 15.
　　　Review of The Homecoming.

1877　_____. The Plays of Harold Pinter, An Assessment. London: Gollancz, 1973.
　　　Basically a review of previous Pinter criticism, most of which is now outdated. Reviewed: See no. 1103.

1878　_____. "Shifting Alliances." Tribune, 18 June 1971, p. 11.
　　　Review of Old Times.

1879　_____. "Students v. the Rest." Tribune, 2 October 1970, p. 15.
　　　Review of Tea Party and The Basement.

1880　TURTON, HENRY. "On the Air." Punch, 4 May 1960, p. 629.
　　　Review of the television version of A Night Out.

1881　_____. "On the Air." Punch, 3 August 1960, p. 174.
　　　Review of the television version of Night School.

1882　TUTAEV, DAVID. "The Theater of the Absurd...How Absurd?" Gambit, No. 2 (n.d.), 68-70.
　　　Looks at the Theatre of the Absurd as an expression of modern Romanticism which will die out.

1883　TYNAN, KATHLEEN. "In Search of Harold Pinter: Is He the Mystery his Critics Allege?" London Evening Standard, Part 1, 25 April 1968, p. 7; Part 2, 26 April 1968, p. 8.
　　　Part 1 contains general comments on Pinter and his career, including the influence of Dylan Thomas on his early poetry, and quotes Alun Owen and Peter Shaffer about Pinter. Part 2 contains additional general comments, with Pinter's reflections on writing.

1884　TYNAN, KENNETH. "At the Theatre. Eastern Approaches." London Observer, 25 May 1958, p. 15.
　　　Review of the first run of The Birthday Party: "the theme is that of the individualist who is forced out of his shell to come to terms with the world at large." Tynan notes that this is not a new theme and that the play could have been shorter.

Tynan

1885   _____. "Dramatists in Perspective." London Observer, 15
        September 1963, p. 27.

1886   _____. "Let Coward Flinch." London Observer, 22 January
        1961, p. 30.
            Review of original production of A Slight Ache.

*1887   _____. "Pinter Came up from the Basement." London Observer.
        Reprinted in: Milwaukee Journal, 26 October 1963, p. 10.
        Cited in Elliott (See no 733), p. 553.

*1888   _____. Right and Left. London: Longmans, 1967.
            A discussion of modern drama. Cited in Imhof (See no.
        1098), p. 19.

1889   _____. "Shouts and Murmurs." London Observer, 21 January
        1968, p. 27.
            Review of radio production of Landscape.

1890   _____. "Shouts and Murmurs." London Observer, 26 May 1968.
            Book review of Mac (See no. 46).

*1891   _____. Tynan on Theater. London, 1964.
            A discussion of modern drama. Cited in Imhof (See no.
        1098), p. 19.

1892   _____. "A Verbal Wizard in the Suburbs." London Observer,
        5 June 1960, p. 16.
            Review of The Caretaker which deals with human relation-
        ships.

*1893   UENO, YOSHIKO. "Drama of Absense: An Essay on Harold Pinter."
        Humanities Bulletin (Tokyo Metropolitan University), No.
        70, March 1969.
            In Japanese. Cited by Tetsuo Kishi in personal
        correspondence.

1894   UHLMANN, WILFRIED. "Neurotische Konflikte und triebgesteuertes
        Sozialverhalten in den Stucken Harold Pinters." Literatur
        in Wissenschaft und Unterricht, 5, No. 4 (1972), 299-312.
            In German.

1895   UNGER, MICHAEL D. "Pinter Plays." Newark Evening News, 10
        December 1964, p. 58.
            Review of New York production of A Slight Ache and The
        Room.

1896 VAMOS, LASZLO, and GYORGY LENGYEL. "Laszlo Vamos and Gyorgy
      Lengyel." Transatlantic Review, No. 18 (Spring 1965),
      107-15.
          Hungarian reaction to Pinter--he is seen as alien.

1897 VANNIER, JEAN. "A Theatre of Language." Tulane Drama Review,
      7, No. 3 (Spring 1963), 180-86.

1898 VERKEIN, LEA. "Von Broadway near Piccadilly." Vlaamsegios,
      45, No. 7 (July 1961), 492-95.
          Production review of The Caretaker. In Flemish.

*1899 VIDAN, IVO. "Komedija nespokpjstava: a forum report."
      Zagreb, 9 (1963), 462-73.
          Cited in Imhof (See no. 1098).

1900 VINSON, JAMES. Contemporary Dramatists. New York and Lon-
      don: St. Martin's, 1973, pp. 608-13. Second edition, 1977.
          Includes Bigsby's "Pinter" (See no. 440).

*1901 VOLKER, KLAUS. "Groteskformen des Theaters." Akzente, 4
      (August 1960), 321-39.
          In German.

1902 von ROSADOR, KURT TETZELI. "Pinter's Dramatic Method: Kullus,
      The Examination, The Basement." Modern Drama, 14, No. 2
      (September 1971), 195-204.
          Reexamines the similarities in treating the subject of
      dominance in these three works in terms of "(1) the use
      of the door, (2) the adaption of the intruder to the room
      and its furniture, and (3) the lapse into silence as an
      instrument to circumvent the owner's privileged position."

1903 WADE, DAVID. "New Poetry in Pinter." The Times (London),
      26 April 1968, p. 9.
          Review of the radio version of Landscape in which
      Pinter uses "another style of writing" and presents in
      Beth a character "utterly different" from previous
      "traditional" Pinter characters.

1904 _____. "Pinter Cutting It Short." The Times, (London), 16
      September 1970, p. 13.
          Review of Night.

1905 WAGER, WALTER. The Playwright Speaks. New York: Delacorte,
      1967. Reprinted: London, 1969, pp. 171-88.
          Includes Bensky's "Harold Pinter: An Interview" (See
      no. 427).

1906   WAGNER, MARLENE S. "The Game-Play in Twentieth-Century
        Absurdist Drama: Studies in a Dramatic Technique." Dis-
        sertation Abstracts International, 32: 4637A. Ph.D. dis-
        sertation, University of Southern California, 1971.
            The dramatic technique of the game in Pinter, Albee,
        Beckett, and Genet is discussed.

1907   WALKER, ALEXANDER. "Brilliant...and Disappointing." London
        Evening Standard, 12 March 1964, p. 10.
            Review of The Caretaker film.

1908   _____. "Dons and Lovers: Vicious When the Jealousy Starts."
        London Evening Standard, 9 February 1967, p. 4.
            Film review of Accident.

1909   _____. Hollywood UK: The British Film Industry in the
        Sixties. New York: Stein and Day, 1974.
            Includes information on Pinter's screenwriting, with
        some interview material.

*1910   _____. Interview with Harold Pinter. Thames TV, 8 January
        1970.
            Reference in Hollywood UK (See no. 1909).

1911   _____. "Magnificent, Yes--and Now I Know Why." London
        Evening Standard, 16 July 1964.

1912   _____. "These Two Will Set You Puzzling." London Evening
        Standard, 9 March 1960, p. 10.
            Review of The Room and The Dumb Waiter.

1913   WALKER, AUGUSTA. "Messages from Pinter." Modern Drama, 10,
        No. 1 (May 1967), 1-10.
            Divides Pinter's work into allegories about life and
        cosmic concerns on the one hand and an examination of the
        drives within relationships between individuals. Dis-
        cusses The Room, The Birthday Party (which Walker admits
        does not fit either category), The Collection, A Slight
        Ache, and The Caretaker.

1914   _____. "Why the Lady Does It." In Lahr, A Casebook on Harold
        Pinter's The Homecoming (See no. 1260), p. 117-22.
            Concludes that Ruth is needed.

1915   WALSH, MICHAEL. "One Fine Hour with Pinter's Lovers." Lon-
        don Daily Express, 29 March 1963, p. 4.
            Review of television production of The Lover.

1916 WALSH, MOIRA. "Films: Accident." America, 116 (3 June
      1967), 821-22.
          A film review of Accident, recommending the film, though
      Walsh sees it as being based on a "thin and shaky frame-
      work."

1917 _____. "Films: Pumpkin Eater." America, 111 (28 November
      1964), 723-24.
          Film review of The Pumpkin Eater, which Walsh finds
      "relevant."

1918 _____. "Films: Spies and Secret Agents." America, 116
      (4 February 1967), 194.
          Film review of The Quiller Memorandum: unconvincing,
      though interesting.

1919 _____. "Films: The Servant." America, 110 (16 May 1964),
      684-86.
          Film review of The Servant in which the Legion of
      Decency ratings are discussed.

1920 WARD, ALFRED CHARLES. Twentieth Century English Literature.
      London: Barnes and Noble, 1964. Reprinted by Methuen.

1921 WARD, DOUGLAS TURNER. "'Ask Pinter.'" New York Times, 5
      February 1967, Sec. 2, p. 3.
          Review of The Homecoming.

1922 WARDLE, IRVING. "The Birthday Party." Encore, 5 (July-
      August 1958), 39-40.
          Review which praises Pinter's theatricality and com-
      pares The Birthday Party with O'Neill's The Iceman Cometh:
      "a man who has withdrawn to protect his illusions is not
      going to be helped by being propelled into the outer
      world."

1923 _____. "The Caretaker." The Times (London), 3 March 1972,
      p. 11.
          Review.

1924 _____. "Comedy of Menace." Encore, 5 (September-October
      1958), 28-33. Reprinted in: The Encore Reader, edited
      by C. Marowitz, T. Milne, and O. Hale (See no. 1404),
      pp. 86-91.
          The image which dominates The Birthday Party is that
      of the womb.

Wardle

1925 _____. "A Director's Approach." In Lahr, A Casebook on Harold
Pinter's The Homecoming (See no. 1260), pp. 9-25.
An interview with Peter Hall about staging The Home-
coming.

1926 _____. "Exiles." New York Times, 19 November 1970, p. 42.
Review of James Joyce's play Exiles with Pinter
directing.

1927 _____. "From Comedy to Sombre Realism." The Times (London),
10 April 1969, p. 7.
Review of Night.

1928 _____. "Harold Pinter." In The Reader's Encyclopedia of
World Drama, edited by John Gassner and Edward Quinn.
New York: Crowell, 1969, pp. 657-58.
Brief biography and overview of Pinter's work.

1929 _____. "Holding up the Mirror." Twentieth Century, 173
(Autumn 1964), 34-43.
The action of contemporary British drama on English
audiences and their reactions to it (nullifying the
shock).

1930 _____. "Keeping Chaos at Bay with Words." The Times (London), 31 July 1975, p. 9.
Disparaging review of No Man's Land which is seen as
structureless and obscure.

1931 _____. "Laughter in the Wilderness." London Observer, 24
June 1962, p. 23.
Review of original stage production of The Collection.
Wardle fears that "evasion of communication" may become
self-imitation.

1932 _____. "New Waves on the British Stage." Twentieth Century,
172 (1963), 57-65.
Pinter has succeeded in surviving the fads of taste of
the English theatre where his imitators have not.

1933 _____. "No Man's Land." The Times (London), 25 April 1975,
p. 13.
Review which concludes that No Man's Land "makes its
effects with total confidence: the objection is that effect
has been raised into a first priority." Wardle is im-
pressed by the use of language of the play (in spite of

its being in part "pastiche Eliot" combined with an "insistent" Beckettian presence), but feels that the work fails to "locate spiritual malaise in some concrete image."

1934 _____. "Old Times." The Times (London), 2 June 1971, p. 6. Review.

1935 _____. "Pinter Propriety." The Times (London), 18 September 1970, p. 6.
A review of Tea Party and The Basement which are both "concerned with the experience of invasion." Generally approving, Wardle does feel that there are some problems in transferring the works from the medium of television to the stage and that the cyclical ending of The Basement is not prepared for.

1936 _____. "Pinter Theatrical Twins in Pools of Solitude." The Times (London), 4 July 1969, p. 7.
Review of Landscape and Silence. Silence is incomprehensible; Landscape, an "elegiac mosaic," is "a theatrical poem to which poetic rather than stage criteria apply."

1937 _____. "Revolt Against the West End." Horizon, 5 (January 1963), 26-33.
Pinter's poetic drama is part of the challenge to conservative audiences put forth by the English Stage Company's original production of The Caretaker.

1938 _____. "The Story Could Go on Forever." The Times (London), 8 April 1976, p. 14.
Review of The Caretaker revival, "Pinter's masterpiece."

1939 _____. "The Territorial Struggle." In Lahr, A Casebook on Harold Pinter's The Homecoming (See no. 1260), pp. 37-44.
Applies the idea of ethnology to Pinter's plays.

1940 _____. "There's Music in That Room." Encore, 7 (1960), 32-34.
Pinter's symbolic The Caretaker creates the formal quality of music similar to Chekhov. Praises play for universality.

1941 WARNER, JOHN M. "The Epistemological Quest in Pinter's The Homecoming." Contemporary Literature, 2 (Summer 1970), 340-53.

Wasson

> In <u>The Homecoming</u> Pinter explores the "epistemological
> possibilities" open to man "in his efforts to overcome
> his crippling alienation from his own self."

1942   WASSON, RICHARD. "Mime and Dream." In <u>Pinter's Optics</u> (<u>See</u>
         no. 311), pp. 7-8.
         Modern drama is moving away from plot towards mime.

1943   WATT, DOUGLAS. "A Midwinter Pinter Festival." New York
         <u>Sunday News</u>, 14 February 1971, Sec. S, p. 3.
         Review of <u>The Birthday Party</u>.

1944   _____. "Pinter's 'Old Times'--A Magical Reverie." New York
         <u>Sunday News</u>, 28 November 1971, Sec. S, p. 3.
         Review.

1945   _____. "Some of Pinter's Magic Turned on at the Forum."
         <u>New York Daily News</u>, 3 April 1970, p. 64.
         Review of <u>Landscape</u> and <u>Silence</u> (New York).

1946   WATTS, RICHARD, JR. "An Absorbing New British Drama." <u>New</u>
         <u>York Post</u>, 5 October 1961, p. 57.
         Review of New York production of <u>The Caretaker</u>.

1947   _____. "An Adventure in Early Pinter." <u>New York Post</u>, 5
         October 1967, p. 55.
         Review of the New York production of <u>The Birthday Party</u>.

1948   _____. "Family Life Portrait." <u>New York Post</u>, 19 May 1971.
         Reprinted in: <u>New York Theatre Critics' Reviews</u>, 14 June
         1971, p. 261.
         Review of <u>The Homecoming</u>.

1949   _____. "Hospitality of a London Family." <u>New York Post</u>, 6
         January 1967, p. 49. Reprinted in: <u>New York Theatre</u>
         <u>Critics' Reviews</u>, 16 January 1967, p. 395.
         Review of <u>The Homecoming</u> (New York), seen as vague
         and repetitious, though still superior to its contempora-
         ries.

1950   _____. "A Pair of Striking Dramas by Britain's Harold
         Pinter." <u>New York Post</u>, 27 November 1962, p. 62.
         Review of <u>The Dumb Waiter</u> and <u>The Collection</u>, New York
         production.

1951   _____. "Pinter Without the Menace." <u>New York Post</u>, 3
         April 1970, p. 38.
         Review of <u>Landscape</u> and <u>Silence</u> (New York).

1952   ____. "Random Notes." New York Post, 25 May 1971, p. 54.
       Some review comments on The Homecoming.

1953   ____. "Revival of a Remarkable Drama." New York Post, 31
       January 1964, p. 30.
       Review of the film version of The Caretaker (The Guest).

1954   ____. "The News of Pinter and Beckett." New York Post, 6
       January 1964, p. 16.
       Review of The Lover (New York).

1955   ____. "Two Plays by Harold Pinter." New York Post, 16
       October 1968, p. 87.
       Review of Tea Party and The Basement (New York), which
are not Pinter's best, but still show him to be a notable
talent.

1956   ____. "Two Remarkable Plays by Pinter." New York Post, 10
       December 1964, p. 46.
       Review of A Slight Ache and The Room.

1957   WEALES, GERALD. "Absolutely As It Is: The Stage." Common-
       weal, 104 (7 January 1977), 20–21.
       Short review of No Man's Land, which is labeled "short
of the best of Pinter."

1958   ____. "Pinter at Work." Commonweal, 89 (6 December 1968),
       350–51.
       Review of Tea Party and The Basement.

1959   ____. "The Stage: Odd Man Out." Commonweal, 95 (17
       December 1971), 278.
       Old Times is called both effective and affective.

1960   ____. "Theatre Survey: New York, Winter, 1962–63." Drama
       Survey, 3 (1963), 123.
       Review of The Collection and The Dumb Waiter.

1961   WEBER, BROM, ed. Sense and Sensibility in Twentieth-Century
       Writing: A Gathering in Memory of William Van O'Connor.
       Carbondale: Southern Illinois University Press, 1970, pp.
       57–74.
       Includes Heilman's "Demonic Strategies: The Birthday
Party and The Firebugs" (See no. 987).

Weightman

1962   WEIGHTMAN, JOHN. "Another Play for Pinterites." <u>Encounter</u>,
       45 (July 1975), 24-26.
         Review of <u>No Man's Land</u>. Weightman obviously does not
       like Pinter and calls him to task for being derivative
       (Sartre, Ionesco, Albee, Kafka, Beckett, Genet, Robbe-
       Grillet), Absurdist, non-structural, etc.

*1963   _____. "The Play as Fable." <u>Encounter</u>, 28, No. 2 (February
       1967, 55-57.
         Themes of homosexuality and alienation discussed. Cited
       in <u>PMLA Bibliography</u>, June 1968, p. 652.

1964   WELLAND, DENNIS. "Some Post-War Experiments in Poetic Drama."
       In Armstrong, <u>Experimental Drama</u> (<u>See</u> no. 374).
         Argues that Pinter's success "would have been impossible
       without the Mercury Theatre's poets."

1965   WELLS, JOHN. "Theatre." <u>Punch</u>, 30 September 1970, pp.
       482-83.
         Review of <u>Tea Party</u> and <u>The Basement</u> (London).

*1966   WELLWARTH, GEORGE. <u>Contemporary Theatre</u>, New York, 1962.
         Cited in Imhof (<u>See</u> no. 1098), p. 19.

1967   _____. <u>The Theater of Protest and Paradox</u>. New York: New
       York University Press, 1964. Revised 1971. <u>See also</u>
       no. 1620.
         Pinter's "Comedy of Allusiveness" is reminiscent of
       the French <u>avant-garde</u>, with traces of Ionesco, Genet, and
       Beckett cited. By the time he had written <u>The Lover</u>, Pin-
       ter had established himself as "the most promising of
       England's young playwrights" with his "most original mind"
       and willingness to "experiment with new dramatic forms
       and techniques."

*1968   WENDT, ERNST. "Burgerseelen und Randexistenzen: uber die
       Dramatiker Harold Pinter und Franz Xavier Kroetz." In
       <u>Moderne Dramaturgie</u>. Frankfurt, 1974, pp. 91-117.
         In German.

1969   WERTHEIM, ALBERT. Discussion leader: "Contemporary British
       Drama: Pinter, Bond, and Stoppard." Modern Language
       Association convention, Chicago, December 1977.

1970   WEST, ANTHONY. "<u>The Birthday Party</u>, 'theatre at its very
       best.'" <u>Vogue</u>, 1 November 1967, p. 134.
         Review of New York production of <u>The Birthday Party</u>.

1971   _____. "The Homecoming, 'a dim crisis.'" Vogue, 1 March
    1967, p. 110.
       A review of The Homecoming (New York), a play about a
    "woman's fall" which lacks "meaning and dramatic interest."

1972   _____. "Tea Party and The Basement, 'perfect little machine.'"
    Vogue, 152 (December 1968), 170.
       Short review of the New York productions of Tea Party
    and The Basement. Stresses the mechanical rightness of
    the Eastside Playhouse for the "fluid stage treatment"
    which "brings the optical vitality of film" to the stage.
    The plays themselves are dismissed as typical Pinter
    productions which build tensions on the ambiguous spaces
    between the banalities spoken by the characters. The
    Basement is seen as another version of J. B. Priestley's
    Dangerous Corner.

1973   WEST, RICHARD. "Extraordinary." London Daily Mirror, 28
    April 1960, p. 26.
       Review of original production of The Caretaker.

1974   WHARTON, FLAVIA. "The Servant." Films in Review, 15, No.
    4 (April 1964), 241.
       Film review; essentially a synopsis.

1975   WHITEMORE, HUGH. "Plays." Queen, 436 (October 1970), 97.
       Review of Tea Party and The Basement (London).

1976   WHITING, JOHN. "Book Reviews." London Magazine, 7, No. 2
    (February 1960), 93-94. Reprinted in: The Art of the
    Dramatist, London: magazine edition, 1970, pp. 184-87.
       Discusses The Caretaker and The Birthday Party and
    Other Plays.

*1977   WICKHAM, GLYNNE. Drama in a World of Science and Three
    Other Lectures. London: Routledge, 1962.
       Reference in Elliott (See no. 733), p. 547.

1978   WIGGIN, MAURICE. "Bubble-gum Reputations." The Sunday Times
    (London), 26 February 1967, p. 50.
       Review of television version of The Basement.

1979   _____. "Crime and Punishment." The Sunday Times (London),
    31 March 1963, p. 39.
       Review of television production of The Lover.

Wiggin

1980   _____. "Gilt-Edged in Golden Square." The Sunday Times
       (London), 13 August 1961, p. 32.
       Review of British television production of The Dumb
       Waiter which has "boredom" as its theme.

1981   _____. "I Have Been Here Before." The Sunday Times (London),
       24 July 1960, p. 36.
       Review of television version of Night School.

1982   _____. "I'll let Mine Cool...." The Sunday Times (London),
       28 March 1965, p. 26.
       Review of television production of Tea Party in which
       the critic admits that he is getting the "hang of this
       strange experience of watching a new Pinter play."

1983   _____. "Rag Trade." The Sunday Times (London), 14 May 1961,
       p. 48.
       Review of British television production of The Collec-
       tion as a parable on the "biblical theme which suggests
       that whoever lusts after a woman with his eyes has
       committed adultery."

1984   _____. "Smaller but Sweeter." The Sunday Times (London),
       27 March 1960, p. 23.
       Review of British television production of The Birthday
       Party: "an exercise of talent in the void; invocation,
       rather than evocation of nameless dreads."

1985   WILLIAMS, RAYMOND. Drama from Ibsen to Brecht. London:
       Chatto and Windus, 1968, pp. 322-25.
       Discusses The Birthday Party.

1986   _____. "Recent English Drama." In The Pelican Guide to
       English Literature, Vol. 7: The Modern Age, edited by
       Boris Ford (See no. 790), pp. 496-508.
       Brief summary, mentioning Pinter.

1987   WILSHER, PETER. "What Happened in Leeds?" The Sunday Times
       (London), 17 June 1962, p. 44.
       Negative review of radio version of The Collection as
       treating a trivial subject in comparison to his previous
       works.

1988   WILSON, CECIL. "Cheers for the Mad Guests." London Daily
       Mail, 20 May 1958, p. 3.
       Review of the first run of The Birthday Party, not com-
       pletely approving in tone.

1989 _____. "Pinter Better in Halves." London <u>Daily Mirror</u>, 9
March 1960, p. 3.
Review of <u>The Room</u> and <u>The Dumb Waiter</u>.

1990 _____. "Why I'm Saying Thank You, Liz, This Morning." London <u>Daily Mail</u>, 10 March 1964, p. 18.
Review of the film version of <u>The Caretaker</u>.

*1991 WILSON, SHEILA. <u>Theatre of the Fifties</u>. London, 1963.

1992 WINEGARTEN, RENEE. "The Anglo-Jewish Dramatist in Search
of His Soul." <u>Midstream</u>, 12, No. 7 (August–September 1966),
40–52.
Examines Pinter and Shaffer and their depiction of a
hostile society and decides that they have little in
common.

1993 WINSTEN, ARCHER. "Reviewing Stand." <u>New York Post</u>, 21
January 1964, p. 44.
Review of the film version of <u>The Caretaker</u>.

1994 WISEMAN, THOMAS. "Harold Pinter's The Caretaker." London
<u>Sunday Express</u>, 15 March 1964, p. 23.
Review of the film version of <u>The Caretaker</u>.

1995 _____. "A Life on the Old Ocean Wave." <u>Time and Tide</u>, 28
June 1962, p. 13–14.
Review of <u>The Collection</u>.

*1996 WOLF, WILLIAM. Review of <u>The Last Tycoon</u>. <u>Cue Magazine</u>,
November 1976.
Film review. Quoted in <u>New York Times</u> advertisement.

1997 WOODFORDE, JOHN. "Shock Around the Clock." London <u>Sunday
Telegraph</u>, 30 October 1966, p. 11.
Review of the film version of <u>The Caretaker</u>.

*1998 WOODROOFE, KENNETH S. "The Plays of Harold Pinter." <u>Thought
Currents in English Literature</u>, p. 40.

1999 WORSLEY, T. C. "The Arts and Entertainment: A New Dramatist
or Two." <u>New Statesman</u>, 31 May 1958, pp. 692–94.
An early estimation of Pinter as an offbeat comic
writer who shows potential, though an excess of symbolism
is the major fault of <u>The Birthday Party</u>.

Worsley

2000 _____. "The Caretaker." London Financial Times, 28 April
       1960, p. 19.
          Review of original production of The Caretaker which
       shows that Pinter has moved "from extraordinary promise
       to extraordinary achievement."

2001 _____. "The Lover and The Dwarfs." London Financial Times,
       20 September 1963, p. 26.
          Review of The Dwarfs and The Lover. The Lover shows the
       "perversion" in "so-called normal sexuality."

2002 _____. "New English Drama." Twentieth Century, 170, No.
       1011 (1961), 169-80. Reprinted in: J. R. Brown, Modern
       British Dramatists (See no. 501), pp. 26-37.
          An overview which mentions Pinter.

2003 _____. "New Pinter Plays, 'Lover' and 'Dwarf,' Offered in
       London." New York Times, 19 September 1963, p. 21.
          Review of The Dwarfs and The Lover.

2004 _____. "A New Wave Rules Britannia." Theatre Arts, 45
       (October 1961), 17-19.
          A brief survey of the English theatre in the early
       sixties.

2005 _____. "The Room: The Dumb Waiter." London Financial Times,
       9 March 1960, p. 17.
          Review of New York production of The Dumb Waiter and
       The Room.

2006 _____. "Three Plays at the Arts." London Financial Times,
       19 January 1961, p. 17.
          Includes a review of A Slight Ache.

2007 WORTH, KATHERINE J. "Harold Pinter." In Revolutions in
       Modern English Drama. London: Bell, 1972, pp. 86-100.

2008 WORTIS, IRVING. "The Homecoming." Library Journal, 92
       (1 April 1967), p. 1508.
          Book review.

2009 WRAY, PHOEBE. "Pinter's Dialogue: The Play on Words."
       Modern Drama, 13, No. 4 (February 1971), 418-22.
          Pinter gives speech "a power and a mystery."

2010   WRIGHT, EDWARD A., and LENTHIEL H. DOWNS. <u>A Primer for Play-</u>
       <u>goers</u>. Englewood Cliffs, N. J.: Prentice-Hall, 1969.
       Includes a discussion of <u>The Dwarfs</u>.

2011   WRIGHT, IAN. "New Films in London." Manchester <u>Guardian</u>, 17
       July 1964, p. 7.
       Film review of <u>The Pumpkin Eater</u>.

2012   _____. "Shooting <u>The Caretaker</u>." Manchester <u>Guardian</u>, 20
       February 1963, p. 7.

2013   W. W. "Two Bafflers." London <u>Daily Worker</u>, 10 March 1960,
       p. 2.
       A negative review of the New York production of <u>The</u>
       <u>Dumb Waiter</u> and <u>The Room</u> which baffle the critic.

2014   WYCISK, MAX M. "Language and Silence in the Stage Plays of
       Samuel Beckett and Harold Pinter." <u>Dissertation Abstracts</u>
       <u>International</u>, 33: 4442A. Ph.D. dissertation, University
       of Colorado, 1973.
       Compares the use of language by Beckett and Pinter to
       show how they are alike and how they are different.

2015   WYNDHAM, FRANCIS. "At the Theatre." <u>Queen</u>, 10 June 1958,
       p. 50.
       Review of <u>The Birthday Party</u>.

2016   YOUNG, B. A. "<u>The Basement</u> and <u>Tea Party</u>." London <u>Financial</u>
       <u>Times</u>, 18 September 1970, p. 3.
       Review.

2017   _____. "The Birthday Party." London <u>Financial Times</u>, 20
       June 1964, p. 9.
       Review of <u>The Birthday Party</u> revival.

2018   _____. "<u>The Homecoming</u>." London <u>Financial Times</u>, 5 June
       1965, p. 7.
       Review of the original production of <u>The Homecoming</u>:
       ending is "a brilliant Pinterian stroke."

2019   _____. "Landscape--Silence." London <u>Financial Times</u>, 4
       July 1969, p. 3.
       Negative review of <u>Landscape</u> and <u>Silence</u>. Pinter has
       moved so far away from reality toward poetry that he is
       no longer writing plays.

2020   _____. "Old Times." London <u>Financial Times</u>, 3 June 1971, p.
       3.
       Review.

Young

2021 _____. "Pinter's 'Homecoming' is Staged in London." New
York Times, 4 June 1965, p. 38.
Review of the original production of The Homecoming.

2022 YOUNG, KENNETH. "Comedy of a Night Club 'Chick': Wry Mr.
Pinter." London Daily Telegraph, 22 July 1960, p. 15.
Review of the television production of Night School.

*2023 ZIEGLER, KLAUS. "Das moderne Drama als Spiegel unserer Zeit."
Der Deutschunterricht, 13 (1961), 5-24.
In German. Cited in Imhof (See no. 1098), p. 20.

*2024 ZIMMERMANN, HEINZ. "Harold Pinter: The Birthday Party
(1958)." In Das zeitgenössische englische Drama: Ein-
führung, Interpretation, Dokumentation, edited by Klaus-
Dieter Fehse and Norbert Platz. Frankfurt: Athenäum,
1975, pp. 43-70.
Cited in 1975 MLA International Bibliography, 1, p.
126.

2025 ZIMMERMANN, PAUL D. "Angry Old Chap." Newsweek, 83 (20
May 1974), 106.
Approving review of the film version of Butley.

2026 _____. "Bag of Tricks." Newsweek, 74, (16 November 1969),
102.
Film review of The Pumpkin Eater.

2027 _____. "Breaking the Bond." Newsweek, 68 (26 December 1966),
72.
Film review of The Quiller Memorandum.

2028 _____. "A Gentleman's Downfall." Time, 83 (20 March 1964),
94.
Film review of The Servant.

2029 No entry.

2030 _____. "Nasties for Noel." Time, 88 (23 December 1966), 75.
Film review of The Quiller Memorandum.

2031 _____. "Sunburn." Newsweek, 78 (16 August 1971), 76.
Highly approving film review of The Go-Between.

2032 _____. "Theatre in the Camera." Newsweek, 82 (3 December
1973), 61-62.
A review of the film version of The Homecoming, stating
that it is even better than the original stage play.

2033   _____. "Who is the Master?" <u>Newsweek</u>, 63 (23 March 1964),
        95-96.
            Film review of <u>The Servant</u>.

2034   _____. "Wife's Tale." <u>Time</u>, 84 (13 November 1964), 125 f.
            Film review of <u>The Pumpkin Eater</u>.

2035   _____. "X-Ray Treatment." <u>Time</u>, 89 (21 April 1967), p. 101.
            Film review of <u>Accident</u>.

2036   ZOLOTOW, MAURICE. "Young Man with Scorn." <u>New York Times</u>,
        17 September 1961.
            A sketch of Pinter's character and an extended biography,
        with synopses of plays <u>The Birthday Party</u>, <u>The Dumb Waiter</u>,
        <u>The Caretaker</u>, and <u>The Collection</u>.

Appendix A:
Chronology of Pinter's Writings

1946-1947   Juvenilia.

1949   "Kullus" is begun.

1950   "New Year in the Midlands" and "Chandeliers and Shadows"
       are published. "New Year in the Midlands" is reprinted
       with "Rural Idyll" and "European Revels" over the name
       "Harold Pinta."
       Work is begun on a novel, The Dwarfs (unfinished).

1951   "One a Story, Two a Death" by "Harold Pinta" is published.

1954-1955   "The Black and White," prose version, is written.

1955   "The Examination" is written.

1957   The Room, The Birthday Party, and The Dumb Waiter are written.

1958   Something in Common (unperformed) and A Slight Ache are
       written.

1959   A Night Out is completed.
           The Caretaker and the revue sketches "Trouble in the
       Works," "The Black and White," "Request Stop," "Last to
       Go," "Special Offer," "That's Your Trouble," "That's All,"
       "Applicant," "Interview," "Getting Acquainted," and
       "Dialogue for Three" are written.

1960   Night School and The Dwarfs are written.
       The Hothouse is finished (unperformed).

1961   The Collection is written.
       "Writing for Myself" is published.

1962   The Lover is written.
        The Servant is filmed.
        The screenplay of The Caretaker (The Guest) is written.

1963   The script is written for The Pumpkin Eater, and the script
            for The Compartment (later published as The Basement).
        A short story version of Tea Party is written.
        "Filming 'The Caretaker'" is published.

1964   Tea Party is written.
        The Homecoming is written.
        "Writing for the Theatre" is published.

1965   "Between the Lines" is published.

1966   The script is written for The Quiller Memorandum, and the
            script for Accident.
        The Basement is written.

1967   Landscape is written.

1968   Silence is written.
        A film version is made of The Birthday Party.
        Mac is published.

1969   The script of The Go-Between is completed.
        Night is written.

1970   The film script of The Homecoming is completed.
        Old Times is written.
        "All of That" is published.

1971   A movie adaptation of Langrishe, Go Down is written.
        "poem" is published.

1972   The film adaptation of Remembrance of Things Past (A la
            recherche du temps perdu) is written.
        Monologue is written.

1973   The film version of Butley is made.

1974   No Man's Land is written.

1975   The film version of The Last Tycoon is made.

Appendix B:
Chronology of First Performances
of Pinter's Works

1957   The Room is first staged at Bristol University by the Drama
         Department, May 15.

1958   The Birthday Party is staged at the Arts Theatre, Cambridge,
         April 28.

1959   The world premiere of The Dumb Waiter takes place at Frank-
         furt-am-Main, the Frankfurt Municipal Theatre, on February
         28, in German.
         "The Black and White" and "Trouble in the Works" are performed
         in One to Another at the Lyric Opera House, Hammersmith,
         July 15.
         A Slight Ache is first broadcast on The British Broadcasting
         Corporation's Third Programme, July 29.
         "Getting Acquainted," "Last to Go," "Request Stop," and
         "Special Offer" are presented in Pieces of Eight at the
         Apollo Theatre, London, September 3.

1960   The Room and The Dumb Waiter (the first performance in English)
         are presented as a double bill at the Hampstead Theatre
         Club, January 21.
         A Night Out is broadcast on the BBC Third Programme, March 1.
         The Caretaker is staged at the Arts Theatre, London, April 27.
         Night School is televised by Associated Rediffusion Television,
         July 21.
         The Birthday Party becomes the first professional performance
         of Pinter in America, Actors Workshop, San Francisco, July
         27.
         The Dwarfs is broadcast on the BBC Third Programme, December
         2.

1961   A Slight Ache is staged as part of a triple bill, Three, at
         the Arts Theatre Club, London, January 18.
         The Collection is televised by Associated Rediffusion Tele-
         vision, May 11.
         A Night Out is staged at the Gate Theatre, Dublin, September
         17.

1962   The Collection is staged at the Aldwych Theatre, London,
            June 18.
        "The Examination" is read by Pinter on the BBC Third Programme,
            September 7.
        The Servant is shown in London in November.

1963   The Lover is televised by Associated Rediffusion Television
            on March 28.
        The Caretaker (film) is shown at the Berlin Film Festival
            on June 27.
        The Lover and The Dwarfs are staged at the Arts Theatre Club,
            London, September 18.

1964   "Applicant," "Dialogue for Three," "Interview," "That's All,"
            and "That's Your Trouble" are broadcast on the BBC Third
            Programme between February and March.
        "Tea Party" is read by Pinter on the BBC Third Programme,
            June 2.
        The Pumpkin Eater is shown.

1965   The Homecoming begins a pre-London tour in March; staged at
            the Aldwych Theatre, London, on June 3.
        Tea Party is televised by BBC-1 in England and throughout
            Europe on March 25.

1966   The Quiller Memorandum is shown in November.

1967   The Basement is televised on BBC-TV on February 28.
        Accident is shown in February.

1968   Landscape is broadcast on the BBC Third Programme, April 28.
        Tea Party and The Basement are staged at the Eastside Play-
            house, New York, October 19.
        The Birthday Party (film) is shown in New York on December 9.

1969   Night is staged in a collection of one-act plays, Mixed
            Doubles, at the Comedy Theatre, London, April 9.
        Landscape and Silence are staged at the Aldwych Theatre, Lon-
            don, July 2.
        Pinter People is televised on NBC's Experiment in Television.

1971   The Go-Between is shown at the Cannes Film Festival.
        Old Times is first staged at the Aldwych Theatre, London,
            June 1.

1973   The Homecoming (film) is shown.
        Monologue is televised, April 10.

1974   Butley (film) is shown.

1975   <u>No Man's Land</u> is staged at the Old Vic, London, April 23.

1976   <u>The Last Tycoon</u> is shown on November 18.

Appendix C:
Productions Directed by Pinter

The Birthday Party, Oxford and Cambridge, 1958.

The Room, Hampstead Theatre Club, London, 21 January 1960.

The Collection, Aldwych Theatre, London, 18 June 1962, co-directed
    with Peter Hall.

The Lover, Arts Theatre Club, London, 18 September 1963, assisted
    by Guy Vassen.

The Dwarfs, Arts Theatre Club, London, 18 September 1963, assisted
    by Guy Vassen.

The Birthday Party, Aldwych Theatre, London, 18 June 1964.

The Man in the Glass Booth (by Robert Shaw), London, 27 July 1967.

Butley (by Simon Gray), London, August 1970.

Exiles (by James Joyce), London, November 1970.

Butley (film), 1974.

Next of Kin (by John Hopkins), London, 31 May 1974.

Otherwise Engaged (by Simon Gray), London, July 1975; New York,
    February 1977.

The Innocents (by William Archibald), New York, October 1976.

Appendix D:
Awards to Pinter

The Evening Standard Award for The Caretaker, 1960.

Page 1 Award of the Newspaper Guild of New York for The Caretaker, 1960.

Berlin Film Festival Silver Bear for The Caretaker (film), 1963.

Edinburgh Festival Certificate of Merit for The Caretaker (film), 1963.

Prix Italia (Naples) for Television Drama for The Lover, 1963.

Guild of British Television Producers and Directors Award for The Lover, 1963.

British Screenwriters Guild Award for The Servant, 1964.

New York Film Critics Best Writing Award for The Servant, 1964.

New York Times listing of The Servant, one of the ten best films of the year, 1964.

British Film Academy Award for The Pumpkin Eater, 1965.

Commander of the Order of the British Empire (C. B. E.) on the Queen's Birthday Honours List, 1966.

Cannes Jury Prize for Accident, 1967.

National Board of Review Award, one of the ten best films of the year, for Accident, 1967.

Antoinnette Perry ("Tony") Award for the best play on Broadway for The Homecoming, 1967.

New York Drama Critics Circle Award for the best play on Broadway, for The Homecoming, 1967.

Whitbread Anglo-American Award for the best British play on Broadway, for The Homecoming, 1967.

American Library Association award, "Notable Books of 1967," for The Homecoming, 1967.

Honorary Fellow, Modern Language Association of America, 1970.

Hamburg University Shakespeare Prize, 1970.

Honorary degree conferred by Reading University, 1970.

Honorary degree conferred by the University of Birmingham, 1971.

Golden Palm (Best Picture) Cannes Film Festival award for The Go-Between, 1971.

Vienna Prize, 1973.

Index